The Readable Julius Caesar: A Modern Retelling Of Caesar's Writings

By: Valerius Vogan

Table of Contents

✦✦✦

Preface

In a world where the echoes of the past reverberate through the annals of history, few figures have wielded as much influence and captured the imagination quite like Julius Caesar. A consummate military leader, political strategist, and chronicler of his own accomplishments, Caesar's legacy continues to shape our understanding of the ancient world and the forces that molded it. "The Readable Julius Caesar" seeks to bring this remarkable story to life, offering a fresh and accessible look at Caesar's writings for a modern audience.

The goal of this book is to make the words of Julius Caesar more approachable, without sacrificing the richness and depth of his accounts. By providing well-crafted translations and insightful commentary, we aim to illuminate the intricacies of Caesar's narratives and shed light on the motivations, decisions, and consequences that shaped his world and, by extension, our own.

In the pages that follow, readers will be taken on a journey through Caesar's military campaigns, from the conquest of Gaul to the Civil Wars and the lesser-known but equally significant Alexandrian, African, and Spanish wars. These accounts reveal not only Caesar's strategic prowess and unyielding determination but also the resilience, courage, and ambition of the people who lived, fought, and died in these tumultuous times.

As you embark on this journey, you will find yourself immersed in the world of the Roman Republic, experiencing firsthand the challenges and triumphs faced by one of history's most enigmatic leaders. Through these carefully crafted translations and introductions, the complexity and nuance of Caesar's accounts are laid bare, allowing readers to engage with the text on a deeper level and appreciate the broader context of the events that transpired.

"The Readable Julius Caesar" is not only a testament to the enduring impact of Caesar's words but also a celebration of the power of storytelling and the importance of preserving history for future generations. By making these seminal works more accessible, we hope to ignite a passion for history and foster a deeper understanding of the forces that shaped the world in which we live.

As you delve into the pages of this book, we invite you to step back in time and explore the vivid tapestry of war, diplomacy, and ambition that defined Julius Caesar's life and the age in which he lived. With each turn of the page, you will be drawn deeper into a world of intrigue, conflict, and transformation, ultimately gaining a greater appreciation for the lessons that the past has to offer and the legacy that Julius Caesar left behind.

So, without further ado, we welcome you to "The Readable Julius Caesar," a journey into the heart of Rome's most intriguing and influential figure, and an exploration of the world that he so indelibly shaped. As you immerse yourself in Caesar's accounts of his exploits, we hope you will gain not only a deeper understanding of the man himself but also of the broader historical context and the timeless themes that continue to resonate today.

From the dramatic conquests in Gaul to the power struggles of the Roman Republic, each chapter of this book offers a window into the past, revealing the complex interplay of ambition, leadership, and destiny that defined an era. "The Readable Julius Caesar" serves as both a tribute to the enduring legacy of one of history's greatest leaders and a reminder of the power of the written word to transport us across time and space, connecting us to the past and offering invaluable insights into the human experience.

May you find inspiration, enlightenment, and perhaps even a renewed appreciation for the vast tapestry of history as you journey through the pages of this book and may the words of Julius Caesar resonate with you long after the final page has been turned.

✦✦✦

Introduction

Julius Caesar was not only a renowned military leader and politician but also a prolific writer. His writings provide valuable insights into his campaigns and the political climate of his time. Here is a list of Caesar's most notable works:

Commentarii de Bello Gallico (Commentaries on the Gallic War): This work is a firsthand account of Caesar's campaigns in Gaul from 58 to 50 BC. It consists of eight books, with the last one possibly written by Caesar's lieutenant, Aulus Hirtius. The Commentaries on the Gallic War is a significant historical source, as it details Caesar's battles, strategies, and interactions with various Gallic tribes.

Commentarii de Bello Civili (Commentaries on the Civil War): This three-book work covers the period from the outbreak of the civil war between Caesar and Pompey in 49 BC until Caesar's victory at the Battle of Pharsalus in 48 BC. The Commentaries on the Civil War provide insight into Caesar's perspective on the events leading up to and during the conflict.

De Bello Alexandrino (On the Alexandrian War): Although the authorship of this work is debated, it is often attributed to Caesar. The text recounts Caesar's campaigns in Egypt in 47-48 BC, including the famous siege of Alexandria and the political intrigue surrounding Cleopatra and Ptolemy XIII.

De Bello Africo (On the African War): This work is likely written by an unknown author, but it is commonly attributed to Caesar. The text details Caesar's campaign in North Africa against the remaining Pompeian forces in 47 BC, culminating in the Battle of Thapsus.

De Bello Hispaniensi (On the Hispanic War): Another work with debated authorship, it is often attributed to Caesar. This text covers Caesar's campaign in the Iberian Peninsula in 45 BC against the last of Pompey's supporters, led by his sons Gnaeus and Sextus Pompeius. The account concludes with Caesar's victory at the Battle of Munda.

◆◆◆

Historical Figures In Julius Caesar's Writings

Below is a list of some prominent historical figures mentioned in Julius Caesar's writings, along with a brief description of each:

Julius Caesar (100-44 BC) - Roman military general, statesman, and author, who played a critical role in the transformation of the Roman Republic into the Roman Empire. He is the author of the works included in this book.

Gaius Cassius Longinus (c. 85-42 BC) - A Roman senator and military commander who was a key figure in the plot to assassinate Julius Caesar.

Marcus Junius Brutus (c. 85-42 BC) - A Roman politician and military leader who was also a central figure in the assassination of Julius Caesar. He is best known as one of Caesar's most trusted friends-turned-assassins.

Pompey the Great (106-48 BC) - A distinguished Roman general and statesman who became one of Julius Caesar's main rivals during the Civil War.

Mark Antony (83-30 BC) - A Roman general and politician who was a close ally of Julius Caesar. After Caesar's assassination, he formed the Second Triumvirate with Octavian and Lepidus to avenge Caesar's death.

Vercingetorix (c. 82-46 BC) - A Gallic chieftain who led a major revolt against Julius Caesar's forces during the Gallic Wars. He was eventually captured and executed by the Romans.

Ambiorix - A leader of the Eburones tribe in Gaul who rebelled against Roman rule during the Gallic Wars.

Ariovistus - A Germanic king who fought against Julius Caesar in the Gallic Wars.

Labienus (c. 100-45 BC) - A skilled Roman officer who initially served under Julius Caesar in the Gallic Wars but later defected to Pompey's side during the Civil War.

Cicero (106-43 BC) - A prominent Roman statesman, orator, and philosopher who was a contemporary of Julius Caesar. Though not directly involved in Caesar's military campaigns, his writings and speeches provide valuable context for the period.

Octavian (later Augustus, 63 BC-14 AD) - Julius Caesar's grandnephew and adopted son who became the first Roman emperor after Caesar's death.

Lepidus (c. 89-12 BC) - A Roman general and politician who became a member of the Second Triumvirate along with Octavian and Mark Antony after Caesar's assassination.

Crassus (c. 115-53 BC) - A Roman general and politician who was part of the First Triumvirate with Julius Caesar and Pompey. He was known for his immense wealth and met his end during the disastrous Parthian campaign.

Lucius Domitius Ahenobarbus (c. 98-48 BC) - A Roman politician and general who opposed Julius Caesar during the Civil War and sided with Pompey.

Gnaeus Pompeius (Pompey the Younger, c. 75-45 BC) - Pompey the Great's son, who continued fighting against Julius Caesar in the Civil War after his father's death.

Titus Labienus (c. 100-45 BC) - A Roman general who served under Julius Caesar in the Gallic Wars but later joined Pompey's side during the Civil War.

Publius Clodius Pulcher (c. 93-52 BC) - A controversial Roman politician known for his populist policies and feuds with prominent figures like Cicero.

Orgetorix - A Gallic nobleman and leader of the Helvetii tribe who planned a mass migration of his people into Roman-controlled lands, ultimately leading to the start of the Gallic Wars.

Diviciacus - A Gallic druid and political leader of the Aedui tribe who allied with Julius Caesar during the Gallic Wars.

Commius - A chieftain of the Atrebates tribe who first served as an ally to Julius Caesar during the Gallic Wars but later joined the revolt against Roman rule.

Quintus Tullius Cicero (c. 102-43 BC) - A Roman general and politician who was the younger brother of the famous orator Cicero. He served under Julius Caesar during the Gallic Wars.

Cato the Younger (95-46 BC) - A Roman senator and statesman known for his unwavering opposition to Julius Caesar's rise to power. He ultimately committed suicide after the Battle of Thapsus.

Scipio Nasica (c. 90-45 BC) - A Roman politician and general who supported Pompey during the Civil War and led the resistance against Julius Caesar in Africa.

Juba I (c. 85-46 BC) - The king of Numidia who supported Pompey's cause during the Civil War and fought against Julius Caesar in Africa.

Ptolemy XIII (62-47 BC) - The pharaoh of Egypt during the time of Julius Caesar's visit. He was involved in the Alexandrian War and eventually lost his throne to his sister Cleopatra VII.

Cleopatra VII (69-30 BC) - The last active ruler of the Ptolemaic Kingdom of Egypt, she was a skilled diplomat, naval commander, and polyglot. Cleopatra famously became Julius Caesar's lover and bore him a son, Caesarion. She later allied with Mark Antony, Caesar's close friend and loyal supporter, which ultimately led to her downfall after the Battle of Actium.

✦✦✦

GALLIC WARS BOOK 1 (58 B.C.E.)

In the annals of ancient Rome, few events have captured the imagination and inspired awe as Julius Caesar's daring and triumphant campaigns in Gaul. The year 58 BCE marked the beginning of a monumental chapter in Roman history, as Caesar embarked on his ambitious quest to subdue the diverse and formidable Gallic tribes. The first book of the Commentarii de Bello Gallico offers an unparalleled glimpse into the strategic genius and unrelenting determination that would come to define Caesar's legacy.

As readers delve into the opening pages of this fascinating work, they are immediately transported to a time of political intrigue, military conquest, and cultural encounters that forever changed the trajectory of Rome and the Western world. Caesar's masterful storytelling brings to life the courage, ingenuity, and resilience of the Romans as they confronted the challenges of a vast and unfamiliar land. The narrative also reveals the complex tapestry of alliances, rivalries, and enmities among the Gallic tribes, providing a rich and intricate portrait of a society on the brink of transformation.

The first book of the Gallic Wars not only chronicles the initial foray of Caesar's forces into Gaul but also establishes the foundation for a series of military adventures that would eventually bring the entire region under Roman control. From the migration of the Helvetii to the legendary battles against the Suebi and the Belgae, these pages bear witness to a pivotal moment in history, one that resonated far beyond the borders of Gaul and Rome.

Gaul: three parts. Belgae live in one, Aquitani in another, Celts (our Gauls) in the third. They differ in language, customs, laws. Garonne separates Aquitani from Gauls, Marne and Seine separate them from Belgae. Belgae bravest because far from civilization and refinement, closest to Germans who they continually wage war. Helvetii also brave as they fight Germans almost daily. Gauls occupy part that begins at Rhone, bounded by Garonne, ocean, and Belgae territories. Aquitania extends from Garonne to Pyrenaean mountains and near Spain.

1:2

Orgetorix was the richest and most respected Helvetian. During the consulship of Marcus Messala and Marcus Piso, he convinced the noble class to join him in a revolt for power. Orgetorix then convinced the people to leave their land with their possessions to easily conquer Gaul due to their superior courage. The Helvetii are vulnerable, surrounded by nature, with rivers hemming them in.

The Helvetians were hemmed in on one side by a deep river from the Germans and on another side by a tall mountain between the Sequani and Helvetii. Lake Geneva and the Rhone River separated them from our Province. These borders made it difficult for their warlike people to expand and attack their neighbors. Despite their reputation for bravery and strength, they were confined to a narrow strip of land, measuring only 240 by 180 miles. This left them feeling regretful and longing for more room to fight.

1:3

Thinking of what they needed for their journey, the Helvetians decided to gather as many wagons and animals as possible and sow as much food as they could. Orgetorix was chosen to make arrangements, and on his travels, he convinced two men to seize power in their own states. He assured them it would be easy with the help of the most powerful nations. They made a promise to each other that they would use their newfound power to conquer all of Gaul.

1:4

The Helvetii, upon receiving word of Orgetorix's plot, made him stand
trial in chains, as was their custom. If found guilty, he would be burned
at the stake. On the day of his trial, Orgetorix called upon his ten
thousand vassals and numerous debtors to join him in court, effectively
avoiding the need for a defense altogether. Outraged, the state
prepared for battle and began to gather their forces. However, before
this could happen, Orgetorix was found dead under suspicious
circumstances, leading many Helvetii to believe he had taken his own
life.

1:5

After he died, the Helvetii still aimed to do what they'd planned,
leaving their domains for good. Once they felt good and ready, they
struck a match to all of their cities-not less than twelve- four hundred
smaller settlements, and every remaining residence. They torched all of
the wheat and grains except what they'd need for the journey,
extinguishing any flicker of hope for their return, thus making
themselves more apt at facing all types of danger. They demanded that
each individual pack up enough grub for three months, all milled
accordingly. They pressed the nearby Rauraci, Tulingi and Latobrigi to
sign on to the plan, and after burning down their own towns, join
them. Indeed, they invited the Boii, former Rhineland dwellers, newly
arrived on Norican soil, having laid siege to Noreia, to unite and join
their mission.

1:6

There were two paths. The first was narrow and hard, through the
mountains by the Rhone river between the Sequani. Only one wagon
could pass at a time and the high peak made an easy ambush. The
second, through our Province, was easier with the help of the ford, as
the Rhone flows between the Allobroges and the Helvetii. Geneva's
bridge connects with Helvetii. They had to persuade or force the not so
friendly Allobroges along the way. Before the 28th of March, in the
consulship of Lucius Piso and Aulus Gabinius, they gathered at the
Rhone for the journey.

1:7

Upon hearing of their attempted passage through our Province, Caesar
quickly departs the city for Further Gaul, arriving at Geneva by swift
marches. Having only one legion in Further Gaul, he commands the
Province to provide as many soldiers as possible and dismantles the
bridge at Geneva. When the Helvetii send ambassadors, including
Numeius and Verudoctius, to request passage through the Province
without harm, Caesar, mindful of previous Hostile actions by the
Helvetii, denies their request. To allow time for his ordered soldiers to
arrive, he grants the ambassadors a return date of April 12th to further
deliberate.

1:8

With his legion and soldiers from the Province, Caesar builds a sixteen-
foot wall and trench for nineteen miles from Lake Geneva to Mount
Jura. He sets up garrisons and fortifies redoubts, ready to intercept any
crossing. When the ambassadors return, he denies passage and warns
against violence, holding firm to Roman customs. The Helvetii try to
force a passage by bridge, raft, and ford, but fail against our strong
works and soldiers' attacks.

1:9

One way remained for them, but it was narrow and required the
consent of the Sequani. Their embassadors turned to Dumnorix, who
had sway over the Sequani and a soft spot for the Helvetii. His desire
for power pushed him to help them out. He convinced the Sequani to
let the Helvetii pass through and made sure they promised not to cause
any harm.

1:10

Caesar heard that the Helvetii planned to march into Santones with war on their minds. He knew this would pose a threat to the Province. Thus, he left Titus Labienus in charge of the fortifications and hastily traveled to Italy to raise troops. After collecting two legions, he mobilized three more and crossed the Alps into Further Gaul. Hostile tribes like the Centrones and Graioceli tried to stop him, but he defeated them in battle. Within seven days, he arrived in the Vocontii region of Further Province, having led his army through the territories of the Allobroges and Segusiani, beyond the Rhone.

1:11

The Helvetii marched through the narrow pass and into the Sequani's land, destroying it as they went along. They had now reached the Aedui's territory, where they continued to ravage their fields. The Aedui, unable to defend themselves or their land, came begging for help, citing their past loyalty to the Roman people. Meanwhile, the Ambarri and the Allobroges also approached Caesar for assistance, claiming they had lost everything to the Helvetii. Faced with these pleas for help, Caesar decided not to wait for the Helvetii to destroy more of his allies' property before taking action.

1:12

The Saone, a lazy river, flows through the land of Aedui and Sequani and meets the Rhone. Helvetii crossed it with rafts and boats, moving three parts of their force, but left one behind on this side. Informed by spies, Caesar marched with three legions during the third watch and attacked them with baggage. The Helvetii were not prepared and suffered severe damage; few found refuge in the woods. This canton, Tigurine, was the one who killed Lucius Cassius, the consul, and made his army pass under the yoke. Immortal gods perhaps let the Helvetian state who had brought calamity upon the Roman people to pay the price first. Caesar thus avenged his own personal wrongs too, as Tigurini killed Lucius Piso, his father-in-law's grandfather, in the same war as Cassius.

1:13

Caesar made a bridge across the Saone to reach the Helvetii's remaining forces. They were surprised by this and sent an embassy led by Divico, who warned Caesar that the Roman people should make peace with the Helvetii or face their characteristic valor. He reminded Caesar not to underestimate them due to his surprise attack on one canton, which was not a display of his valor.

1:14

Caesar was not hesitant. He remembered the Helvetian embassadors' circumstances and was angered as the Roman people didn't deserve it. They were deceived because they didn't think they'd done any wrong. Caesar couldn't forget their earlier outrage, nor could he ignore their recent wrongs. The Helvetii boasted about their victory and were amazed that they hadn't been punished yet. But Caesar knew that the gods punish those who do wrong with greater prosperity and longevity, only for consequences to be more severe later. The Helvetii would need to give Caesar hostages and satisfy the Aedui and Allobroges for their past wrongs to make peace. Divico said that the Helvetii were trained to receive, not give hostages.

1:15

On the next day, they moved their camp as did Caesar. He sent his cavalry, numbering four thousand, from all over the Province and from the Aedui and their allies to keep a lookout for the enemy's movements. The Helvetii's cavalry, buoyed by their previous night's victory, attacked our cavalry in a vulnerable location resulting in few casualties. The Helvetii took pride in their victory and started attacking our men from their rear. However, Caesar didn't let his men engage in the fight just yet. He chose to prevent the enemy from causing harm and destruction. For almost two weeks, their van followed the enemy's rear with just five to six miles difference in between.

1:16

Caesar kept asking the Aedui for the promised corn, but they kept delaying it, saying it was being collected on the road. The cold weather had made the corn in the fields and the fodder scarce. Caesar couldn't use the corn he had, as the Helvetii had diverted their march. With the day to serve out the corn fast approaching, Caesar reprimands the Aedui chiefs for not assisting him in such a critical moment. He complains bitterly of being forsaken, especially as he had undertaken the war at their urging.

1:17

Liscus finally spills the beans to Caesar after he hears the man's persuasive words. Liscus admits to Caesar that some powerful folks are convincing the people to withhold the corn they owe, while inciting them with provocative language. They claim that losing to the Gauls is better than being governed by Romans. Liscus warns Caesar that these same people also leak information about their plans to the enemy, making it difficult to keep things under wraps. Despite knowing the danger of his admission, Liscus shares this information with Caesar to help the cause.

1:18

Caesar figured out that Liscus was pointing to Dumnorix with his speech, but he wasn't ready to talk about it in front of everyone. He quickly dismissed the council and kept Liscus to ask him about what he said earlier. When they were alone, Liscus spoke more openly. Caesar also asked others privately and found out that everything Liscus said was true. Dumnorix was a daring man who was well-liked by the people for his generosity. He wanted a revolution and had been making money for years by bidding low on taxes that no one dared to compete with him. He had lots of cavalry at his disposal, and he was influential not only at home but in neighboring states. He was connected to the Helvetii and hated Caesar and the Romans. Caesar also learned that Dumnorix had led the cavalry that fled in the recent failed engagement - a revelation that dismayed the other cavalry.

1:19

Julius Caesar heard the rumors, and the proof was clear. Dumnorix, without orders from Caesar or his own state, had led the Helvetii through Sequani land and arranged for hostages. The Aedui's magistrate reprimanded him, and Caesar had reason to punish him. But he also valued Dumnorix's brother, Divitiacus, who was faithful and just. Caesar consulted with Divitiacus and asked him to judge his brother's case without causing offense.

1:20

Divitiacus grabbed hold of Caesar, tears in his eyes, pleading with him not to inflict harsh punishment upon his brother. He admitted the charges were true and that Dumnorix had caused him much pain. Caesar reassured him that he held him in high regard and forgave Dumnorix at his request. Dumnorix was warned to avoid suspicion, but Caesar set spies on him to keep watch.

1:21

On the very same day, Caesar's scouts informed him that the enemy had set up camp at the base of a mountain, eight miles from his own camp. He dispatched a team to investigate the mountain's characteristics and potential paths up the slopes. The scouts returned with news that the ascent was simple. By the third watch, Caesar commanded his praetorian lieutenant, Titus Labienus, to lead two legions up to the mountain's peak, guided by those who had examined the terrain. Caesar explained his strategy, then rushed to meet them on the same path the enemy had taken and sent the cavalry ahead of him. The experienced military man, Publius Considius, who had served under Lucius Sulla and Marcus Crassus, was sent forward with scouts.

1:22

As the sun crept up the mountainside, Titus Labienus held the summit and Caesar's army was a mere mile and a half from the enemy camp. Unbeknownst to our men, Considius charged towards them on horseback, claiming the mountain was already swarmed with Gallic arms and ensigns. Caesar swiftly led his troops to the next hill and set them up in battle formation. Labienus, following orders not to engage the enemy until Caesar's army was present, held back and waited for our warriors to arrive. After a long day of waiting, spies reported that the mountain was secure and that our enemy had moved camp. It was revealed that Considius had been gripped by fear and falsely reported the enemy's position. Caesar kept his distance and followed them, finally setting up camp three miles away.

1:23

The day after, with only two days left until he had to distribute corn to his troops, and being just eighteen miles from Bibracte, the largest and most stocked town of the Aedui, Caesar diverted his path to secure a good supply. Word of this change of direction was betrayed to the enemy by some Gallic horsemen who deserted Lucius Aemilius. The Helvetii, perhaps under the impression that the Romans were retreating or that they could be cut off from provisions, altered their course and pursued Caesar's army from behind.

1:24

Caesar sees the enemy coming and retreats to the next hill. He sends his cavalry to fend off the attack while he positions his four tried-and-true legions in a triple line in the middle of the hill. On top of the summit, he places his two newly raised legions from Hither Gaul and his auxiliaries. He orders his men to cover the entire mountain and protect the baggage with those in the top line. The Helvetii bring all their wagons to one place, and they form a tight phalanx as they advance on our front line after defeating our cavalry.

1:25

Caesar hid his own horse and those of his men to make the danger
equal and discourage any thoughts of escape. He then led his soldiers
into battle, easily breaking the enemy's phalanx with their javelins. The
Gauls were hindered by their bucklers pierced by Roman javelins,
which left them entangled and unprotected. After a long fight, they
gave way and retreated to a nearby mountain. The Boii and Tulingi
attacked the exposed flank of the Romans, causing the Helvetii to
renew the battle. The Romans faced their enemies in three divisions,
ready to take on those defeated and those just arriving.

1:26

The fight was long and tough, with no clear winner. One enemy
division headed for the mountains while the other went to their
wagons. They used the wagons as a shield to throw weapons at our
men. Even though no one turned their backs, the battle continued into
the night. Our men eventually took control of the enemy's camp and
captured Orgetorix's daughter and son. The enemy marched non-stop
throughout the night, reaching Lingones' territory on the fourth day.
Our men had to take a three-day break due to injuries and burials.
Caesar ordered the Lingones not to help the enemy or face the same
consequences as the Helvetii. After the break, Caesar and his forces
pursued the enemy.

1:27

The Helvetii, in dire straits, sent envoys to him seeking surrender. They
met him on the way, begged and wept for peace. Caesar told them to
stay put until he arrived. He then demanded hostages, weapons, and
runaway slaves. While rounding up these items the next day, 6000
Verbigene men, either scared or hopeful, slipped away in the night
towards the Rhine and Germany.

1:28

Caesar found out and ordered those who aided the Helvetii to bring them back before him as enemies. Others were allowed to surrender, as long as they gave up hostages, weapons, and deserters. The Helvetii, Tulingi, and Latobrigi were sent back to their own lands, but with nothing to eat. To prevent the Germans from taking over these lands, Caesar ordered the Allobroges to give the Helvetii plenty of food and rebuild their destroyed towns. The Aedui asked to settle the Boii in their territory since they were brave, and they were given freedom and the same rights as the Aedui.

1:29

Greek lists found in the Helvetii camp, detailing the numbers of men, women, boys, and the elderly. The figures were staggering: 368,000. But only 92,000 men could fight for their survival. Caesar ordered a census and when the count was taken, only 110,000 returned home.

1:30

After beating the Helvetii, ambassadors from all parts of Gaul, including the state leaders, gathered to congratulate Caesar. They acknowledged that while he may have sought revenge for Rome's past grievances, Gaul benefited from the outcome as well. The Helvetii intended to conquer all of Gaul and enslave its people, choosing the most fruitful lands for their own use. With Caesar's blessing, they asked to convene a general assembly to address some important matters. They swore to keep the meeting confidential, sharing information only with those the assembly selected.

After the assembly disbanded, the chiefs returned to Caesar and asked for a private meeting about their safety. They begged for their conversation to be kept secret, as they feared torture would follow any disclosure. Divitiacus the Aeduan spoke and said that there were two parties in Gaul, and the Germans were called in by the Arverni and Sequani. More were brought over, and now there were 120,000 of them in Gaul, causing conflict with the Aedui. After a great calamity and being forced to give hostages to the Sequani, Divitiacus fled to Rome to seek aid. A king of the Germans, Ariovistus, had taken the territory of the Sequani and ordered them to depart, with the threat of all Germans crossing the Rhine. The Gauls could not compare to the Germans in land or living habits.

1:32

After Divitiacus spoke, the people cried out for Caesar's help. But the Sequani just stared at the ground, saying nothing. Caesar asked them why they were silent, but they remained sad and still. Finally, Divitiacus spoke again, explaining that the Sequani were too afraid to speak out against Ariovistus, even in secret. They had let him into their land, and now he had all their towns under his control. The Sequani were in a worse situation than any other group, and they couldn't even run away.

1:33

Upon receiving these reports, Caesar lifted the spirits of the Gauls with his words, promising that he would address this issue with hopes that Ariovistus would put an end to the oppression. He dismissed the assembly and pondered the situation, realizing that this must be dealt with as the Germans posed a threat to the Roman people. He knew wild men would not be likely to restrain themselves, and Ariovistus had grown unbearable. It was evident that action needed to be taken quickly to prevent further danger.

1:34

Caesar decided to send people to Ariovistus for a talk. He said it was important and official. Ariovistus refused, saying that he wouldn't come to Caesar if he needed anything, so Caesar had to come to him. Also, he didn't want to risk traveling without an army. He also thought it was weird that Caesar and the Romans wanted anything to do with his land that he won in a fight.

1:35

Caesar sent ambassadors with a message for the man who had been treated with kindness by Rome. The message was simple, advising the man not to cross the Rhine into Gaul anymore, to restore the hostages he had taken, and to stop attacking Rome's allies. If he followed through, Rome would consider him a friend. If not, Caesar would make sure Rome's interests were protected.

1:36

Responding as Hemingway might:

Ariovistus said they had the right of war, to govern those they conquered as they see fit. Romans also ruled conquered nations with their own discretion. The Aedui, defeated in war, became tributaries to him. Caesar arriving made this less valuable. Ariovistus won't restore Aedui hostages but won't make war if tribute is paid annually. No one ever challenged him without being ruined. Caesar could try, but well-trained Germans who had not been indoors for 14 years would show their valor.

1:37

The message arrived for Caesar, and with it, embassadors from the Aedui and Treviri. The Aedui complained of the Harudes who were ravaging their land and Ariovistus, who refused their hostages for peace. Meanwhile, the Treviri reported a hundred cantons of the Suevi attempting to cross the Rhine, led by Nasuas and Cimberius. Caesar feared the reunion of Ariovistus and this new band, and quickly gathered supplies to march against him.

1:38

Caesar traveled for three days when he got word that Ariovistus was advancing to Vesontio, the biggest town of the Sequani. Vesontio had everything that could be used in war, and its location was good enough to keep the war going. With the Doubs river surrounding the town and a tall mountain almost covering the remaining space, Vesontio was easy to defend. Caesar marched day and night and took control of the town, stationing his army there, which made it the perfect stronghold.

1:39

As Caesar lingered in Vesontio, waiting for provisions, rumors of the fierce and mighty German warriors spread among the troops. Panic set in, even among experienced soldiers and leaders, some of whom begged to leave. This cowardice infected the camp, with even the brave talking of the dangers of the narrow roads and vast forests. Some warned Caesar that the soldiers were too scared to move forward. Tears were shed and wills were sealed. The enemy was not the cause of their fear, but their own trembling hearts.

1:40

Caesar saw what was happening and gathered the centurions for a council. He scolded them for questioning their direction and purpose. Ariovistus had been friends with the Romans, so why would he suddenly turn on them? Even if he did, Caesar knew his soldiers were brave and had defeated formidable enemies before. The Gauls were beaten by Ariovistus only because he tricked them, not because he was strong. Caesar planned to leave that night with the tenth legion but hoped others would follow. He trusted this legion because they were brave and loyal.

1:41

After his speech, all the soldiers felt the fire to fight burning within them. The tenth legion was the first to thank him for his confidence in them. The others made excuses, but Caesar forgave them. Divitiacus led them on a safer route, and after seven days of marching, scouts spotted Ariovistus' army only twenty four miles away.

1:42

Ariovistus sends messengers to Caesar inviting him to talk. Caesar
didn't refuse and thought Ariovistus had come to his senses. They
agreed to meet on the fifth day. But Ariovistus demanded that Caesar
didn't bring any foot-soldier with him, only cavalry. Caesar didn't trust
Ariovistus and decided to take away all the horses from the Gallic
cavalry and let the legionary soldiers ride them, just in case. One of the
soldiers joked that Caesar did more than he promised.

1:43

On a plain stood a mound, far enough from both sides. Caesar and
Ariovistus agreed to meet there. Caesar positioned his cavalry and
legions on one side, and Ariovistus placed his cavalry on the other.
Ariovistus requested to speak on horseback with 10 men beside him.
Caesar began by reminding him of the kindness and gifts he had
received from the Roman senate, for which he had not earned. He also
mentioned the longstanding relationship between the Romans and the
Aedui, Gaul's dominant tribe. Caesar demanded that Ariovistus stop
his attacks on the Aedui and their allies, give back the hostages, and
keep his troops from crossing the Rhine.

1:44

Ariovistus answered Caesar's demands, boasting of his own virtues. He
claimed that he had settled in Gaul at the invitation of the Gauls, and
that he had only taken tribute as was customary for conquerors. He
also argued that he was protecting himself, not attacking Gaul.
Ariovistus warned Caesar that keeping his army in Gaul could lead to
suspicion, and that he must either depart or be seen as a foe. In fact,
many of the nobles and leading men of the Roman people would
welcome Caesar's death. However, if Caesar were to depart and
relinquish control of Gaul to Ariovistus, he would be rewarded greatly
and the wars would end peacefully.

1:45

Caesar said many things to show why he couldn't abandon his allies or give up Gaul to Ariovistus. The Romans had won their sovereignty in Gaul through war and had pardoned the Arverni and the Ruteni, not imposing tribute on them. According to Caesar, the Romans had a just claim to Gaul, but if the Senate's decree was to be followed, then Gaul should be free.

1:46

Caesar heard Ariovistus' cavalry was getting closer, throwing rocks at Caesar's men. He stopped talking and went to his soldiers, telling them not to fight back. Although Caesar's legion could handle the cavalry, he didn't want to appear sneaky after the conference. The common soldiers were angry at Ariovistus' arrogance and attack, so they were ready to fight.

1:47

Ariovistus sent his people to Caesar to ask for a conference, but Caesar saw no reason for it. The Germans had been violent the day before, so it was not safe to send one of his own officers. Instead, he sent a brave young man who knew the Gallic language and was unlikely to inspire violence. Ariovistus, however, accused the men of being spies and put them into chains.

1:48

He moved camp towards a hill and set up six miles from Caesar. The following day he marched past Caesar's camp and camped two miles farther from him. This was to cut off Caesar from his supplies. Caesar drew out his forces in battle order for five days in a row, hoping to provoke Ariovistus to engage. But Ariovistus kept his army in camp and only allowed cavalry skirmishes. The Germans had a unique battle method with 6,000 horse and active foot, where each horse selected a foot soldier for protection. In battle, the horse and foot worked together, and they were swift enough to keep pace with the horses.

1:49

Ariovistus kept himself cooped up in the camp. So Caesar selected a spot beyond the German encampment to pitch his own, about 600 paces away. He lined up his troops in three rows and set out to the position. The first two rows must be ready, the third to build the fortifications. Ariovistus dispatched a light troop battalion, plus all of his riders, to deter our boys and impede the fortification work. But as planned, Caesar directed two rows to drive off the enemy and the third to finish the job. The camp fortified, he left two legions and some of the resources behind and marched the rest of the four legions back into the larger camp.

1:50

The next day, Caesar did as usual and led his troops out from both camps. He positioned his troops a little further from the bigger camp, offering the enemy a chance to fight. But seeing that they didn't show up, he returned his army to the camp at noon. Only then, Ariovistus decided to send some of his men to attack the smaller camp, and the fierce battle dragged on until evening. Many wounds were dealt and taken on both sides until the sunset, and then Ariovistus retreated to his camp. Caesar questioned his prisoners about why Ariovistus didn't engage, and he learned that among the Germans, their matrons used lots and divination to determine if they should fight or not. The matrons had said, "the Germans would not win if they engaged in battle before the new moon."

1:51

The next day, Caesar left a guard to protect both camps and gathered his auxiliary troops before the smaller camp to bolster his appearance of strength against the enemy. In three lines, he advanced towards the enemy camp. The Germans were forced to draw their forces out, dividing themselves into equal groups with their chariots and wagons surrounding them. Women, in tears and with disheveled hair, begged the soldiers not to deliver them into Roman slavery as they went into battle.

1:52

Caesar made lieutenants and questors for each legion so they could see the bravery of his soldiers. He led the battle on the right wing, where the enemy was weakest. Our men attacked with javelins, but the enemy quickly closed in for hand-to-hand combat. The Germans formed a phalanx, and our soldiers leaped on top to attack from above. Though the left wing of the enemy fled, their large numbers still pressed on our men from the right. P. Crassus, commanding the cavalry, sent the third line to help our struggling soldiers.

1:53

The fight continued and the enemy fled all the way to the Rhine, over fifty miles away. Some were able to swim across or find a boat, but Ariovistus, with his two wives and daughters, was not so lucky. Our horse chased and killed the rest of them. Luckily, Caesar found C. Valerius Procillus, his friend, and rescued him from the enemy's grasp. Procillus was almost killed three times by the enemy, but luck was on his side. Another soldier, M. Mettius, was also found and brought back to Caesar.

1:54

A battle was reported across the Rhine. The Suevi retreated home, but the Ubii chased and killed many of them. Caesar finished two big wars in one campaign and took his army to winter quarters early. Labienus was in charge of the quarters while Caesar went to Hither Gaul for court.

✦✦✦

GALLIC WARS BOOK 2 (57 B.C.E.)

As the epic tale of conquest and valor continues in the Gallic Wars Book 2, Julius Caesar turns his gaze to the fierce and resourceful tribes of the Belgae, setting the stage for another year of relentless campaigning in 57 BCE. Building upon the foundations laid in the first book, Caesar's narrative shifts to chronicle the ever-evolving challenges, strategies, and alliances that marked this next phase of the Roman conquest of Gaul.

The second book of the Gallic Wars not only expands upon the military exploits of Caesar and his legions but also offers a deeper understanding of the Gallic peoples, their culture, and their way of life. Through the lens of Caesar's narrative, we witness firsthand the trials and tribulations of a society grappling with the reality of Roman domination and the loss of their ancestral lands and traditions.

As you embark on this enthralling journey through the pages of Gallic Wars Book 2, prepare to be captivated by the timeless tale of ambition, courage, and resilience that lies at the heart of Caesar's conquests and the indelible mark they left on the course of history.

2:1

While Caesar was in Hither Gaul during winter, he received reports and letters from Labienus. They informed him that the Belgae, who constituted one-third of Gaul, were banding together against the Romans. The reasons behind this alliance were twofold: they feared that after Gaul was subdued, the Romans would turn their attention towards them, and some were influenced by various Gauls. Additionally, certain Belgae saw an opportunity for a power shift as it was more difficult to take control under Roman rule.

2:2

Caesar got worried and raised new legions in Hither Gaul after hearing bad news. He sent his lieutenant, Q. Pedius, to lead them into Gaul before joining the army himself in summer. He commissioned the local Gauls to keep an eye on what the Belgae were up to. They reported that an army was gathering in one place. So, Caesar decided to move toward the Belgae without hesitation, prepared with supplies. After about 15 days, they arrived in the territories of the Belgae.

2:3

Unexpectedly and ahead of schedule, the Remi, closest to Gaul of the Belgae, dispatched Iccius and Antebrogius to surrender themselves and their land to Rome's protection. They had not joined the other Belgae or conspired against Rome, would provide hostages, obey commands, offer their towns, and give aid. All other Belgae bore arms, even the Suessiones, brothers with the same rights, laws, government, and magistrates. The Germans on this side of the Rhine had also joined them. The folly of their unification knew no bounds.

2:4

When Caesar asked about who was fighting and what they were capable of, he was told this: the Belgae came from German lineage, settled in the fertile land across the Rhine, and drove out the Gauls to maintain their territory. They were the only ones who stopped the Teutones and Cimbri from entering their land, making them very proud and skilled in war. The Remi, their neighbors and allies, knew the exact number of fighters promised from each Belgae state for the war. The most powerful of them were the Bellovaci, with 100,000 fighters and 60,000 chosen for battle. They wanted to lead the whole war. The Suessiones were also ready to fight, as were the Nervii and the Atrebates.

Their closest neighbors were plentiful and prospering. Divitiacus, once the most powerful man in Gaul and Britain, reined over the land in the memory of many. Now Galba led the charge with the approval of all who trusted his good sense and unblemished character. Twelve towns promise an army of 50,000. The Nervii, Atrebates, Ambiani, Morini, Menapii, Caleti, Velocasses, and Veromandui will double that number. The Germanic Condrusi, Eburones, Caeraesi and Paemani could bring 40,000 to the battlefield.

2:5

Caesar talked nice to the Remi and then had the whole senate come to him. He wanted the chief men's kids as hostages and they gave them up. He told Divitiacus from Aeduan that they needed to split up the enemy forces. He wanted the Aedui to go mess up the Bellovaci's place. Then the Belgae forces got close, so Caesar moved his army over the river and set up camp. He made a big wall and trench, and left Q. Titurius Sabinus with some cohorts on the other side of the river.

2:6

The town of Remi, named Bibrax, was attacked fiercely by the Belgae eight miles from our camp. The siege was sustained with difficulty that day. Gauls besiege like Belgae, by drawing men around the fortifications and throwing stones at the walls. They then form a testudo, advance to the gates, and undermine the wall. On this occasion, it was easy to do so as the defenders lacked sufficient strength after stones and darts were thrown. Iccius, commander of the town and one of the Remi, sends messengers to Caesar at night, seeking assistance as he cannot hold out any longer. Iccius is a man of high rank and among those who came to Caesar as an ambassador for peace.

2:7

At midnight, Caesar led armed Numidian, Cretan archers, and Balearian slingers, guided by the same messengers from Iccius, to help the Remi townspeople. Their arrival infused the Remi with a desire to resist and defend their town, causing the enemy to abandon their hope of taking it. Upon burning any nearby villages and buildings, the enemy camped close to Caesar's camp, extending more than eight miles in breadth with fires and smoke.

2:8

Caesar considered refusing battle with the enemy due to their superior numbers and valor. However, through frequent cavalry actions, he discovered that his men were just as capable. Taking advantage of the natural terrain, he created a cross trench and forts on either side of the hill where his camp was, equipping them with military engines to guard against a flank attack. Leaving two legions as a reserve, he arranged the other six in battle formation in front of the camp. The enemy also brought out their forces from their camp.

2:9

A marsh stood between us and the enemy, both of us itching for a fight. Our cavalry clashed in the meantime, but neither side made a move to cross the marsh. Seeing our horses had the upper hand, Caesar led our army back to camp. The enemy quickly fled to the Aisne River and tried to ford it. Their plan was simple: storm Q. Titurius' fort and cut off the bridge, or failing that, destroy the lands of the Remi and stop our men from foraging.

2:10

Titurius warns Caesar, who rallies his cavalry, Numidians, slingers and archers, and charges towards the enemy. A fierce battle ensues, with our men attacking the disordered foe in the river and cutting down many of them. The enemy, overwhelmed by our missile barrage, attempt to cross the river, but are surrounded and slaughtered by Caesar's cavalry. Realizing that their plan to take the town and cross the river has failed, the enemy decides to return to their respective countries and gather forces to defend against the Roman invasion. They are also motivated by the need to protect their own provisions and territories, as they learn of the approaching Aedui. Despite attempts to convince them to stay, they leave to aid their own people.

2:11

They marched out of their camp at night, with much clamor and disarray. No one gave commands or followed any order; each man sought his own spot at the front, hoping to reach home quickly. Caesar feared an ambush, so he kept his troops in the camp, waiting for more information. When scouts confirmed that the enemy was indeed retreating, Caesar sent out his cavalry to pursue them. Three legions followed closely behind, attacking the rear and killing many. The enemy at the front broke rank and ran, while those in the back bravely defended themselves. Our men killed many until nightfall, then returned to camp.

2:12

The day after, without pause, Caesar marched his army to the Suessiones, a neighboring tribe. Their town, Noviodunum, was his target. He tried to take it by storm but failed. His camp fortified, he prepared for a siege. Meanwhile, the Suessiones regrouped and returned to the town. The Romans built mounds and towers with such precision and speed that the Gauls surrendered upon witnessing the magnitude of their works. All thanks to the persuasion of the Remi who asked Caesar to spare the Suessiones.

2:13

Caesar got hostages and weapons, made Suessiones surrender, and fought against the Bellovaci. They went into Galled Bratuspantium while Caesar was a bit away. Old men came out and said they wanted protection, and the town surrendered. Women and boys also asked for peace.

2:14

Divitiacus begged for mercy. He explained how the Bellovaci, who had always been friends with the Aedui, turned against them and declared war on Rome. The Bellovaci were urged by their leaders, who fled to Britain after realizing the damage they caused. The Aedui and the Belgae begged Caesar to show kindness to the Bellovaci. If he did, the Aedui would gain more influence among the Belgae who had always aided them in times of war.

2:15

Caesar respected Divitiacus and the Aeduans. To spare them, he took them under his protection. The Belgae had a large influence and population, so he demanded 600 hostages. After they surrendered and gave up their weapons, he moved on to the Ambiani's territory, who surrendered without hesitation. The Nervii were adjacent to their land. Caesar asked about their customs and learned that they were wild, brave, and rejected luxury items like wine that weaken the spirit. They berated other Belgae who gave up their independence to Rome and refused to accept any peace conditions or send messengers.

2:16

After three days' march through their land, prisoners revealed to him that the river Sambre lay just ten miles from his camp. The Nervii, Atrebates, and Veromandui, joined forces, waiting for the Romans on the other side of that river. They convinced both of their neighbors to go to war with them. Aduatuci's army was on the way to their aid. They secured their women and the elderly, useless for war, in a place surrounded by marshes, out of any army's reach.

2:17

After figuring out some things, he sends out soldiers to find a good spot for the camp. A bunch of Belgians and other Gauls follow him too. They saw how the army marched and told the Nervii. They said it would be easy to attack the first legion when they were dealing with baggage. Then, the other legions would be too scared to fight. The Nervii don't have good cavalry, so they made hedges out of trees and thorns a long time ago. It was like a wall that nobody could get through. The Nervii believed the advice was good since it would be hard for our army to get past those hedge-walls anyway.

2:18

Our men's camp was set upon an even hill, sloping down to the Sambre river. Across the water, a similar hill rose up, heavily wooded in the upper part, rendering the view of the innermost part a mystery. The foe was tucked away in the woods, but a handful of horse soldiers bravely paraded along the open ground beside the stream. The river was shallow, approximately three feet deep.

2:19

Caesar sent his cavalry ahead, then followed with his forces, marching differently than the Belgae had claimed. His vanguard was six legions without baggage, followed by the baggage train, and lastly, two legions protected the rear. The enemy's horse attacked ours, retreating into the woods only to come back out and strike us again. While this happened, the six legions constructed a fortified camp. Once the Nervii saw our baggage train, they charged at our horses, causing them to scatter. The Nervii approached quickly, seeming to emerge from the woods, the river, and our location at once - and stormed our camp.

2:20

Caesar had it all to do at once. He had to show the standard, which means get ready to fight. He had to signal with the trumpet and call in the soldiers from their work. They had been gathering materials for the rampart. He had to organize the battle and give the soldiers a pep talk. He also had to give them a secret word to use. But time was short, and the enemy was coming. Luckily, Caesar had trained his soldiers well, and they knew what to do without being told. Also, Caesar had ordered his lieutenants to stay put until the camp was fortified. They didn't wait for Caesar's permission and did what they thought was best.

2:21

Caesar gave orders and hurried around, wherever fate led him, to inspire the troops. He came upon the tenth legion and encouraged them briefly, reminding them to remember their courage and stand strong in the face of the enemy's assault. When the enemy was only a short distance away, he signaled for battle to begin. As he went to encourage another group, he found them already fighting. The enemy was so determined to fight and time was so short that soldiers didn't have time to put on proper gear or even show their proper insignia. They fought where they were and stood with whatever group they found first, not wanting to waste any time in seeking out their own company.

2:22

The troops were positioned haphazardly on the sloping terrain, more out of necessity than strategy. Legions fought the enemy from different angles, obscured by thick hedges. There were no reserves or centralized commands, and chaos reigned. As a result, fortune played a significant role in the unpredictable outcome.

2:23

The ninth and tenth legions swiftly drove the Atrebates into the river, relentless in their pursuit despite the obstacles. Though they found themselves in a disadvantageous position, they still emerged victorious, putting their enemies to flight once more. Meanwhile, the eleventh and eighth legions fought from a position of strength, perched on the banks of the river. But the Nervii, under the command of Boduognatus, saw an opening and took it, surrounding the exposed legions and attacking from all sides.

2:24

Our horsemen and light-armed infantry were with those who were routed by the enemy's first assault. They tried to escape into the camp, but they met the enemy face to face and sought flight in another quarter. The camp-followers, who had seen our men pass the river as victors, panicked and fled when they saw the enemy parading in our camp. Meanwhile, the baggage train arrived with cries of alarm, and they, too, scattered in every direction. All of these circumstances caused the cavalry of the Treviri, renowned for their courage among the Gauls, to become distressed. They saw our camp filled with a large number of the enemy and the legions hard pressed and surrounded. Realizing that our situation was dire, they fled and reported to their state that the Romans were defeated and conquered, and the enemy was in possession of our camp and baggage-train.

2:25

Caesar left the tenth legion and went to the right wing. There, he saw
his men were struggling, and the twelfth legion's standards were
causing trouble with the crowded army. Many centurions had died or
were wounded, and some soldiers were retreating. The enemy was still
advancing, but Caesar could not find any reserves. He took a shield and
told the soldiers to keep fighting. This gave the soldiers hope, and they
fought harder. The enemy's advance slowed down.

2:26

Caesar saw the seventh legion struggling and ordered the tribunes to
unite the legions and attack the enemy from two sides. With
reinforcements, the soldiers gained courage and fought bravely.
Meanwhile, the two legions guarding the baggage-train rushed to help,
and Labienus sent the tenth legion to assist as well. They acted fast
upon hearing of the danger and did everything they could to help the
camp, the legion, and the commander.

2:27

Their arrival changed everything, inspiring even the wounded to
continue fighting. The unarmed camp-retainers attacked the dismayed
enemy, while the horsemen tried to make up for their previous flight.
Though the enemy fought fiercely and bravely, using fallen warriors as
makeshift shields, they were eventually overthrown. Even as they fell,
however, they continued to fight, using their bodies as mounds to
launch weapons from. These were men of great courage who did not
make the reckless decision to cross a broad river and climb high banks
without reason; their valor made the difficult seem easy.

2:28

The Nervii were almost annihilated after the battle, their old men and
women hiding in fenny places and marshes. When they learned that
Caesar's army was unstoppable, they surrendered themselves to him.
They told Caesar that their senators were reduced from 600 to three
and only 500 were fit to fight. Caesar spared the remaining inhabitants
and ordered their neighbors not to harm them.

2:29

The Aduatuci marched to help the Nervii but turned back when they heard of their defeat. They left everything and took their possessions to a town fortified by nature. The town was surrounded by high rocks and steep cliffs except for a small, gently sloping area that was fortified with two walls, heavy stones, and sharpened stakes. They were descendants of the Cimbri and Teutones who left 6,000 men to guard their belongings. After their countrymen were destroyed and they were harassed by their neighbors, they made peace and settled in this place.

2:30

Upon our arrival, the enemy made small attacks on us. They kept themselves within the town when we enclosed them with a twelve-foot rampart in a circuit of fifteen miles. As we built a tower, they mocked and insulted us, questioning the purpose of such a construction and how puny Romans could handle its weight. Their taunts referred to our small stature, something they often mocked about us.

2:31

The sight of the moving machine approaching their walls startled them, prompting them to seek peace with Caesar. They conceded that the Romans had divine aid to move such contraptions and fight from close quarters. They surrendered themselves and their possessions to him, but begged that they be allowed to keep their arms. It was better to face any fate from the Romans than to be tortured by their jealous enemies whom they once ruled.

2:32

Caesar answered them and said that he had a habit of sparing the state rather than rewarding them for their bravery. If they surrendered themselves before the battering-ram touched the wall, they could be spared. However, he made it clear that they could only surrender if they handed over their arms. Caesar promised to treat them the same way he treated the Nervii and ordered their neighbors not to harm those who surrendered to the Romans. The townspeople agreed to follow his orders. They threw their arms from the wall into the trench before the town. The heaps of arms almost reached the top of the wall and rampart. However, they secretly kept about a third of their arms hidden in the town. They opened the gates and peacefully enjoyed the day.

2:33

Caesar shut the gates and sent the soldiers out of the town at night to protect the townspeople. The Aduatuci made a surprise attack with concealed weapons and bark shields, hoping to take advantage of the lowered guard. The Romans fought fiercely, defending their ramparts and towers against the desperate enemy. Despite being outnumbered, the Romans prevailed, forcing the remaining Aduatuci back into the town after causing 4,000 casualties. The next day, Caesar entered the town and took all the spoils, selling 53,000 people as slaves.

2:34

He heard from P. Crassus, who had commanded a legion against the coastal Veneti, Unelli, Osismii, Curiosolitae, Sesuvii, Aulerci and Rhedones, that they now submitted to Rome.

2:35

When Caesar subdued all of Gaul and barbarians were impressed, sending messengers to make peace treaties and pledges to him, he ordered them to return in the next summer. After leading his legions to winter quarters near his battle regions in Carnutes, Andes, and Turones, he departed for Italy. Upon receiving Caesar's letter, a fifteen-day thanksgiving was given to honor his achievements; a first of its kind.

✦✦✦

GALLIC WARS BOOK 3 (56 B.C.E.)

As the saga of Caesar's conquests continues in the enthralling Gallic Wars Book 3, the narrative shifts to the year 56 BCE, bringing new challenges and adversaries to the forefront. In this riveting account, Caesar expands his campaign further into Gaul, navigating the intricacies of tribal politics, military strategy, and diplomacy to secure Roman dominance in the region.

In this installment, readers are transported to the heart of Caesar's strategic operations, witnessing firsthand the relentless determination and martial prowess of the Roman legions as they confront an array of formidable foes. As the narrative unfolds, we are introduced to the diverse tribes and landscapes of Gaul, offering a rich and nuanced understanding of the people and places forever altered by the march of the Roman army.

3:1

Caesar sent Galba with his men to open the dangerous passage through the Alps, where Roman merchants usually travel. Galba fought hard and successfully against the Nantuates, Veragri, and Seduni. After receiving embassadors from all the parts and taking hostages, he decided to station his two cohorts among the Nantuates while wintering in Veragri. The village is located in a valley bounded by high mountains, consisting of two parts to be divided between the Gauls and cohorts. The cohorts settled in the unoccupied village part, which Galba fortified with a rampart and a ditch.

3:2

In winter quarters, after days had passed and corn was brought in, Caesar received word from his scouts that the Gauls had abandoned the town he left to them and were joined by a large Seduni and Veragri force in the mountains. The Gauls plotted to start another war and take down Caesar's legion because they underestimated the small number of soldiers and thought they were vulnerable due to absence and detachment of cohorts.

Despite their initial assault from the mountains and their anger over their children being taken as hostages, the Romans were unable to maintain their position due to the disadvantageous terrain. The Gauls believed that the Romans sought to claim control over the nearby province and the mountain peaks, perpetually securing their grasp on the area.

3:3

Upon receiving the message, Galba had a crisis on his hands. The winter-quarters and fortifications were not ready for war, and they didn't have enough food. He was caught off-guard, and he knew that he faced serious trouble. Galba called a meeting of his leaders, and everyone was nervous. They were surrounded by an army of armed men, and they couldn't get supplies or reinforcements. Some of the leaders advised leaving everything behind and retreating. Others thought it was better to stay and fight until the last, even though they didn't have much hope.

3:4

In quick time, the foe charged upon us, raining stones and arrows upon our fortification. Our warriors resisted valiantly, hurling their own weapons with accuracy from their elevated position. Whenever a weak point was identified, our soldiers rushed to its defense, offering aid. Yet they were outnumbered, unable to leave the battlefield when fatigued or injured, unlike their opponents who continuously rotated fresh troops.

3:5

After six long hours of nonstop fighting, our men were spent, with no strength left and dwindling weapons. The enemy, pressing on harder, was breaking through our rampart and filling up our trench. Our men were on the brink and saw no way out. But P. Sextius Baculus, a brave but wounded centurion, and C. Volusenus, a skilled and valiant soldier, came to Galba with a last-ditch plan: a sally. Galba quickly gathered his centurions and ordered the soldiers to rest and collect weapons before launching a desperate charge from the camp. They put all their hope in their own courage.

3:6

They followed orders and charged from every gate. The enemy didn't know what hit them. Surrounding the barbarians, they killed more than a third of a 30,000-strong army. The rest fled in a panic, with no chance to regroup. Our men didn't give them a moment's rest. With the enemy vanquished and stripped of their weapons, Galba made a wise decision to not risk his men's lives again. He burned the village as punishment and returned to the province with the legion, encountering no resistance. Winter settled in, and they made camp with the Nantuates and then the Allobroges.

Caesar thought the war in Gaul was over after defeating the Belgae, expelling the Germans, and defeating the Seduni. He decided to visit Illyricum in the winter to gain knowledge of their countries. However, a sudden war erupted when P. Crassus and the seventh legion needed more corn and provision in the Andes. Several officers of cavalry and military tribunes were sent out among the neighbouring states including T. Terrasidius to the Esubii, M. Trebius Gallus to the Curiosolitae, Q. Velanius and T. Silius to the Veneti.

3:8

This state's got the most sway on the sea coast, no doubt. They're called the Veneti, and they're the best sailors around. They know these waters like the back of their hand. They've got a ton of ships, too - more than anyone else. And since there aren't many ports on this wild and windy coast, they've got all the other traders tributary to 'em. It all started with Silius and Velanius, who these guys took hostage, hoping to get their own hostages back from Crassus. Then the other nearby tribes followed suit - these Gauls don't mess around. They made a pact, agreed to only act together, and reached out to other states, saying they'd rather stay free like their ancestors than become Roman slaves. And pretty soon, all the coastal tribes were in on the plan. They sent a message to P. Crassus, telling him to give up their hostages if he ever wanted to see his officers again.

3:9

Crassus tells Caesar of the situation. Caesar builds war ships on the Loire River and gets rowers, sailors, and pilots. He heads to the army when the season permits. The Veneti and other states know of his arrival and prepare for war since they detained the embassadors. They rely on their navy since they know the land passes are cut off, the sea approach is difficult, and the Romans don't know the area. They fortify towns, get corn and allies, and call for auxiliaries from Britain.

3:10

Caesar faced difficulties in waging war, yet he was compelled to do so by the insult to the state, rebellions, and confederacies formed by multiple states. He knew that ignoring these actions would set a precedent for other nations to follow. The Gauls were always eager to revolt, and freedom was a universal human desire. He decided to distribute his army in order to prevent more states from joining the confederation.

3:11

Thus, Caesar sends Labienus and his cavalry to the Treviri near the Rhine to prevent Germans summoned by the Belgae from crossing the river. Crassus heads to Aquitania with twelve cohorts and cavalry to prevent auxiliaries from joining the fray. Titurius Sabinus is sent with three legions to keep separate the Unelli, Curiosolitae, and Lexovii, while Brutus is put in charge of the fleet and directs it towards the Veneti. Caesar rushes with land forces to join the fray.

3:12

Their towns were tricky to conquer. Built on jutting land, they were cut off when the unforgiving tide rolled in or ebbed out, rendering approach impossible. Even when we excluded the sea with mounds and dams, those sly Veneti would abscond with their property and defend themselves elsewhere. Our powerful works could only do so much as their ships vastly outnumbered ours, all while storms and the vast open sea made navigation exceedingly difficult.

3:13

Their ships were strong and sturdy, built of oak to endure any force. The keels were flat, allowing them to navigate shallow waters, and the prows and sterns were designed to withstand the ocean's powerful currents. Instead of sails, they used treated animal skins, and their anchors were secured with iron chains. In battle, their strength and height made them nearly impenetrable, and they could weather fierce storms with ease. Our fleet may have been faster, but in such treacherous waters, their ships were better suited for survival.

3:14

Caesar took many towns but found the enemy's flight could not be
prevented. He waited for his fleet to arrive, fully equipped and ready to
clash with the enemy's. It wasn't clear what approach to take as the
Gauls had a higher ship advantage. Our men had sharp hooks which
caused the enemy's sails to fall rendering their ships useless. Courage
was the deciding factor, and our men had the advantage as the whole
battle was under the gaze of Caesar and the whole army.

3:15

The enemy ships had their sail yards down and were surrounded by
two or three of our own. Yet our soldiers, with great vigor, fought to
board the vessels. The barbarians, seeing their defeat, fled for safety.
But the wind suddenly calmed and trapped them in place, giving us a
chance to finish the battle. Our men pursued and captured the enemy
ships, leaving only a few to escape in the cover of darkness. The battle
raged from early afternoon until sunset.

3:16

The Veneti and the coastal war ended in one blow, as all the young and
notable fighters assembled for that final battle, and had nowhere else to
go when they lost. Caesar took full advantage of his victory and
punished them severely, executing their senate and enslaving the
remaining survivors. This was a lesson to all barbarians to respect the
rights of ambassadors in the future.

3:17

Amidst the Veneti's turmoil, Q. Titurius Sabinus arrived in the
territories of the Unelli with Caesar's troops. Viridovix held dominion
over these lands and commanded those states that had rebelled against
Rome. The Aulerci and the Sexovii, having murdered their own Senate
for refusing to join the war, had shut their gates and allied with
Viridovix, along with a horde of outlaws and raiders from all over
Gaul. Sabinus kept himself in his camp, while Viridovix taunted him by
bringing out his forces daily and daring him to a fight. Sabinus
refrained because he knew that, as a lieutenant, it was imprudent to
engage such a mighty host without favorable circumstances or
advantageous ground, especially in the absence of the commander-in-
chief.

3:18

He suspected one of the crafty Gauls was a coward, and with heavy
incentives convinced him to switch sides and betray Caesar. The Gaul
informed the enemy of the Romans' frailty, convincing them to attack
the camp. The Gaul's words were reinforced by the failure of Sabinus
to attack and a lack of provisions. The enemy was elated by their
perceived victory and began to fill the trenches with brushwood.

3:19

The camp sat on a gentle rise, a mile up from the bottom. They hurried
there, not wanting the Romans to gather and arm themselves. Sabinus
gave his men the signal they wanted and a sudden sally was made from
two gates. The enemy, carrying burdens, were caught off guard and
unskilled. Our soldiers, experienced from past battles, attacked with
great vigor, causing the enemy to turn and flee. The cavalry chased
after them, leaving only a few who managed to escape. With the naval
battle won and news of Sabinus' victory, all the states immediately
surrendered to Titurius. The Gauls were impetuous in starting wars but
weak in enduring hardships.

3:20

P. Crassus arrived in Aquitania to wage war, a region where many Roman troops had been previously killed or defeated. He prepared carefully by gathering supplies, troops, and cavalry, including brave soldiers from nearby states. But upon arriving, the Sotiates launched a surprise attack with their cavalry, followed by infantry forces that had been hiding in a valley. The battle was chaotic and fierce.

3:21

The fight was a long and tough one. The Sotiates believed their past victories were enough to secure the safety of Aquitania. Our men, led by a young commander without their general and other legions, aimed to prove their mettle. After much bloodshed, the enemy finally turned and fled. Crassus marched towards the Sotiates' principal town, laying siege to it after they put up a valiant resistance. The Aquitani, skilled in mining, tried to attack our rampart and vineae, but their efforts were in vain. Eventually, they sent ambassadors to Crassus and surrendered, delivering their weapons as instructed.

3:22

As our men were focused on one task, Adcantuanus, who had control, made a move with 600 loyal followers known as soldurii. They enjoyed the luxuries of those they were devoted to and shared their fate. If one was killed, they all died. Although Adcantuannus attempted to break through, a battle ensued, and he was forced to retreat. Crassus still granted him the same surrender terms as others in the town.

3:23

After receiving their arms and hostages, Crassus marched into the
territory of the Vocates and Tarusates. Barbarians were alarmed and
began to send embassadors to combine forces and summon aid from
neighboring states. Experienced leaders were chosen from among
those who had fought with Q. Sertorius. Roman tactics were adopted
in selecting advantageous positions, fortifying the camp, and cutting off
enemy provisions. With their forces small and the enemy growing in
number, Crassus knew he could not delay in giving battle. At the
council, all agreed and the fight was scheduled for the next day.

3:24

At dawn, with his forces fully assembled and arrayed in two rows,
Caesar stationed the auxiliaries at the center and waited, keeping a
watchful eye for the enemy's next move. Although the enemy had the
advantage of greater numbers and boundless war experience, they
preferred securing victory by blockading the passes and cutting off the
supplies. Once the Roman soldiers due to lack of resources would
begin to withdraw with their hogs, they would attack them while
maneuvering and feeling despondent. The Roman authorities and
soldiers agreed to the enemy's proposition, but it accomplished
nothing. Crassus, observing the enemy's inaction, knew that their delay
had bolstered his troops' spirits and determination to fight. Hearing
such utterances from the soldiers, he spurred them on and stormed the
enemy's camp, causing his own soldiers to embrace and cheer with joy.

3:25

As the ditch was being filled and darts were thrown at the rampart, the
auxiliaries supplied weapons to the soldiers and brought turf to the
mound. The enemy fought with courage and their high position made
their weapons effective. The horse reported to Crassus that the
enemy's camp was vulnerable from the Decuman gate.

3:26

Crassus tells the horse commanders to promise rewards, then orders them to take the four cohorts to the enemy fortifications. They make it there unobserved, knock down the fortifications, and storm into the enemy camp. This sudden attack inspires our soldiers and they fight harder. The enemy realizes their hopeless situation and tries to run away by jumping off the ramparts. Our cavalry chases them all the way to the open fields, leaving only a quarter of the original 50,000 enemy troops alive. The cavalry gets back to our camp late at night.

3:27

News of the battle reached Aquitania and most surrendered to Crassus. They sent hostages including the Tarbelli, Bigerriones, Preciani, Vocasates, Tarusates, Elurates, Garites, Ausci, Garumni, Sibuzates, and Cocosates. However, a handful of more distant tribes, feeling safe due to the impending winter, did not follow suit.

3:28

At the end of a summer when almost all of Gaul was subdued, Caesar took his army to fight the Morini and the Menapii who had refused to make peace. These tribes were different from the others, hiding in their forests and swamps with their belongings, seeing that the larger nations were defeated. When Caesar built his camp and the enemy didn't show, they suddenly attacked from all directions. Our men quickly fought them off, killing many but losing a few in the dense woods.

3:29

Caesar cut the forests to protect his soldiers from surprise attacks. He piled the timber to form ramparts on both sides. Our men quickly cleared a vast area, capturing enemy cattle and baggage. But a fierce storm halted the work, forcing soldiers out of their tents. Caesar then burned their homes and villages before settling in for winter with the Aulerci and Lexovii.

GALLIC WARS BOOK 4 (55 B.C.E.)

Julius Caesar in his fourth book of the Gallic Wars recounts the battles he fought and the lands he conquered, with straightforward prose that spares no sentiment. The tribes of Gaul, a savage and proud people, met the might of the Roman legions and were vanquished. The battles were brutal, the victories hard-won, the losses mourned in silence. Caesar's writing is like the man himself - tough, unyielding, and full of steely resolve. He tells the story of war without artifice or adornment, with impeccable clarity and precise words, leaving nothing to the imagination.

4:1

That winter, while Cn. Pompey and M. Crassus were consuls, the Usipetes and Tenchtheri invaded Gaul by crossing the Rhine where it meets the sea. Their motivation was to escape war with the Suevi and find more hospitable land for farming. The Suevi were the most fearsome and numerous of all the German tribes, with a hundred cantons that each sent a thousand soldiers to war. They lived a nomadic life, moving every year and subsisting mainly on milk and meat while hunting for their food. This constant physical activity and freedom from discipline made them tall and strong, and they cared little for clothing even in the coldest weather. They even bathed in the open rivers.

4:2

Merchants deal in war booty, not imported goods. Gauls treasure pricey, subtle oxen, but Germans prefer local, scruffy ones. They toughen those animals up by using them every day. In fights, the Germans leap from their horses and fight on foot, then return to their horses which wait patiently for them. They never use horse covers. Even outnumbered, they bravely face any mounted cavalry without fear. Wine makes people weak and unmanly, so they don't allow it in their land.

4:3

They boasted of their power by pointing out the vast, empty lands surrounding their territory. The Suevi claimed it proved their dominance over other nations who couldn't withstand them. These desolate lands stretched for about six hundred miles. On the other side of their border were the Ubii, a more refined Germanic tribe with a prosperous state due to their proximity to the Rhine and exposure to Gaulish culture. Even though the Suevi failed to push them out in multiple wars, they subdued the Ubii into being their tributaries, weakening their power.

4:4

The Usipetes and Tenchtheri, a fierce duo who struggled against the
Suevi for years, were driven out of their land and forced to wander
across Germany. They eventually made their way to the Rhine, where
they encountered the Menapii. The Menapii were frightened by their
arrival and placed guards to prevent their crossing. After many
attempts to cross, the Usipetes and Tenchtheri pretended to leave only
to return and ambush the Menapii in the night. They took over their
houses and supplies and remained there for the winter.

4:5

Caesar, upon learning of these matters, feared the Gauls' fickle nature
and their tendency towards change. He believed that they could not be
trusted with anything, as it was their habit to stop travelers and inquire
about any news or information they may have come across. In towns,
common people would crowd around merchants, forcing them to
reveal where they came from and what they knew. These reports and
stories often led to rash decisions, which they inevitably regretted later.
The Gauls tended to believe answers that matched their desires, rather
than the truth.

4:6

Caesar knew their custom, so he headed to the army earlier in the year
to avoid a tougher war. He found out that embassies had been sent to
the Germans by some states, promising them everything they desired if
they left the Rhine. Lured by hope, the Germans raided farther into
Eburones and Condrusi's territories, which were under Treviri's
protection. Caesar summoned Gaul's chiefs, pretended ignorance of
what he knew, raised some cavalry, and decided to wage war against the
Germans.

4:7

With his cavalry selected and provisions in tow, he headed towards the Germans. In a matter of days, emissaries arrived with a message: The Germans do not start wars, but will fight when provoked. It is a legacy passed down for generations, to resist any and all attackers without compromise. They admitted reluctance in coming to this place, having been forced out of their homeland. If the Romans were wise, they would embrace their offer of friendship and allyship. These Germans were not to be underestimated, except perhaps by the mighty Suevi. They claimed to be able to conquer all other peoples on this earth.

4:8

Caesar said he couldn't team up with them while they were still in Gaul. He didn't think it was likely that a group that couldn't protect their own land could take others'. Plus, there weren't any unoccupied lands in Gaul that could be handed out to such a big group without hurting someone else. If they wanted, they could move to the Ubii's turf where there were already ambassadors asking for Caesar's help against the Suevi.

4:9

The embassadors spoke and promised to report back to their people. After three days of discussion they would come back to Caesar, but asked him not to move his camp any closer. Caesar could not comply for he knew they had sent their cavalry to pillage and gather supplies. He suspected they were waiting for their return, causing delay.

4:10

From Le Vosge, in the Lingones' land, flows the Meuse. It joins with the Waal, a branch of the Rhine, and creates Batavi Island before emptying into the ocean, just eighty miles away. The Rhine, on the other hand, begins among the Lepontii, living in the Alps, and swiftly runs through the Sarunates', the Helvetii's, the Sequani's, the Mediomatrici's, the Tribuci's, and the Treviri's territories. The river splits into different streams as it approaches the ocean, forming extensive islands inhabited by barbaric folks - some live on fish and bird eggs. Eventually, it flows into the ocean with its many mouths.

4:11

Caesar was close to the enemy, and the ambassadors returned to him. They requested him not to advance, but he continued. They pleaded with him to stop his troops from engaging and allowed them three days to negotiate. Caesar thought this was just an excuse so that their horse could return. He agreed to meet the ambassadors the next day to hear their demands, but ordered his officers not to provoke the enemy into an engagement.

4:12

The enemy spotted our 5000-strong cavalry while they only had 800 horses left. They attacked, catching our army off guard, and chaos ensued. They stabbed our horses and caused our soldiers to flee. Even Piso, a brave Aquitanian descended from an illustrious family, fell in battle. He fought valiantly to protect his brother, but ultimately perished surrounded by enemies. His brother charged into the fray but paid the ultimate price as well.

4:13

Caesar thought the enemy shifty and didn't want to wait for their cavalry to return. He didn't trust the Gauls either. He told his guys the plan and then some Germans came in to play nice but he saw through it and captured them. Caesar then led his troops out, with the cavalry at the back.

4:14

With his army in three lines, Caesar marched eight miles and caught the Germans by surprise. The enemy had no time to prepare or arm themselves, confused and uncertain whether to fight or flee. Chaos ensued, and Caesar's soldiers, still bitter over the previous day's betrayal, stormed the camp. The Germans fought back briefly but were ultimately overwhelmed, with only women and children escaping into the woods. Caesar's cavalry chased after them.

4:15

The Germans saw their families being slain and ran away, dropping their weapons and flags. They fled to the Meuse and Rhine river and many gave up, throwing themselves into the water. The survivors were exhausted and afraid. Our soldiers returned safely from this great war with 430,000 opponents. Caesar allowed those he had captured to leave, but they feared retaliation from the Gauls and chose to stay with him. Caesar agreed.

4:16

After the German war, Caesar decided to cross the Rhine. He wanted to scare the Germans into thinking about their own land, instead of gallivanting over to Gaul. A bunch of cavalry from the Usipetes and Tenchtheri who were into pillaging and getting some food had fled over to the Sigambri, beyond the Rhine. When Caesar asked them to give up the guys who'd led the attack, they told him the Rhine was the boundary of Roman rule, and it was unfair to demand their land but forbid them from crossing into Gaul.

The Ubii were the only folks from outside the Rhine who had sent representatives to Caesar. They'd even promised hostages and asked for his help against the Suevi. At least, they wanted Caesar to ferry his army across the Rhine since his reputation was tops after he beat Ariovistus then the others. They were happy to offer loads of vessels for the transport.

4:17

Caesar decided to cross the Rhine, but he didn't want to risk it with ships. So, he built a bridge even though it was difficult due to the width, speed and depth of the river. He used piles and beams to construct the bridge, which he joined in different directions for extra strength. He also placed piles as buttresses to prevent the force of the stream. This would also protect the bridge from trees or vessels that might be sent down the river by the barbarians.

4:18

In ten days, the timber was gathered and the army crossed the bridge. Caesar stationed guards at both ends of the bridge and quickly marched towards the Sigambri's land. Along the way, ambassadors requested peace and alliance, to which Caesar responded kindly and demanded hostages. However, the Sigambri fled as soon as the bridge was built, taking all their belongings and hiding in the wilderness with the help of Tenchtheri and Usipetes.

4:19

Caesar stayed in their lands for a while and burnt down their homes, destroyed their crops. He then went to aid the Ubii and learned from them that the Suevi had prepared for the Romans' arrival by gathering their troops and possessions to a central location. After accomplishing his mission, Caesar returned to Gaul, having spent eighteen days beyond the Rhine.

4:20

In the remaining bit of summer, Caesar, despite the early winters in the north where Gaul lies, intended to venture into Britain. He knew that our foes in Gaul had been aided by the Britons in most of the wars fought. Even if time didn't permit him to wage war, just by setting foot in the land, gaining insights into the people's character, and the knowledge of their territories, ports and landing sites that the Gauls were ignorant of, it would be of great benefit to him. That place was unknown to everyone except tradesmen who had no familiarity with anything except the seaside and those areas facing Gaul. After inviting traders from all parts, he still couldn't glean the size of the island, the count or size of the groups living there, the type of warfare tactics they used, their way of life, or which harbors were most suitable for a significant number of large ships.

4:21

Before he set foot on the island, Caesar sent Caius Volusenus along with a warship to gather information about the place. He trusted this as a sensible measure. Volusenus was instructed to thoroughly look into everything and report back as soon as possible. Meanwhile, Caesar marched forward to Morini with his entire force. He asked neighboring countries to send him ships along with the fleet he built the previous summer for the war. When the Britons discovered his plans, they sent him ambassadors who promised to give hostages and submit to Roman authority. Caesar listened to them intently, urged them to keep their promise, and sent them back home with Commius who he had made king of Atrebates. Caesar believed Commius was courageous, trustworthy, and held much influence in the region. He directed him to visit as many states as possible, persuade them to protect the Roman people, and tell them that he would soon arrive. Volusenus, having viewed the island from his ship, returned to Caesar five days later to report his observations.

4:22

Caesar stays in the area to get ships. Morini ambassadors come to him, apologizing for their "uncivilized" behavior and promising obedience. Caesar takes it as a stroke of luck, not wanting to leave an enemy behind or wage war this time of year, and takes some hostages. He secures 80 transport ships for two legions, giving warships to others. 18 burden ships with horses are left behind. He sends lieutenants to the Menapii and other Morini lands, and leaves a garrison in the harbor.

4:23

He set sail for the further port with his horse, followed by a tardy squadron. Arriving in Britain at dawn, he found the enemy armed and in position on the hills. The sea was trapped by close mountains, making it unfit for landing. He waited for the others to arrive, and gathered the officers to share his plan, insisting on swift and decisive action. When the wind and tide turned in his favor, he moved the fleet to a flat shore, seven miles away.

4:24

The Roman plan was sensed by the barbarians who then sent forth their fighters on horses and chariots, which they use heavily in battle. They tried to prevent the Romans from landing while bringing the rest of their warriors. But the main problem for the Romans was that their large-sized ships could only dock in deep waters. Additionally, their soldiers, burdened with heavy armor, had to disembark in unknown territories, fight off the barbarians, and stand in the waves. On the other hand, the barbarians were comfortable throwing their weapons and riding their horses as they knew the territory. The Romans, taken aback by this, didn't show the same enthusiasm as before, as they weren't accustomed to fighting in such conditions.

4:25

Caesar saw the enemy's fear of our warships, strange to them with their ready motion and service. He ordered them to draw back and to be rowed toward the open flank of the enemy. There they fiercely attacked with slings, arrows, and engines. The barbarians, unaccustomed to our style, stopped and retreated. Caesar's men hesitated, fearing the deep sea, until the carrier of the tenth legion's eagle cried out, "Leap, fellow soldiers, unless you wish to betray your eagle to the enemy. I, for my part, will perform my duty to the commonwealth and my general." He leaped from the ship, and soon others followed. Those in nearby vessels saw and joined in the fight.

4:26

The battle raged with intensity, both sides fiercely engaged. Our men struggled to keep formation, stumbling on unsteady ground with no clear leader or standard in sight. Meanwhile, the enemy, masters of the shallows, attacked swiftly and without mercy, picking off our stranded soldiers one by one. But Caesar, ever the sharp observer, rallied to their aid, sending soldiers on boats up the shore. Our men, strengthened by reinforcements, launched a successful counterattack, routing the enemy. Yet, they were unable to pursue the fleeing horsemen, who had relied too heavily on their sea legs. This would be Caesar's only setback in an otherwise storied career.

4:27

The enemy was beaten, but they quickly sent messengers to Caesar to discuss peace. They promised hostages and to obey whatever he commanded. Commius, who had been sent by Caesar to Britain, came with these messengers. The enemy had captured him, even though he was an ambassador with the general's authority, and after the battle, returned him hoping for forgiveness. Caesar was displeased, as they turned to war without cause, and yet wished to make amends. He pardoned them, took hostages, some of who were given at once, while the remainder would be delivered soon from faraway lands. They advised their people to leave and the leaders came to surrender themselves and their regions to Caesar.

4:28

A treaty agreed, four days after arrival in Britain. The eighteen ships, carrying cavalry, departed from the upper port with a gentle breeze. Upon nearing the camp a violent storm hit, leaving none of the ships able to navigate. Some returned to their starting dock, while others, in perilous danger, were pushed towards the western side of the island. After anchoring, they set sail on a stormy night, escaping to the continent as the ships filled with water.

4:29

It was a full moon that night, raising the tide in the ocean, a fact unknown to our men. The warships Caesar provided to ferry the army were onshore, filling with water. The storm camouflaged the burdened ships, causing chaos in the army due to the lack of options to manage or repair them. Most were wrecked, with others missing cables and tools to sail. Winter corn hadn't been stored, as they planned to winter in Gaul. All hope seemed lost.

4:30

Upon discovering the lack of cavalry, ships, and corn amongst the Romans, the British chiefs held a conference. They noted the limited number of soldiers and the small extent of the camp. Caesar had brought his legions over without baggage, which made the camp even more restricted. The chiefs saw an opportunity to cut off the Romans from provisions and prolong the war. They conspired to bring their people from the country parts and slowly departed from the camp.

4:31

Caesar didn't know their plan yet, but he figured it out from the damaged ships and the lack of promised hostages. So he got ready for the inevitable. He brought in food, used damaged ships to fix the others, and got whatever else they needed from the mainland. The soldiers did their part, and even with twelve lost ships, they could still make the journey.

4:32

As stuff was happening, one gang of soldiers headed out to get some food. No one thought a big fight was coming. Some people hung out in the country, while others went back and forth to the camp. Then, some guards at the camp's gates told Caesar that a lot of dust was heading toward them from the direction where the gang went. Caesar guessed that the barbarians were up to no good. He told two other groups of soldiers to take over guard duty, and he went with two more to check things out. The rest of the soldiers got ready and followed them. A little ways out from the camp, they saw that their buddies were in trouble. The enemy had them surrounded and was chucking weapons at them. All the corn had been picked, except for the soldiers' spot. During the night, the bad guys hid in the woods and waited for the soldiers to show up. When they did, the bad guys attacked, and the soldiers got all jumbled up. Some got killed, and others ran around trying to figure out what to do. The enemy's cavalry and chariots let them close in on the soldiers.

4:33

Their way of fighting involved using chariots to break the ranks of the enemy with the fear of the horses and the noise of the wheels. After creating chaos, they would jump out on foot to engage in direct combat. The charioteers would position themselves nearby for a quick escape if things went badly. They combined the speed of horses with the stability of infantry and were highly skilled in maneuvering their chariots. They were able to control their horses even on steep terrain and move with great speed and precision.

4:34

Our men feared the new way of battle, but Caesar came and paused the enemy. He waited for a better time to fight and withdrew the legions into camp. The Britons fled and bad weather kept them at bay. The enemy sent messengers to gather a larger force and attacked the camp.

4:35

Caesar expected the enemy to flee once again if they were defeated, but he was ready with thirty horsemen provided by Commius the Atrebatian. Caesar arranged his legions in battle formation and engaged the enemy. They quickly retreated and our men pursued, killing many. Afterwards, they destroyed everything in sight and returned to camp.

4:36

On that day, the foe's messengers arrived to discuss peace with Caesar. He asked for twice the amount of hostages he previously demanded, and requested they be brought to the mainland. With winter fast approaching and his ships in need of repair, he set sail at midnight. Most of his fleet made it safely, but two cargo ships were carried downstream.

4:37

300 soldiers marched to camp from two ships when the Morini attacked. Caesar had left them at peace, but they were eager for loot. The Morini surrounded the troops and demanded they surrender their arms or face death. The soldiers formed a defensive circle and fought back fiercely for more than four hours. The enemy summoned 6000 men to the fight, but our soldiers inflicted heavy casualties. When Caesar arrived with cavalry, the enemy fled and many were slaughtered.

4:38

The next day, Caesar dispatched his lieutenant Labienus with the legions he had retrieved from Britain to squash the Morini rebellion. The Morini, with their marshes all dried up, lacked refuge, and hence, were quickly captured by Labienus. Meanwhile, Caesar's other lieutenants had destroyed Menapii's land and burned their homes before returning because the men had disappeared amidst the dense woods. Caesar stationed his troops among the Belgae for winter, and just two British states offered hostages, while others ignored his demands. The Senate lauded Caesar's achievements, dedicating twenty days for thanksgiving.

✦✦✦

GALLIC WARS BOOK 5 (54 B.C.E.)

In Gallic Wars Book 5, the narrative takes a riveting turn as the year 54 BCE sees Caesar face a new array of challenges and adventures. With the backdrop of a second expedition into Britain and the brewing unrest among the Gallic tribes, this captivating account brings to life the complexities of Caesar's military campaigns and diplomatic maneuvers. As you delve into this next chapter, prepare to be immersed in a world of strategic ingenuity, fierce resistance, and the undying resilience of both the Romans and the Gauls, as they navigate the ever-shifting sands of conquest and rebellion during this critical period in history.

They came, they saw, they conquered. This was the essence of the Gallic Wars, as experienced by Julius Caesar in 54 BC. In his fifth book on the subject, he details the battles, strategies, and sacrifices that led to the victory of the Roman army over the Gauls. The brutality of the war is matched only by the tactical genius of Caesar, who employed unconventional methods to secure his triumph. Yet even in the midst of victory, Caesar is aware of the cost of war, both in terms of lives lost and the toll it takes on the human spirit.

5:1

Domitius and Claudius being consuls, Caesar leaves his winter quarters in Italy and commands his lieutenants to build ships and repair the old ones. He plans them to be lower for easier loading and unloading due to the changing tides. He also makes them wider to carry more horses and burdens. He orders them to be light and fast. He goes to Illyricum to stop the Pirustae and makes them bring hostages for their actions. He orders the damages to be estimated and compensated.

5:2

With the assizes complete, he heads back to Gaul and then to the army. At the winter quarter, he sees six hundred ships and twenty-eight warships built with scarce materials and extreme enthusiasm from soldiers. He praises their work and orders the ships to gather at port Itius, which was the shortest passage to Britain - just thirty miles from the mainland. He leaves enough soldiers for the mission and takes four legions without baggage and 800 horse into Treviri lands. The Treviri didn't attend general diets and supposedly deal with Germans beyond the Rhine.

5:3

The strongest state in Gaul for cavalry, and with a great many infantry forces, bordered on the Rhine. Two men, Indutiomarus and Cingetorix, battled for power there. Cingetorix pledged his loyalty to Caesar upon hearing of his arrival, but Indutiomarus gathered cavalry and infantry for war, hiding those too old to fight in the Arduenna forest. Some of the state's leaders turned to Caesar to protect their interests, as they feared for the state's safety. Indutiomarus sent envoys to Caesar, claiming he stayed away from his people to keep them in line and would come to Caesar's camp if he agreed to protect him and his state.

5:4

Caesar knew the real reason behind Indutiomarus' words and the situation that prevented him from carrying out his plan. He called for Indutiomarus to come to him with hostages, including his own son and relatives. Caesar consoled Indutiomarus and asked him to continue his loyalty. But he also reconciled the leaders of Treviri with Cingetorix, whom he admired greatly. This made Indutiomarus angry and diminished his influence among his people, making him more hostile towards Caesar.

5:5

Caesar went to port Itius with his legions after things were sorted out. He found out that 40 ships, built in the country of the Meldi, had returned to the same port due to a storm. The remaining ships were ready with everything needed for sailing. 4,000 cavalry of all Gaul and chief persons of all states assembled there as well. Caesar decided to leave few of them in Gaul whose loyalty he discerned and took the rest as hostages for fear of commotion in Gaul when he was absent.

5:6

Dumnorix, the Aeduan, was one of them, and Caesar wanted him with him. Dumnorix liked change, power, and had influence among the Gauls. He even claimed that Caesar had given him sovereignty over the state which made the Aedui upset. Caesar learned of this and tried to convince him to stay in Gaul, but Dumnorix refused. He then tried to persuade other Gauls to stay on the continent and fear that Caesar would kill all of Gaul's nobility. People reported this to Caesar.

5:7

Caesar discovered Dumnorix's disloyalty and, in order to protect the commonwealth, detained him while still gathering information. After a delay caused by unfavorable wind, Caesar ordered his soldiers to board ships, but Dumnorix left with the Aedui cavalry without warning. Caesar halted his expedition and sent his own cavalry to bring Dumnorix back, with orders to use force if necessary. Due to Dumnorix's blatant disobedience, he was killed upon capture, although he fought fiercely and begged for help. The Aedui horsemen returned to Caesar.

5:8

Labienus stayed back with the others to hold the harbor, watch for danger, and get food, whilst Caesar, with five legions and a few horses, sailed on a southwest wind that slowed and left them lost in the current until sunrise. In a moment of luck, they spotted Britain on their left and turned the tide to reach the shores where they landed without any enemy present, save a few troops who later scattered from fear of the massive number of our ships.

5:9

Caesar set up camp and learned the enemy's position from prisoners. Leaving men to protect his ships, he moved towards the enemy in the dark. The enemy attacked with cavalry and chariots, but were pushed back by Caesar's forces. They retreated to a fortified spot in the woods, but the seventh legion set up a rampart and took the position. Caesar didn't pursue them far, wanting time to fortify his camp.

5:10

At dawn the next day, Caesar dispatched infantry and cavalry divisions in pursuit of the fleeing enemy. As they closed in on the rear, Quintus Atrius' riders rode up to report a fierce storm that had wrecked their ships, causing widespread destruction and chaos. Anchors and cables proved powerless against the ferocity of the tempest, and sailors and pilots were helpless to stop the barrage of crashing vessels. The calamity dealt a serious blow to their campaign.

5:11

Knowing these things, Caesar ordered the troops to stop marching and return to the ships. He saw what he had expected, with only some ships lost, and the others badly damaged. Caesar chose men to repair the ships, asked others from the continent to come, and directed Labienus to construct as many ships as he can. Although it was difficult, Caesar decided the best way forward, to bring all the ships to shore, fortify the camp, and leave the same forces as before guarding the ships. After ten days of strenuous labor by the soldiers, Caesar left for the same place where he returned from. When he arrived, he found Cassivellaunus leading a greater force of Britons, who had placed him in charge of the entire war.

5:12

Britain, land of two peoples: inlanders said born there, maritimers from Belgae here for loot and war, bearing names of their homelands. They stayed, built like Gauls, had tons of cattle. Coins weighed in brass or iron, tin made inland, iron in the sea, but brought mostly from elsewhere. Not much timber, no beech or fir. Hares, cocks, and geese no good for eat, but bred for fun. Milder colds.

5:13

The island is shaped like a triangle, with one side facing Gaul. One part, in Kent, points east towards most ships from Gaul, while the other side faces south. This side is 500 miles long, and another side faces Spain and the west, where Ireland is located, estimated to be half the size of Britain. Mona, an island lies in the middle of the journey, while multiple small islands are believed to exist there, with some accounts claiming thirty consecutive days of darkness during the winter solstice. Upon further investigation, we discovered that nights are shorter on the island than on the mainland. According to them, this side measures up to 700 miles. The third side faces north, to which no land is opposite, and a corner of it primarily looks towards Germany. This side measures up to 800 miles long. All in all, the island's circumference is approximately 2,000 miles.

5:14

The people of Kent are the most civilized among all, dwelling solely by the sea, they are similar to the Gallic ways. The inland people, on the other hand, do not plant seeds but rely on milk and meat for sustenance. Their garments are made of skin. All Britains smear themselves with wood dye, giving them a fierce persona during battles. They keep their hair lengthy while shaving their bodies, except for the head and upper lip. Brothers share their wives, even up to a dozen, as well as parents having relationships with their children. The offspring of these unions are attributed to their virgin husbands.

5:15

The enemy put up a good fight in their chariots and on horseback, but our men were victorious and drove them away. Our men became overeager and pursued them too far, resulting in some losses. Later, the enemy attacked again when our men were busy fortifying the camp. They fought fiercely, and even the best of our legions had trouble with their unusual tactics. They retreated safely, but not before killing Q. Laberius Durus, a tribune of our soldiers. We sent more cohorts against them, and ultimately repelled their attack.

5:16

Our men faced a tough enemy in an open field. They couldn't chase the retreating Britons or leave their positions, burdened by heavy armor. Even the cavalry fought with danger, as the Britons would retreat and switch to foot combat. They fought in small groups with great distance between them and often had backup ready to relieve their fatigue. This was a dangerous system for both sides.

5:17

The next day, the enemy stopped on the hills, far from our camp, appearing in small groups and with less enthusiasm than before. At noon, Caesar sent three legions and all the cavalry with Lieutenant C. Trebonius to forage. The enemy attacked the foragers suddenly from all directions. Our men boldly attacked and repulsed them, pursuing until they drove them away. The horse did not give the enemy a chance to regroup, rally or leap from their chariots. After this retreat, the auxiliaries left and the enemy never engaged with us in large numbers again.

5:18

Caesar finds out their plan, leads his army across the Thames River at a difficult ford, and sees the enemy forces on the other side. The bank is defended with sharp stakes, and under the water, they hide the same type of stakes. He learns this information from prisoners and deserters. Caesar sends cavalry ahead and orders the legions to follow. With incredible speed and determination, the soldiers charge forward despite the water reaching their heads. The enemy can't handle the attack and flees.

5:19

Cassivellaunus gave up the battle and let go of his soldiers. He kept only 4,000 charioteers who kept an eye on us and attacked when we spread out to plunder. Caesar restricted our troops to raid only within marches' reach, and the enemy's land remained untouched beyond that.

5:20

Meanwhile, the Trinobantes, one of the most powerful states in the
area, sent ambassadors to Caesar, seeking his protection. Mandubratius,
whose father had been killed by Cassivellaunus, and who himself had
fled, had sought Caesar's help earlier. The Trinobantes promised to
submit to Caesar's rule, requesting his protection for Mandubratius and
the appointment of a leader for their state. Caesar asked for forty
hostages and food for his troops in return. The Trinobantes promptly
fulfilled these demands, sending the exact number of hostages and
food ration as expected.

5:21

The Trinobantes were safe from the soldiers, so the Cenimagni,
Segontiaci, Ancalites, Bibroci, and Cassi gave up to Caesar. They told
him about Cassivellaunus' capital town that was protected by woods
and swamps, filled with a lot of men and cattle. Caesar led his legions
there and found the place was well defended. But he attacked from two
sides anyway, and the enemy didn't hold up for long. They fled and left
behind a lot of cattle and enemy soldiers dead on the ground.

5:22

As all of this happened, Cassivellaunus ordered messengers to Kent
where four kings reigned over the sea. They were to gather their men
and launch a surprise attack on the naval camp. Our men fought back,
defeating the enemy and even capturing their leader. Cassivellaunus,
shaken by the losses and the desertion of his allies, sent ambassadors to
Caesar requesting surrender. Caesar, intending to stay the winter on the
continent, demanded hostages and tribute from Britain. He forbade
Cassivellaunus from warring with Mandubratius or the Trinobantes.

5:23

He received hostages, led his army back to the shore, and found the ships repaired. Since he had many prisoners and lost some ships in the storm, he decided to bring his army back in two trips. Despite many voyages with many ships, no soldiers were lost. However, very few empty ships made it back, and most of the newly built ones were driven back. With the equinox approaching and many ships missing, Caesar tightly packed his soldiers and set sail in calm weather, arriving at land safely at dawn.

5:24

Ships docked and Gauls gathered at Samarobriva for a meeting due to the drought that harmed the corn that year. Caesar had to adjust his army's winter quarters, splitting the legions amongst various states. Each legion was given a different destination. One legion was sent to Eburones, near Meuse and Rhine, under Ambiorix and Cativolcus' control. Caesar commanded his lieutenants, Q. Titurius Sabinus and L. Aurunculeius Cotta to take charge. The legions were placed within a distance of 100 miles, except for L. Roscius' peaceful placement. Caesar stayed in Gaul waiting for the confirmation of the fortified winter-quarters.

5:25

One Carnutes man named Tasgetius, from a long line of rulers, was helped by Caesar, who got him back his family's power because of his bravery and loyalty. But, bad people who didn't like him killed him after he had been king for three years. Caesar got worried and thought the state might rebel, so he told Lucius Plancus to go with some soldiers and catch anyone who might have helped kill Tasgetius. At the same time, all the people Caesar put in charge of his armies said they were staying in winter quarters and the place was safe.

5:26

After two weeks in winter-quarters, Ambiorix and Cativolcus stirred up trouble. Even though they had traded with our soldiers and helped supply our winter-quarters, they listened to the messages of Indutiomarus and riled up their people against us. They ambushed our soldiers gathering wood and attacked our camp with a large force. But our men quickly armed themselves and defended the rampart, even winning a cavalry battle. The enemy eventually gave up and asked for a meeting to resolve their grievances.

5:27

C. Arpineius, a Roman knight and friend of Q. Titurius, along with Q. Junius, arrived for a conference with Ambiorix, a person from Spain known to Caesar. Ambiorix expressed gratitude towards Caesar and confessed that he was indebted to him for freeing him from a tribute he owed to the Aduatuci and for returning his son and his brother's son, both held captive by the Aduatuci. He stated that he didn't attack Caesar's camp by choice but under pressure from his people. His government model was such that the people had as much authority over him as he had over the people. The reason for the war was the sudden combination of the Gauls, who couldn't resist it due to their weakness. Ambiorix urged Titurius to consider the safety of his and his soldiers' lives, as a large force of Germans was hired and would arrive in two days. He suggested that they should quickly withdraw to Cicero or Labienus, who were about fifty miles away, assuring them of safe passage through his territories.

5:28

Arpineius and Junius shared what they had heard with the lieutenants. The news was unsettling, even if it was from an enemy. It seemed improbable that the lowly Eburones would dare to attack the mighty Roman people. The council debated the matter. L. Aurunculeius and other high-ranking soldiers argued against hasty action. They believed a fortified winter camp and patience would suffice. After all, they had already fought off the German attack and had enough supplies. They couldn't let the enemy dictate their moves.

5:29

Titurius warned that the enemy would become stronger and more dangerous if they delayed their attack. He believed that Caesar had left for Italy and that the Carnutes and Eburones would not have dared to oppose them if Caesar were still present. The Germans were angry and Gaul was in turmoil, but Titurius believed they could either reach the nearest legion or act quickly if necessary. He questioned the advice of Cotta and the others, saying that even if there was no immediate danger, the risk of famine during a prolonged siege was very real.

5:30

The argument went back and forth between Cotta and Sabinus, both sides holding their ground. "Alright," resigned Sabinus, his voice booming so the surrounding soldiers could hear him. "It's your call. But I'm not the one here who's trembling at the thought of death. Those who are will know it, and they'll hold you accountable when things don't go well. The soldiers who might end up stranded and out of supplies, isolated from the rest of us, they're the ones who'll suffer the most. But if you let them join the nearest winter-quarters in three days, they'll stand a better chance at surviving whatever comes their way."

5:31

They rose from the council, stopping both, begging that they not cause a great danger with their disagreement and stubbornness. If they all agreed on the same thing, whether to stay or leave, the matter was simple. However, they saw no safety in disagreement. They debated until midnight, and Cotta ended up giving in to Sabinus' opinion. They proclaimed that they would march at daybreak, and the soldiers spent the rest of the night inspecting their belongings, deciding what to bring and what to leave behind. They tried to justify their departure, citing danger and lack of sleep. At dawn, they left camp with a lot of baggage, convinced that Ambiorix's advice was not that of an enemy, but of a friend.

5:32

The enemy heard the Romans leaving and planned an ambush in the woods two miles away. They attacked when the Romans were in a vulnerable spot, in a valley. It was a tough fight and not favorable to our men.

5:33

Titurius panicked in the moment, scrambling to organize his troops without a plan in place. This was no surprise - those who consult during action inevitably falter. Meanwhile, Cotta's prior forethought allowed him to lead and inspire his soldiers with skill that befit both a general and a soldier. However, the officers commanding the troops in various locations were unable to coordinate well, their efforts hampered by the march's distance, leading to the order to abandon baggage and form a formation. Though reasonable in the circumstances, the soldiers lost hope upon seeing the fearful tactic, and the enemy became more eager to engage. Chaos erupted with many of the soldiers abandoning their ensigns in favor of valuable baggage, causing uproar and lamentation throughout the field.

5:34

The barbarians showed good judgment. Their leaders ordered the soldiers to stay in their place and reminded them that they would get the spoils of victory. The barbarians were just as brave and numerous as the Romans. Even though they were abandoned by their leader and luck, they relied solely on their courage to save themselves. Whenever a cohort of Romans attacked, many enemies fell. Ambiorix saw this and ordered his men to throw weapons from a safe distance and not get too close. They should retreat in the direction where the Romans attacked, and when the Romans went back to their standards, they should follow and attack them.

5:35

The command was followed carefully. When the cohorts charged, the enemy fled. The Roman army was left unprotected, and were attacked from their open flank. If they tried to hold their position, they couldn't fight back or escape the weapons. Despite these disadvantages, they fought bravely, withstanding the enemy for most of the day. T. Balventius, Q. Lucanius, and L. Cotta were all wounded or killed fighting valiantly.

5:36

Q. Titurius, uneasy about the situation, sent his interpreter Cn. Pompey to speak to Ambiorix, who was urging his men from afar. Pompey asked for mercy for Titurius and his soldiers. Ambiorix said they could talk and that he hoped the people could help. He swore no harm would come to them. Titurius wondered if it would be wise to retreat and talk to Ambiorix. Cotta, wounded, refused to go and stood firm in his decision.

5:37

Sabinus tells his soldiers to follow him, including the centurions at the front. They approach Ambiorix who orders them to throw down their weapons. Sabinus complies and orders his men to do the same. Ambiorix drags out the negotiations and eventually kills Sabinus while he's surrounded. The Gauls shout "Victory" and attack, breaking our soldiers' ranks. Many men, including L. Cotta, die fighting. The survivors retreat to the camp they left, but are attacked again. They fight until nightfall, but losing hope, they take their own lives. A few make it to Labienus and recount the story.

5:38

Ambiorix was elated by the victory. He rode swiftly with his cavalry to the border of his kingdom, the Aduatuci. They did not stop for rest, as he ordered his infantry to follow closely. The following day, he told the tale of their victory to the Nervii, urging them to take this chance to fight for their freedom and take revenge against the Romans. He informed the Nervii that two lieutenants had been slain in the fight and a large portion of the army has perished. The legion wintering with Cicero could be easily defeated, he promised to assist. The speech easily won over the Nervii.

5:39

Messengers were sent promptly to various governing tribes. They rallied and attacked Cicero's winter-quarters without warning. Cicero was unaware of Titurius' death. Soldiers gathering timber for fortifications got trapped by the enemy's horsemen. The legion's adversaries, including the Eburones, Nervii, and Aduatici and their allies, began their onslaught. Our soldiers quickly armed themselves and mounted the ramparts. They had a tough time that day since the enemy aimed for a quick victory. The enemies were confident that they would reign forever if they won.

5:40

Messengers set out with letters to Caesar at once, Cicero promising great rewards if they succeeded. All the passes were blocked, and the messengers caught. Overnight, 120 towers were built from collected wood with incredible speed. The enemy amassed greater forces and attacked the camp, filling in the ditch. Our men resisted like before and continued for days. All night, work never ceased, even for the sick and wounded. Preparations were made for the next day's assault by burning stakes and obtaining pikes. Towers, battlements, and parapets were constructed from hurdles. Though weak, Cicero himself worked throughout the night, only stopping when the soldiers begged him to rest.

5:41

The Nervii leaders, who were Cicero's pals, needed to chat with him. They shared the same intel that Titurius heard from Ambiorix, mainly that Gaul was rebelling, Germans had crossed the Rhine, and Caesar and his peeps were under attack. Sabinus was also dead. They pointed to Ambiorix for proof that they weren't lying. But Cicero shut them down, saying Romans don't take deals from armed enemies. If they want help, they gotta lay down their weapons and send delegates to Caesar. Cicero hoped Caesar's fairness would grant the Nervii's requests.

5:42

The Nervii, unable to fulfill their hopes, besieged the winter-quarters by building a rampart and ditch using military tactics they had learned from us. As they had no iron tools, they resorted to using their swords and cloaks to cut turf and empty out earth. Despite this, they managed to construct a ten-mile circumference fortification in under three hours, revealing the vast number of men involved. They then proceeded to build towers and other siege equipment, taught to them by our prisoners.

5:43

On the seventh day of the attack, the wind grew fierce and the Gauls began hurling hot balls and javelins at our thatched huts. The fire quickly spread, and though the enemy believed they had won, they soon discovered the courage and presence of mind our soldiers possessed. Despite being scorched and besieged, our soldiers fought valiantly and fiercely, refusing to abandon their post. It was a calamitous day, but also the deadliest for our enemy. Though the flames eventually died down and a tower was brought to the rampart, our centurions and soldiers did not retreat. Instead, they called the enemy to enter and then cast stones from all directions, dislodging them and setting their tower ablaze.

5:44

Two brave centurions in a legion, T. Pulfio and L. Varenus, often argued over who was the best. During a fierce fight, Pulfio calls out to Varenus, telling him this is their chance to prove themselves. Pulfio charges towards the enemy and Varenus follows. Pulfio pierces the enemy with his javelin, but gets trapped by his own shield with a javelin in his belt. Varenus rushes in to help, causing the enemy to turn their attention to him. Varenus fights his way through but slips and falls. Pulfio comes to his aid and they both fight off many enemies before retreating to safety. It was impossible to decide who was the better of the two.

5:45

As the attackers grew fiercer each day and the defenders grew fewer, more messengers sought out Caesar with urgent letters. But many of these messengers were captured and brutally executed in front of our warriors. However, a brave Nervian named Vertico, who had already pledged his allegiance to Cicero, devised a plan. He promised his slave freedom and riches if he could sneak a letter to Caesar, which the slave did by hiding it on his javelin and posing as a Gaul. Thanks to Vertico's efforts, Caesar learned of Cicero's peril and the impending doom of our legion.

5:46

Caesar got the letter late in the day. He sent a messenger to Crassus, who was 25 miles away, telling him to come quickly. Crassus left with the messenger. Caesar also sent a message to Fabius to lead his legion to the Atrebates' land. He asked Labienus to come with his legion to the Nervii borders if it was good for the commonwealth. He didn't wait for the rest of the army, just gathered 400 horse from nearby winter-quarters.

5:47

Crassus was coming, so Caesar moved twenty miles that day, leaving his baggage, hostages, documents, and corn with Crassus. Fabius joined him immediately as commanded. Meanwhile, Labienus feared leaving his winter-quarters and facing the enemy after the death of Sabinus and destruction of the cohorts. He sent a letter to Caesar telling him of the danger and the enemy's closeness.

5:48

Caesar, not getting his desired three legions, settles for two and places his only hope in urgency. He marches through Nervii and learns of Cicero's troubles from prisoners. Caesar bribes a Gallic horseman to deliver a letter to Cicero in case he cannot enter the camp. The letter, written in Greek to avoid enemy discovery, informs Cicero of Caesar's quick arrival and urges him to "maintain his ancient valor." The Gaul throws the spear as ordered, it lands in a tower unnoticed for two days. A soldier eventually spots it and delivers it to Cicero who reads it aloud to his men. The sight of fires in the distance confirms the arrival of Caesar's legions, bringing joy to all.

5:49

When the Gauls found out they were discovered, they ditched the blockade and headed straight to Caesar with 60,000 men. Cicero saw his chance and asked Vertico to deliver a letter to Caesar. He warned him to be careful and said that the enemy had turned their full force against him. Caesar got the message at midnight and told his troops about it, filling them with courage. Early the next day, he moved his camp and saw the enemy's forces on the other side of a valley and a stream. They were in a dangerous position, but he knew that Cicero was rescued and he could slow down. He fortified a tiny camp with only 7,000 men and no baggage, hoping to make the enemy think they were weak. He sent scouts to look for a way to cross the valley.

5:50

That day, cavalry skirmishes happened by the river, with both sides staying put, waiting. The Gauls expected more forces, while Caesar hoped to lure the enemy to clash in front of his camp on this side of the valley by pretending to be scared. Failing that, he planned to cross the valley and river more safely, after researching the passes. As day broke, enemy cavalry attacked our horses, but Caesar ordered a retreat, deliberately. Back at camp, he had the gates blocked, raised the rampart and made it seem like we were panicked to confuse the enemy.

5:51

The enemy attack with poor strategy as our men wait atop the ramparts. They approach nonetheless and hurl weapons at us from all sides. They even go so far as to invite any willing Romans or Gauls to join their cause before a certain hour. They underestimate us, for their attempts to break through the gates fail, and they resort to trying to tear down our ramparts and fill our trenches. But Caesar, leading the charge and unleashing our cavalry, puts them to rout. None remain to fight, and many are slain and disarmed.

5:52

Caesar arrived at Cicero's place, unscathed, thanks to the woods and marshes that stopped him from chasing the enemy. The enemy still had their towers and fortifications up, and Caesar was surprised to find the tenth of the enemy troops wounded. He praised Cicero and his legion for their courage in the fight. Caesar learned of the death of Sabinus and Cotta from prisoners, and addressed the soldiers individually, showing his appreciation for their bravery. At the assembly, he told the story of what happened and provided comfort to his troops. Caesar suggested that they should bear the loss calmly because the gods were on their side, and the enemy's pleasure won't last long, nor will their grief.

5:53

The report of Caesar's victory spreads through the Remi's land with great speed. Despite being sixty miles away, Labienus receives the news before midnight. Indutiomarus, who planned to attack Labienus' camp the next day, retreats with his troops once he hears of Caesar's victory. Caesar sends Fabius and his legion back to winter-quarters, while he stays with three legions near Samarobriva in different quarters. With the Gauls debating war, Caesar receives continuous reports of their commotions throughout the winter. L. Roscius, Caesar's lieutenant over the thirteenth legion, reports that large Gaul forces from Armoricae, just eight miles away, plan to attack him. However, upon learning of Caesar's triumph, the Gauls retreat, their departure resembling a flight.

5:54

Caesar gathered the leaders of Gaul and scared some of them into loyalty and encouraged others. But the Senones, a powerful state, tried to kill their king, Cavarinus, who Caesar put in power. When he escaped, they chased him out and refused to follow Caesar's orders. This caused many to turn against Rome except for the Aedui and Remi, who had always been loyal. It's not surprising though, since the Gauls were once fierce warriors and now had to obey Rome.

5:55

The Triviri and Indutiomarus begged across the Rhine all winter, promising riches and asserting the Roman army was weak after many losses. But no German States dared cross, having already failed in past wars. Indutiomarus raised troops and bribed outlaws, gaining great influence throughout Gaul and receiving embassies seeking his favor.

5:56

He saw that they came to him of their own accord, the guilty Senones and Carnutes, and the Nervii and Aduatuci preparing for war against the Romans. He called an armed gathering, as Gaulish tradition dictated, where all youths came in arms, and the last to arrive was killed after suffering all kinds of torture. There, he declared his son-in-law and former ally, Cingetorix, an enemy and took his property. He proclaimed that the Senones and Carnutes had invited him to march through Remi's territories before attacking Labienus' camp, and he explained what he wanted to do before it happened.

5:57

Labienus was holed up in a heavily fortified camp and didn't fear for himself or his men. He wanted to make sure he didn't miss out on any opportunities to win the war, so he sent messengers to nearby states and called for horsemen to join him on a set date. Meanwhile, Indutiomarus and his cavalry circled around Labienus' camp every day, sometimes to gather intel, sometimes to talk or to scare him. But Labienus kept his men within the walls and did what he could to make the enemy think he was scared.

5:58

Labienus kept his men close and guarded to prevent the Treviri from knowing their plight. Indutiomarus taunted them all day, but the Romans remained silent. At night, the enemy dispersed in disarray. Labienus quickly dispatched the cavalry, warning them not to kill anyone but Indutiomarus. The plan succeeded - Indutiomarus died and his forces retreated, giving Caesar some well-deserved peace in Gaul.

GALLIC WARS BOOK 6 (53 B.C.E.)

As readers venture into Gallic Wars Book 6, the narrative delves into the tumultuous events of 53 BCE, where Caesar faces a formidable challenge: the widespread revolt of the Gallic tribes. In this gripping account, Caesar's strategic acumen and relentless determination are tested as he strives to quell the uprising and maintain Roman dominance. Prepare to be captivated by the unfolding drama, as the complex interplay of military might, diplomacy, and the indomitable spirit of both the Romans and the Gauls come to life in this crucial chapter of Rome's conquest of Gaul.

6:1

Caesar plans for an uprising in Gaul and calls for M. Silanus C. Antistius Reginus, and T. Sextius to gather troops. He also asks Cn. Pompey to send the troops he had previously enlisted in Cisalpine Gaul to join him. This move is to prove to the Gauls that Rome has enough resources to sustain any losses during the war. Pompey agrees, Caesar quickly gathers his troops, and doubles his lost cohorts under Q. Titurius. The Gauls learn through his actions the power and discipline of the Roman people.

6:2

Indutiomarus died and his relatives gained power. The Treviri begged the Germans for help and promised them money. Some agreed and formed an alliance with Ambiorix. Caesar learned of this and saw that war was brewing, so he prepared for battle earlier than expected.

6:3

As winter lingered, Caesar gathered his four closest legions and marched with swiftness into Nervii territory. Without warning, he seized cattle and men, laying waste to the land and leaving the spoils to his soldiers. The Nervii had no choice but to surrender and offer hostages in hopes of survival. Quickly completing his mission, he led his troops back to winter quarters. In the spring, he called forth the council of Gaul, but sensing war and rebellion on the horizon, he moved the council to a new location, Lutetia of the Parisii. Without hesitation, Caesar advanced toward the Senones with his legions, taking long strides and arriving among them soon after.

6:4

Acco led the effort but found out the Romans were near. Fearing the worst, they sent guys to beg for mercy via the Aedui. Caesar, being the wise guy he is, forgave them and handed over hostages as a sign of trust. The Carnutes tried to do the same thing with the help of the Remi, but got the same result. Caesar just wanted to wrap things up and get ready for the summer war, so he made the states provide cavalry. Council adjourned.

6:5

This part of Gaul was calm now, and Caesar was focused on the war with the Treviri and Ambiorix. To avoid any trouble caused by Cavarinus' bad temper or his hatred of the state, Caesar orders him to march with him and the cavalry of the Senones. Knowing that Ambiorix would not want to fight, Caesar watches his other plans closely. The Menapii lived near the Eburones, protected by morasses and woods. They had never asked for peace like the rest of Gaul, and Caesar knew that they had a bond with Ambiorix, who had allied with the Germans via the Treviri. Caesar wanted to cut off the Germans and avoid a war with Ambiorix, so he sent the baggage to Labienus and ordered two legions to join him. With five lightly-equipped legions, Caesar marched against the Menapii, who had not called for any support and retreated to the woods and morasses, taking all their possessions with them.

6:6

Caesar split his troops with Fabius and Crassus, built bridges in a hurry, and attacked the enemy. He burned homes and villages, and took many cattle and prisoners. The Menapii, afraid, offered peace by sending their ambassadors to Caesar. He demanded that they don't give refuge to Ambiorix or his messengers within their land. Caesar left Commius the Atrebatian and some cavalry as protectors among the Menapii and rode on towards the Treviri.

6:7

Caesar was busy doing his thing when the Treviri, with a lot of soldiers and horses, planned to attack Labienus and his legion, who were camping nearby. But Labienus found out about their plans and decided to go after them with his cavalry and 25 cohorts. There was a river separating them but Labienus didn't think the enemy would cross it. He talked to his people about moving camp since they heard the Germans might help the Treviri. But he was just pretending to be scared so he could act like he was retreating. This tricked the enemy and they reported back to their own camp that it looked like the Romans were running away.

6:8

Barely had the rear left the fort when the Gauls, eager to seize the anticipated loot, crossed the river and attacked. Labienus, anticipating their move, tricked them and ordered his troops to form a line of battle. They quickly threw their javelins and charged towards the Gauls with threatening banners. The scared Gauls were put to flight, and Labienus pursued them with his cavalry, slaying a large number and taking several prisoners. A few days later, he gained control of the state, as the Germans who were to aid the Treviri, retreated due to the skirmish. The perpetrators of the revolt, including Indutiomarus' relatives, fled their own state. Cingetorix, who remained loyal from the start, was granted the supreme power and government.

6:9

Caesar went to the Treviri then decided to cross the Rhine. He didn't want the Treviri to get help from Ambiorix and he needed a plan if Ambiorix tried to run. After the soldiers built the bridge, he left some behind, and led the rest of the forces and cavalry over. The Ubii said they didn't help the Treviri and begged Caesar to spare them. After investigating, Caesar found out that the Suevi had sent help to the Treviri. Caesar accepted Ubii's apology and asked more about the Suevi's travel routes.

6:10

Meanwhile, the Ubii informed him that the Suevi were gathering their forces and enlisting cavalry and infantry from other nations under their command. Knowing this, Caesar provisioned his troops and found a suitable spot to make camp. He urged the Ubii to remove their livestock and belongings from the countryside to the cities, hoping this would force the Suevi, who were ignorant of such tactics, into unfavorable combat. The Ubii sent scouts to gather intelligence about the Suevi, who in a few days vanished with their allies, retreating to the dense Bacenis forest to serve as a natural protection against the Cherusci and the Romans. There they awaited Caesar's arrival.

6:11

Since arriving, it seems fitting to share the ways of Gaul and Germany. In Gaul, factions arise in every state, canton, division, and even family. The leaders, esteemed for their influence, hold power over all affairs. This was established long ago to prevent the common people from being oppressed. No leader allows their party to be mistreated. Gaul is divided into two factions, and this policy permeates throughout the land.

6:12

Caesar came to Gaul where the Aedui and Sequani vied for power. The Sequani, weaker on their own, made allies of the Germans and Ariovistus to strengthen their position. After defeating the Aedui in battle and taking their nobility, they gained control of the region. Aedui leader, Divitiacus went to Rome for help, but returned empty-handed. Caesar's arrival changed everything. The Aedui regained their hostages, influence and power, while the Remi became allies with Caesar. The Sequani lost their grip on power, and the Remi took their place.

6:13

In Gaul, there exist two orders of men who hold rank and dignity. The common folk live as slaves and have no say in important decisions. They become vassals to the nobles when they can't pay their dues. There are the knights and the Druids. The Druids conduct both public and private religious ceremonies and are highly revered by the young men who seek them for teaching. They are the judges in almost all disputes and violation of their decrees lead to great punishment. There is one supreme authority figure among the Druids and when he dies, others succeed him. The Druids gather every year in a sacred place in the Carnutes to make decisions on disputes submitted to them from all parts of Gaul. This institution is said to have originated in Britain and those desiring to study it more, visit Britain.

6:14

The Druids avoid battle and taxes while having special privileges. Some choose the profession themselves while others are sent by family. They memorize countless verses without writing them down, thinking it will make them more diligent and attentive. They also teach their beliefs that souls are reborn after death and this inspires bravery. Additionally, they educate youngsters on the workings of the stars and gods.

6:15

The knights are a different lot. They only know war. Before Caesar, the knights would engage in war every year either to inflict injury or to repel them. The most distinguished knights have the most vassals and dependents. Birth and resources mean nothing to them, only power and influence matter.

6:16

The Gauls are a superstitious lot, devoted to strange rites. When they face grave illnesses or dangers of war, they often offer human sacrifice. The Druids - their priests - lead the macabre ceremonies that are believed to placate the gods. The Gauls hold that only by offering a man's life can they secure the favor of divine forces. They carry out these sacrifices regularly as part of national customs. Sometimes, they construct giant effigies, fill their reed-made frames with people, then set them ablaze. They believe this form of sacrifice pleases the gods more if the victims have committed crimes. But when they cannot find enough offenders, they resort to offering the innocent.

6:17

They worship Mercury above all else. They think he invented everything and guides them in their travels. Apollo, Mars, Jupiter, and Minerva are also gods they believe in. Just like everyone else, they think Apollo prevents diseases, Minerva's good for invention, and Jupiter rules over all gods. Mars is the god of war and they vow to him on the battlefield. If they win, they sacrifice the animals they captured and leave the rest in piles. These piles are sacred and no one dares to take anything from them. If someone tries, they'll be punished harshly.

6:18

"The Gauls claim descent from Dis the god, passed down to them by Druids. Their calculation of seasons is by nights, not days, and birthdays and beginnings of months and years follow the day after the night. Unlike others, they hold off on revealing their children until they can fight. It'd be wrong for a boy to be seen in public by his father."

6:19

Husbands in Gaul receive dowries from their wives, and then contribute an equal amount from their own estates to keep the money together. They keep track of these funds and any profits they make, and if one spouse dies, the other inherits all of it. These husbands have power over life and death for their family, including their wives. If a prominent man dies in suspicious circumstances, there is an investigation into the wives, and if they are found guilty, they are tortured and killed. Gaul funerals are grand and expensive, with everything the person loved thrown in the fire, including live animals. In the past, they would even burn slaves and dependents who were close to the deceased after the typical funeral rites were done.

6:20

In smart states, the law says if someone hears a rumor about the commonwealth, they gotta tell the magistrate and not blab to anyone else. Dumb guys get fooled by fake news and screw everything up. Rulers keep tight-lipped about secrets, but let people know what's needed. Only talk about the state in council.

6:21

The Germans don't keep with our rituals. They don't follow druids or value sacrifices. They only recognize the sun, fire, and the moon as gods that give purpose. They live by the hunt and war, starting from their childhood. Among their people, those who are chaste for the longest time are praised for their growth, strength, and physical power. To have been with a woman before turning twenty is deemed dishonourable. They have no shame in bathing publicly in rivers with only deer skin cloaks covering parts of their body.

6:22

Agriculture isn't their top priority, so they survive on milk, cheese, and meat. No one has a specific plot of land, but the officials and the important folks decide each year how much land each tribe and family gets. Then, they make them leave the next year. They got reasons for doing this. They don't want people to forget about war and just farm instead. They don't want the rich to steal from the poor. They don't want people to make fancy houses. They don't want people to fight over money. They want everyone to be content with what they have.

6:23

The states take pride in having vast deserts around them and laid waste frontiers, proving their strength. They intimidate their neighbors by pushing them off their land and creating a secure boundary. During a war, the magistrates in charge hold power of life and death. When at peace, provincial and canton chiefs handle justice and disputes among their people. Robberies committed outside their state are not shameful because they believe it trains their youth and fights idleness. Those who refuse to follow their chosen leader during an assembly are seen as traitors and disregarded. Guests are treated with respect and their houses are always open with free provisions.

6:24

The Gauls once ruled over the Germans, waging war with great might, and even colonizing beyond the Rhine due to their large population and limited land. The Volcae Tectosages settled in the most fertile parts of Germany around the Hercynian forest, known as Orcynia to the Greeks. They remained there, respected for their valor and honor, yet still encountering the same hardships and scarcity as the Germans. Despite their proximity to the Province and introduction to luxuries from distant lands, the Gauls were ultimately outmatched by the Germans, losing many battles and surrendering their once great prowess.

6:25

The Hercynian forest, mentioned earlier, takes a nine-day trek for those in a hurry. There are no measures for roads and it begins at the Helvetii, Nemetes, and Rauraci borders, extending straight along the Danube River to the territories of the Daci and Anartes. It bends left away from the river, touching many neighboring nations, and no one from this part of Germany claims to have reached its end, even after sixty days of travel. Many unusual creatures are found in this forest, beasts different from any other and worth documenting.

6:26

An ox, stag-like in form, bears a horn that towers and stays true to form, unlike any of its kind. Alongside it, limbs extend like palms, stretching far and wide. The males and females appear alike, both with equally sized horns and the same visage.

6:27

Elks, like roes in shape and skin, but bigger and without horns. Legs without joints, no lying down or standing up. They sleep slightly reclined against trees which serve as their beds. Hunters track them to their tree leanings and cut the trees down to trap the elks. They fall down too.

6:28

The Germans hunt an animal called uri, which looks like a bull but is smaller than an elephant. Their strength and speed are impressive, and they attack anyone they see. The Germans trap and kill them, and the young men become strong and skilled by practicing this hunting. The ones who kill the most are celebrated and receive great praise. However, even when they are captured young, they cannot be tamed. The horns of these animals are different from our oxen, and the Germans treasure them. They bind them with silver and use them as cups at their best parties.

6:29

Caesar, knowing the Suevi had gone into the woods, anticipated a shortage of corn and decided not to pursue further. However, he didn't want the barbarians to think he was gone for good, so he destroyed 200 feet of the bridge and fortified the area with towers and guards. He left a young man in charge and later set out for war with Ambiorix, travelling through a vast forest. Caesar sent Basilus and the cavalry ahead to scout the area and ordered no fires be made to avoid detection. He promised to follow soon after.

6:30

Basilus follows orders, marching quickly and exceeding expectations. He takes those who were not expecting him by surprise and advances towards Ambiorix himself. Luck plays a big role in the art of war. By a remarkable chance, Basilus finds Ambiorix unguarded and unprepared, before anyone even knew he was there. Though Ambiorix's weapons and horses are taken, he manages to escape death due to the protection of his wooded dwelling. His followers fight off our horse for a moment, but one of them gets Ambiorix on a horse and he flees to safety in the woods. Ambiorix was fortunate both in his encounter and his escape from danger.

6:31

It's uncertain whether Ambiorix deliberately avoided battle or was just caught off guard by our cavalry's sudden appearance. Regardless, he quickly sent messengers out to instruct his people to flee and fend for themselves. Some ran to the forest, others to the marshes. Some hid on the islands the tide creates. Many left their homes, entrusting their lives and belongings to strangers. Cativolcus, who had joined forces with Ambiorix, couldn't bear the strain of war or escape and committed suicide with yew-tree juice after cursing out Ambiorix.

6:32

The Segui and Condrusi, Germans located between the Eburones and Treviri, requested Caesar's mercy, claiming they were not at war nor had they aided Ambiorix. Caesar checked the truth with his prisoners and ordered the return of any Eburones found fleeing to them. As a reward, he promised not to harm their lands. Next, Caesar split his forces into three parts and stationed the baggage of all his legions at Aduatuca, a stronghold where Titurius and Aurunculeius had wintered. The spot's existing defenses let Caesar save his soldiers' labor. To guard the baggage, he chose the fourteenth legion, one of three new forces from Italy, and put Q. Tullius Cicero in charge with 200 horse.

6:33

With the army split, T. Labienus is to head toward the Menapii with three legions; C. Trebonius with the same amount will wreck the district by the Aduatuci; he shall lead the remaining three to the river Sambre, which joins the Meuse, and to Arduenna's furthermost parts where he's been told Ambiorix went with a few horse. He promises to return by the end of the seventh day, the day corn is due to the garrisoned legion. If all goes well, Labienus and Trebonius are to return on the same day, and with the enemy's plans uncovered and their measures shared, they can begin a new type of attack.

6:34

No army, no town, no safe place to hide. People scattered far and wide, taking refuge in hidden valleys and woody spots. To keep the soldiers safe, they had to be split up, making it hard to attack with force. Caesar needs more men and sends messengers out to nearby lands to get them. The goal is to destroy those who wronged them, but only at minimal cost to their own forces. Soon, a large army is gathered, ready to fight.

6:35

Things were happening all over the territory of the Eburones, and the seventh day was close, the day Caesar wanted to return to his legion and baggage. It showed how much luck ruled in battle and how bad things got. The enemy was scattered and scared, so there wasn't much to fear. The news spread beyond the Rhine to the Germans that the Eburones were being looted, and everything was up for grabs. The Sigambri, who lived close to the river, got together 2,000 horse and sailed across the Rhine, 30 miles downstream from where Caesar left his bridge and garrison. They got to the Eburones and caught a lot of fleeing people and cattle. The Sigambri wanted more, so they asked their prisoners where Caesar was. They learned that Caesar had moved further away and that the whole army had gone. A prisoner told them that they could grab a lot of Roman treasure if they went to Aduatuca, where the army had left all the good stuff. The Germans went for it, leaving their plunder behind, and following the guide who had told them about the treasure.

6:36

Cicero kept his soldiers in check, as instructed by Caesar, but then grew suspicious upon hearing that Caesar may have been absent for longer than agreed. Cicero's tolerance was tested by those who wished to leave the camp, so he sent a group to forage nearby. About 300 recovered invalids and numerous attendants joined, along with beasts of burden.

6:37

At that moment, by pure coincidence, the German cavalry arrived and made a quick attempt to attack our camp at the Decuman gate. Their approach was unseen due to the nearby woods, and they nearly reached the camp before the merchants could retreat within its walls. Our soldiers were caught off guard by the sudden attack, causing a panic in the entire camp. Some believed that it had already been taken, while others imagined strange superstitions that led them to envision the worst possible outcome. This confusion made the enemy believe that there was no garrison within the camp, and they attempted to breach its defenses.

6:38

P. Sextius Baculus, a fearless leader in Caesar's army, had been left injured and hungry for five days in the garrison. He emerges from his tent without weapons, fully aware of the imminent danger from the enemy. Without hesitation, he grabs weapons from his comrades and stands guard at the gate. The other centurions join him, and they fight fiercely for a brief moment. Despite receiving several wounds, Sextius does not back down until he faints. His fellow soldiers save him, but this gives the others the strength to continue defending their position.

6:39

The soldiers finished foraging when they heard a shout. The horses went ahead to check the danger, but there was no fortification for them. The new soldiers looked to their leaders for orders. Everyone was rattled by the surprise. The barbarians saw our standard in the distance and stopped their attack, thinking our larger legion had returned. But then they realized our small group was vulnerable and attacked from all sides.

6:40

The camp-followers flee to the nearest high ground. When that fails, they huddle among the soldiers, increasing their fear. Some suggest breaking through the enemy's charge by forming a wedge, others propose standing firm on a hill. But the experienced soldiers with Caius Trebonius as their leader refuse both options. Encouraging each other, they charge through the enemy ranks and make it back to camp unscathed. The cavalry and camp attendants follow their lead and are saved. The soldiers who stayed on the hill lacked the skill and experience to defend themselves or act with speed. The promoted centurions fought bravely but died in combat. Some soldiers make it back to camp alive, while others are killed by the enemy.

6:41

The Germans couldn't take the camp by force, so they left with their loot. Our men were ready on the fortifications. Fear lingered even after they were gone. C. Volusenus came with cavalry, but no one believed that Caesar was with his army. Fear made their minds go crazy, thinking that the cavalry was the only force left. Caesar came and the fear disappeared.

6:42

He returned and knew the cost of war. He complained that the cohorts left the outposts for even the smallest danger. Luck played a big part in the enemy's arrival and their retreat from the camp. What's most surprising is that the Germans, who came to rob Ambiorix, ended up helping him instead by showing up at the Roman camp.

6:43

Caesar marched once more to attack the enemy, gathering many auxiliaries from nearby countries, and sent them out in different directions. They set fire to all the villages and buildings they saw, taking away anything of value. The cattle and men ate all the corn and the storms made it fall to the ground. Those who had hidden would soon have nothing left when Caesar's army left. Sometimes, the prisoners said they had seen Ambiorix, and Caesar's men tried hard to catch him. They almost succeeded, but Ambiorix escaped at night with only four guards.

6:44

After leaving destruction in his wake, Caesar marches his army back to Durocortorum with the loss of two cohorts. He calls a council of Gaul to deal with the treacherous Senones and Carnutes. Acco, the mastermind of the plot, receives the harsh punishment of our forefathers. Some cowards escape before facing trial and are barred from basic needs. For winter, two legions are sent to the borders of Treviri and Lingones, and six to Agendicum in Senones' lands. With provisions secured, Caesar heads to Italy for his trials, as planned.

GALLIC WARS BOOK 7 (52 B.C.E.)

As the epic tale of Caesar's conquests reaches its climax in Gallic Wars Book 7, the year 52 BCE bears witness to the fiercest and most decisive confrontations in the struggle for Gaul. In this riveting account, Caesar grapples with the formidable rebellion led by the charismatic Gallic chieftain, Vercingetorix. Prepare to be enthralled by the dramatic narrative, as the fate of Gaul hangs in the balance, and the relentless pursuit of power, courage, and determination of both the Romans and the Gauls culminate in a series of legendary battles that would forever shape the course of history.

7:1

Gaul was at peace, so Caesar headed back to Italy for business. He got
news that Clodius was dead and the Senate decreed that all Italian
youth had to take up arms. So, he decided to recruit from the province.
This news quickly spread to Transalpine Gaul where they made up
rumors that Caesar was stuck in Rome because of civil unrest. The
Gauls saw this as a chance to revolt against Rome. Gaul leaders held
secret meetings, discussing the death of Acco, the possibility of the
same fate befalling them, and the wretchedness of being under Rome's
power. They wanted to start a war to regain their freedom no matter
the cost. They suggested killing Caesar before he could reach his army,
seeing as he had no guard for the journey, and the legions wouldn't
leave their winter quarters unguarded. They'd rather die in the battle
than not fight for their ancestors' freedom.

7:2

As these plans were being made, the Carnutes profess that they're ready
for any danger to protect their people. They pledge to be the ones to
start the war. They can't exchange hostages now, so they demand a
promise by oath and honor. They bring together their military banners,
a sure sign that they take this matter seriously. The rest of the Gauls
cannot abandon them once the call to battle is made.

7:3

On the day they had agreed upon, the desperate Carnutes, led by
Cotuatus and Conetodunus, gathered in Genabum and killed the
Roman traders who had settled there. One of them was a prominent
knight named Caius Fusius Cita, who had been tasked by Caesar with
overseeing the provision department. The news traveled fast
throughout Gaul, as it always did whenever something important
happened. The people would shout out the news across the land,
passing it from one neighbor to another. In this case, the events in
Genabum were heard in the territories of the Arverni before the first
watch had even ended, which spanned over 160 miles.

7:4

The young Vercingetorix, son of Celtillus the Arvernian, roused his followers to take up arms against their oppressors. Expelled from his hometown, he gathered a group of desperate men and convinced more to join their cause. With his newfound army, he defeated his enemies and was crowned king. He demanded hostages and weapons from surrounding states and ruled with an iron fist, punishing even the slightest infraction with mutilation or death.

7:5

Gathering a fierce army from among the punished, he dispatches Lucterius, a man of incredible boldness from the Cadurci, with a portion of the forces to the Ruteni lands. Meanwhile, he marches into the Bituriges' land with his own soldiers. The Bituriges urgently plead with the Aedui, their protectors, to come to their aid to resist the enemy. The Aedui, following the advice of Caesar's lieutenants, send horses and foot troops to help the Bituriges. However, at the Loire River, which separates the Bituriges from the Aedui, the reinforcements delay and ultimately return home due to fear of the treacherous Bituriges. Soon after, the Bituriges join forces with the Arverni. Whether the Aedui's fear was justified or borne from treachery, we cannot confirm without evidence.

7:6

News of these events reached Caesar in Italy while he learned that Cneius Pompey had calmed the situation in the city. So Caesar made his way to Transalpine Gaul. But once he got there, he was unsure of how to join his army. If he called them to his province, they would have to fight without him. On the other hand, if he tried to reach them alone, he would be foolish to rely on those who seemed to have calmed down.

7:7

Lucterius of the Cadurcan, sent to convert the Ruteni, converts them to the Arverni. He goes to the Nitiobriges and Gabali and takes some hostages. Then, Lucterius marches bravely to Narbo with his powerful force. Caesar learns of this and decides that he needs to move to Narbo before anything else. He gets to Narbo and builds up the defenses and encourages his soldiers. Some forces go to rendezvous among the Helvii near the territories of the Arverni.

7:8

With Lucterius vanquished and danger lurking near Roman garrisons, Caesar sets out to the Helvii's land. The frosty mountain of Cevennes barring his way, he braves through six feet of snow with his men. Upon reaching the Arverni's territory, the enemy is taken aback; the snow having never before thawed enough for anyone to travel here, let alone an army. Caesar commands his cavalry to create chaos and alarm among the defenders. News of this chaos quickly spreads to Vercingetorix, who moves to preserve his people's land and property.

7:9

Caesar waited two days, expecting Vercingetorix to act as he planned. Then, he left to raise more troops, leaving Brutus in charge. Caesar ordered the cavalry to range widely, and promised to return within three days. He marched tirelessly to Vienna, arriving unexpectedly when he found more cavalry there. Fearing for his safety, he advanced quickly to the Lingones' territory, where two legions were wintering. Caesar gathered his army together before the Arverni could learn of his arrival. Vercingetorix retreated to the Bituriges' country, before attacking Gergovia.

7:10

Caesar was in a quandary about his plans because he feared that keeping his legions in one place during winter would lead to a revolt in Gaul. He also worried that moving them too soon would result in a lack of provisions. Despite the hardships, he chose to endure them rather than risk losing the support of his allies. After reminding the Aedui to provide him with supplies and urging the Boii to remain loyal, he left two legions and the army's luggage at Agendicum and marched towards the Boii.

7:11

On day two, he came to Vellaunodunum, a Senones town, ready to attack for food and strategic reasons. On day three, after embassadors came to discuss a surrender, he demanded weapons, cattle, and hostages. Leaving Caius Trebonius to their fate, Caesar continued to march towards Genabum. Upon reaching the town, he camps and waits for the right moment to attack. With the town connected via a bridge, he orders two legions to keep watch in case of escape. The people of Genabum attempted to cross the river quietly before midnight. However, Caesar proved too cunning and set fire to the gates, thus gaining the advantage. He seized the town entirely, leaving very few enemies alive. After taking the loot, he destroyed the town and continued his march into the Bituriges territories.

7:12

Upon learning of Caesar's arrival, Vercingetorix abandoned the siege of Gergovia and marched to meet him. Caesar had already started besieging Noviodunum when ambassadors from the town came to plead for mercy. Caesar demanded their weapons and horses, and took hostages. However, upon sending soldiers to collect the weapons and horses, they spotted Vercingetorix's cavalry approaching. The townsmen took this as a sign of hope and prepared for battle. But the centurions in the town, realizing the Gauls' intentions, took control of the gates and successfully protected their men.

7:13

Caesar, calling for his horse to be brought forth from the camp, charged into battle with his cavalry. As his men faced great distress, Caesar dispatched the four hundred German horse, which he had initially kept with himself, as reinforcements. The Gauls, unable to resist their attack, were forced to flee, having lost many soldiers. Upon their defeat, the townspeople, intimidated once more, seized and presented to Caesar the individuals whom they believed had stirred up the mob, submitting themselves to him. With these affairs settled, Caesar led his army to Avaricum, the largest and most fortified town in the Bituriges' territories, located in a remarkably fertile region. He was confident that taking control of Avaricum would bring the state of the Bituriges under his rule.

7:14

Vercingetorix gathered his men after losing at Vellaunodunum, Genabum, and Noviodunum. He convinced them to change tactics by preventing the Romans from gathering food. Vercingetorix planned to destroy the homes and villages in the Romans' path with the help of his cavalry. He encouraged his men to prioritize the safety of all instead of personal property. Vercingetorix believed that the Romans would either give up or put themselves in danger by venturing further from their camp. Burn the unfortified towns and remove any temptation for desertion or Roman plunder. Sacrifices were necessary to prevent guaranteed slavery or death.

7:15

The Bituriges agreed by all to burn over twenty towns in one day. Though regrettable, they believed that with certain victory, they could swiftly recover. They argued the fate of Avaricum in council, whether to defend or set it ablaze. The Bituriges begged the Gauls not to force them to destroy their beautiful city, preferring to protect it with ease from attack with its natural defenses of a river and marshes. Vercingetorix opposed their idea, but eventually relented, moved by their plight and the soldiers' empathy. The town was fortified with a fitting garrison.

7:16

Vercingetorix trailed Caesar with shorter marches, stopping to camp in a fortified spot defended by woods and marshes fifteen miles from Avaricum. From there, he kept a close eye on everything happening in Avaricum through scouts who reported back every hour. He even launched surprise attacks on our men when they went out for supplies, causing significant damage. But we eventually found a solution, by changing our routines and using different routes.

7:17

Caesar set up his camp on the unprotected side of the town, a narrow path led his way. He struggled for supplies and never stopped asking the Boii and Aedui for more corn, but they were of little help. His army suffered greatly from hunger, resorting to cattle for sustenance, yet they still stood tall in pride and held their heads high. When Caesar spoke to the legions, threatening to end the siege, they begged to continue fighting to avenge their fallen comrades in Genabum. They knew no defeat and would never back down from a challenge.

7:18

As the towers neared the walls, Caesar learned from some captives that Vercingetorix had destroyed the forage and set up camp near Avaricum. Caesar then sneaked out of his own camp at midnight and arrived at the enemy's camp early in the morning. Upon learning of Caesar's arrival, the enemy hid their belongings in the woods and gathered their forces on an open space. Caesar ordered his men to pile up the baggage and prepare their arms.

7:19

A hill rose gently from the bottom, but a marsh surrounded it, narrow and impassable, except at a few guarded fords. The Gauls, organized by tribe, had taken the hill and cut down the bridges. They were ready to overpower the Romans from the higher ground, for they knew the marshes and all its guarded passages. Though it seemed like the armies were evenly matched, it was an empty show of courage, and Caesar made this clear to his soldiers. He reminded them that victory would come at a great cost, and he held their lives more important than his own glory. After consoling them, he led them back to camp, determined to prepare for the siege.

7:20

Vercingetorix returned to his men and was charged with treason. They claimed he moved his camp nearer to the Romans, took all the cavalry, abandoned the forces without a commander, and enabled the Romans to seize them. Vercingetorix responded by pointing out that he moved his camp because of a lack of forage, got close to the Romans due to the terrain, and sent the cavalry where it would be useful. He left no one in command accidentally to prevent the eagerness of the multitude from risking an engagement. He had no desire for power from Caesar because he could win it through victory. Furthermore, he had tortured some Romans and learned that they were planning to flee. His actions had prevented the Romans from finding any food in the area.

7:21

The crowd roared and clashed their weapons as was their custom, showing their approval for Vercingetorix's speech. They hailed him as an exceptional general, praising his leadership during the war. A select group of ten thousand men were chosen to venture into the town, and the Bituriges were not the only ones entrusted with safeguarding the general safety, since they knew that the Bituriges would claim all the glory if they successfully defended the town.

7:22

Our soldiers fought bravely but the Gauls were clever and skilled in
making devices. They used nooses to trap our hooks and undermined
our mound with their knowledge of mining. Their wall was covered in
turrets with skins and they launched frequent attacks on us day and
night. They matched our towers and countermined our mines with
sharp stakes, boiling pitch, and heavy stones. It was a tough battle.

7:23

Gallic walls were made in a simple and effective way. First, beams were
placed on the ground with equal distance between them. They were
then mortised and covered with earth, and finally closed off in the
front with large stones. More rows were added with the same distance
and space between them, and stones were added to hold everything in
place. This created a strong and sturdy wall that was both beautiful and
useful for defense, not to mention protected from fire and battering
rams.

7:24

The siege faced many obstacles, including mud, cold, and showers, but
soldiers worked tirelessly for 25 days to raise a mound near the enemy's
walls. One night, while Caesar was keeping watch, the enemy set the
mound on fire and launched a surprise attack. Chaos ensued with
torches, pitch, and dry wood raining down. Thankfully, Caesar had
ordered two legions to keep watch and react quickly in case of an
attack. They were able to respond swiftly and extinguish the flames
while others fought off the attackers and repaired the ramparts.

7:25

The battle raged on into the night, with the enemy constantly renewing their hopes of victory. Our exposed position left us unable to easily provide assistance, and the enemy took advantage, constantly relieving their tired men. The safety of Gaul hung in the balance. In my view, a brave Gaul fell dead while throwing balls of tallow and fire into the enemy's fire. His comrades, undaunted, continued to take his place, one after the other, even as they were struck down by the enemy's bolts. The post was never left unguarded until the fire was extinguished and the enemy retreated, putting an end to the fighting. This tale, worthy of remembrance, could not be overlooked.

7:26

The Gauls tried everything, but nothing worked. They decided to escape the town at night after Vercingetorix ordered them to do so. The women tried to stop their husbands from fleeing because they couldn't run as fast and didn't want to abandon their children. When the men didn't listen, the women cried out and alerted the Romans. This scared the Gauls, and they gave up their plan to run to avoid Roman punishment.

7:27

The following day, Caesar, with the tower advanced and his plans set, saw a violent storm emerging. He considered this a perfect opportunity to strike since he noticed the guards on the walls were too carefree. Therefore, he instructed his men to appear as if they were working less efficiently and showed them what he wanted to achieve. He then secretly placed his soldiers within the vineae and encouraged them to gain a proportional victory to their hard efforts. Caesar promised to reward those who scaled the walls first and signaled for the attack. Without warning, the soldiers rushed out from all sides and swiftly conquered the walls.

7:28

The enemy, surprised by the attack, scattered from the walls and gathered in the market, ready to fight. Seeing no attackers, they dropped their weapons and ran. Some were killed by the infantry at the gates, some cut down by the cavalry outside. No one bothered with plunder. Exhausted from the siege and incited by the massacre at Genabum, they spared no one, not even the elderly, women, or children. Of the forty thousand, only eight hundred made it to Vercingetorix's camp. He received them in silence, fearing dissent from his already strained troops. After separating them, they were directed to their respective states in the camp.

7:29

Vercingetorix rallied his soldiers with brave words. He advised them not to be disheartened by their loss, and reminded them that the Romans were not invincible in combat. He believed the Romans only triumphed through sneaky tactics, which they were not familiar with. Although he did not think defending Avaricum was a wise decision, he promised to regain the loss with his superior strategies. Vercingetorix planned to unite Gaul and make it a force to be reckoned with. He urged them to fortify their camp and prepare for any surprise attacks from the Romans to ensure their safety.

7:30

The Gauls didn't mind the speech because their leader, Caesar, wasn't discouraged by the loss. He didn't hide from the people and they thought he was wise for wanting Avaricum burned and then abandoned. This made Caesar more respected, whereas other generals lose respect after a loss. The Gauls also began to believe in Caesar's plan to unite the states. They even started fortifying their camps, despite being unaccustomed to hard work.

7:31

Vercingetorix ain't slackin' on his efforts to gain more states to his side. He sends out the right people to woo the nobles with gifts and promises. He's makin' sure the folks who joined him after Avaricum get equipped proper with weapons and clothes. Vercingetorix orders every state to bring him a certain number of soldiers by a certain date, while also collectin' all archers from every corner of Gaul. With all this in place, he quickly gets his troops back to full strength. Teutomarus, son of Ollovicon - king of the Nitiobriges who the Senate considers a friend - shows up with a bunch of horsemen he hired from Aquitania.

7:32

Caesar rested at Avaricum, resting and refueling his army with plenty of food. With winter ending, he saw an opportunity to strike against the enemy, either by drawing them out or blockading them. The Aedui nobles asked for his help, as their state was in turmoil with two magistrates each claiming the throne. If left unattended, the state would fall into civil war. Caesar was called to action to use his power to prevent it.

7:33

Caesar didn't want the state to turn to violence due to internal dissensions, so he left the war and went to the Aedui. He called for the senate and those involved in the dispute to meet him at Decetia. When they assembled there, he found out that one brother had been declared magistrate by the other, which was against the laws. Caesar forced Cotus to resign and made Convictolitanis the supreme authority.

7:34

He made a decree, urging the Aedui to forget their feuds and join the war. He promised them rewards for their service and asked for their cavalry and ten thousand foot soldiers. He separated his army, giving Labienus four legions to conquer the Senones and Parisii. He kept six legions to conquer the Arverni, heading towards Gergovia along the banks of the Allier. He split the cavalry between Labienus and himself. Vercingetorix got wind of their move, destroyed the bridges, and moved his army to the other bank of the Allier.

7:35

As the opposing armies made camp across from each other and distributed scouts to prevent surprise, Caesar faced a challenge. The river Allier was impassable until autumn, and he feared being trapped on the wrong side. So he left some cohorts behind and led the rest of his troops to what he believed was an abandoned encampment. There, he quickly rebuilt a bridge that had been destroyed, crossed the river, and chose a strategic location for his army. Vercingetorix, having learned of Caesar's movements, moved swiftly to avoid confrontation.

7:36

Caesar marched for five days to Gergovia. Though he engaged in a slight cavalry skirmish, he couldn't take the city by storm, as it sat atop a mountain that was difficult to climb. Vercingetorix, however, had a strong position: he divided his forces up by state and placed them across the nearby hills, with a council of state leaders at his side. Almost daily, he staged cavalry actions to test his men. Caesar hoped to gain control of a nearby hill, which would give him access to water and free foraging rights. He took it by night, routing the weak garrison that held it and setting up two legions there. Then, he dug a double trench to keep his troops secure from potential ambushes.

7:37

While Gergovia was busy with its own business, Convictolanis, the noble Aeduan who was made magistrate by Caesar, accepted a hefty bribe from the Arverni. He met with a group of young men, including Litavicus and his brothers, and urged them to seize their freedom and rule. Convictolanis convinced them that the Aedui were the only thing keeping the Gauls from victory, and that by joining forces with the Arverni, they could drive the Romans out of Gaul. Litavicus and his brothers, easy to persuade with bribes and speeches, agreed to lead the plot. They hatched a plan for Litavicus to take charge of the ten thousand soldiers on their way to Caesar and for his brothers to go before him. They worked out the details and prepared to carry out their scheme.

7:38

Litavicus, commander of the army and 30 miles from Gergovia, assembled his soldiers and wept, telling them that their knights and nobles had perished, accused of treason and killed without trial by the Romans. Others confirmed this brutal act and urged revenge. Litavicus seized provisions, tortured and killed Roman citizens, and spread the same false story to Aedui, urging them to join in vengeance.

7:39

Eporedirix, an Aeduan of high birth and influence, rode in at Caesar's summons alongside Viridomarus. Despite being raised from lowly origins, he was their equal in status. They tussled over precedence in the ongoing feud between magistrates, each backing a different candidate. In the dead of night, learned of Litavicus's plans, Eporedirix shared his concern with Caesar. He begged Caesar to keep their state allied with Rome, as he foresaw that the safety of many could be jeopardized by the foolish decisions of a few misguided youth.

7:40

Caesar was anxious upon hearing the news, as he had always favored
the Aedui. Without hesitation, he took four light-armed legions and all
the cavalry from the camp. He didn't have time to contract the camp,
as the situation demanded immediate action. Leaving his lieutenant
behind with two legions, Caesar marched forward twenty-five miles
with his soldiers. They came across the Aedui, and Caesar directed his
cavalry to slow their advance. He commanded his soldiers not to kill
anyone and ordered the two traitorous brothers to address their
friends. The Aedui fell to their knees in surrender and laid their
weapons down. However, Litavicus and his clansmen, who follow the
old ways of the Gauls, fled to Gergovia, rather than forsake their
loyalty to their patrons.

7:41

Caesar sent messengers to tell the Aedui that he let the people live that
he could have killed in war. He gave his army three hours to rest before
marching to Gergovia. Halfway there, Fabius' horsemen arrived to
warn him that the camp was being attacked by a powerful army. The
soldiers were tired and wounded from defending the rampart. Fabius
blocked most of the gates and added breastworks to prepare for
another attack. Caesar and his soldiers hurried to the camp before
sunrise.

7:42

As Gergovia bustles with activity, the Aedui don't bother confirming
news from Litavicus. Their greed, wrath and inherent gullibility lead
them to take even the slightest rumor as truth. Roman citizens are
massacred, enslaved and their property plundered. The situation
worsens with Convictolitanis inciting more attacks. They lure Marcus
Aristius, a military tribune, from Cabillonus with the promise of
security and force all traders to follow suit. They attack constantly,
taking away their belongings and besieging those who resist. As
casualties pile up, they incite others to take up arms.

7:43

In the meantime, news arrived that Caesar had captured all their soldiers. They ran to Aristius, claiming they acted without public authority. Litavicus and his brothers' properties were seized, and the tribe sent messengers to Caesar to clear their name. They aim to retrieve their soldiers, but their guilt and greed for plunder led them astray. They started making war plans and riling up neighboring states. Caesar knew of their plot but remained calm when speaking with the messengers. He didn't hold the mob's fickleness against the state and wouldn't abandon his respect for the Aedui. Caesar then planned a return from Gergovia, anticipating more unrest, to avoid appearing to flee.

7:44

As he pondered, opportunity presented. While securing the works in the smaller camp, he noticed the enemy's hill devoid of men. Deserters confirmed the hill's back was wooded and narrow, exposing a pass to the other side of town. They feared losing it would result in being surrounded and without resources. All were summoned by Vercingetorix to fortify this place.

7:45

Caesar hears the news and sends troops of horse to the area, causing a commotion in every direction. At dawn, he brings out a large amount of baggage and muleteers disguised as horsemen to ride around the hills with a few cavalry. The Gauls couldn't tell what Caesar was up to from their distant view. Caesar sends one legion to the same hill, and then moves them to lower ground and hides them in the woods. This increases the Gauls' suspicion and they march to defend the area. Caesar sees the enemy camp abandoned and transferred his soldiers to the less camp while advising his lieutenants to hold back from fighting and instead focus on surprising the enemy. The Aedui are also sent to ascend from the right. Then, the signal is given for action.

7:46

At 1200 paces from the plain, a wall towered straight up, with a circuit that increased the route's length. Gauls had built a six-foot wall, made with massive rocks, as a blockade to the foot of the ascent. The natives had filled the upper part of the hill with their close-packed camps right up to the town's wall, leaving all space below empty. On the signal, the soldiers surge forward to the fortification, seize the separate camps, and take them. They are so agile in their attack that even King Teutomarus, of the Nitiobriges, caught unawares as he rested in his tent at noon, barely escapes with his upper body bare and his horse lacerated.

7:47

Caesar achieved what he wanted and ordered a retreat, with the tenth legion following his orders. The other legions, unable to hear the trumpet sound, were still held back by the tribunes and lieutenants. Fueled by the thought of victory, they chased down the fleeing enemy towards the town's wall and gates. A sudden shout from the city panicked those who were far away, and they fled, throwing clothes and silver over the wall in hopes of mercy. Some even surrendered to our soldiers. Lucius Fabius, a centurion of the eighth legion, climbed the wall with the aid of his comrades and took them up in turn.

7:48

Meanwhile, those who had defended the other part of town had heard the Roman victory cries and rode their horses over in a hurry. They joined their fellow fighters, standing beneath the wall, increasing their numbers. The Gallic women, who once reached out to the Romans, now begged their own people for mercy. They displayed their children and their messy hair. But the contest was not equal: the Romans were better positioned and had more soldiers. After a long fight, the exhausted Gauls couldn't hold off the fresh troops.

7:49

Caesar saw unfavorable ground and the enemy's growing strength in battle. To ensure his troops' safety, he sent orders to Lieutenant Sextius to lead cohorts down the hill towards the enemy. Caesar waited nearby with his legion, uncertain of the battle's outcome.

7:50

As our men fought fiercely in close combat and the enemy relied on their numbers and position, Caesar sent the Aedui to create a diversion by attacking our exposed flank. The resemblance of their weapons scared our soldiers, despite seeing their bare right shoulders, a symbol of peace. They suspected a ploy by the enemy. The centurion Lucius Fabius and his team, who had scaled the wall with him, were killed and thrown off the wall. A centurion from the same legion, Marcus Petreius, was also overpowered, wounded and unable to save himself, he led his men to retreat to the legion while he fought the enemy. He killed two of them and bought his men time to retreat. He died fighting, but saved his comrades.

7:51

Soldiers surrounded, lost position, lost forty-six centurions. Tenth legion saved by flat ground, thirteenth cohorts also helped. Legions arrived, stopped, fought back. Vercingetorix retreated. Nearly seven hundred soldiers gone.

7:52

The next day, Caesar called a meeting to reprimand his soldiers for their recklessness and greed. They disregarded the advice of their leaders and charged ahead without regard for the disadvantageous terrain. Caesar commended their courage but condemned their arrogance, insisting that a soldier needed not only bravery but also self-restraint. He shared a story of when he had given up a sure victory to avoid unnecessary losses due to position.

7:53

After a fiery speech, keeping up the morale of his soldiers, Caesar
marched his troops forward, anticipating a battle. But Vercingetorix,
refusing to come down to flat ground, only drew Caesar's cavalry into a
minor skirmish before retreating back to camp. The next day, Caesar,
satisfied with his efforts to humble the Gauls and uplift his own army,
moved his camp towards the Aedui. With no chase from the enemy, on
the third day he restored the Allier river bridge and guided his entire
army across.

7:54

After chatting with Viridomarus and Eporedirix the Aeduans, he heard
that Litavicus took all the cavalry to gather the Aedui. He knew the
Aedui were conniving in multiple ways, and if he let them go, they
would provoke the rebellion. But if he detained them, they might get
insulted or sense his fear. So, he let them go and reminded them how
he elevated their demoralized tribe from loss of land, power, and
supplies to a superior position in history. Then, he bade them goodbye.

7:55

Noviodunum sat on Loire's banks, a town of the Aedui, which Caesar
had filled with hostages, corn, money, and horses purchased in Italy
and Spain for the war. Upon learning about Litavicus' admission into
Bibracte and the senate's embassy to Vercingetorix for peace
negotiations, Eporedirix and Viridomarus saw a chance they couldn't
miss. They slaughtered Noviodunum's garrison and anyone trading
there, divided the spoils, relocated state hostages to Bibracte, and
burned the town. They then took whatever corn they could, tossing the
rest into the river or setting it ablaze, erected guards and garrisons
along the Loire's banks, and flaunted their cavalry to scare the Romans
while gathering more forces. The Loire's swelling from melting snows
made it hard to cross and added to their advantage.

7:56

Caesar heard of the enemy's movement and thought it best to hurry and cross the bridge, risking it all, before the enemy could gather more troops. No one liked his plan to march into the Province, what with the shame and hard roads, and worries for the safety of those he sent ahead. So, he and his army marched quickly day and night to the Loire River, and surprised everyone by finding a shallow enough ford for them to cross. The cavalry dispersed to weaken the current and confuse the enemy. Once across, they found food for the army and marched into the Senones territory.

7:57

While Caesar did his work, Labienus left new soldiers to guard the supplies at Agendicum and led four legions to a Parisii town, Lutetia. The enemy got wind of their arrival and brought in reinforcements from nearby. Camalugenus, an experienced military leader, was put in charge by the Aulerci despite being old. Seeing a marsh blocking their path, he decided to camp there and keep us from crossing.

7:58

Labienus tried to make a road through the marsh using hurdles and clay, but found it too hard. He moved silently from his camp in the third watch and made it to Melodunum. He got hold of fifty ships and scared the town's people with his sudden arrival, so he took over the town easily without a fight. Then, he fixed the broken bridge and led his army towards Lutetia along the riverbank. The enemy got news of this and set Lutetia on fire, breaking down the bridges. They went to the banks of the Seine, opposite Labienus' camp.

7:59

News arrived that Caesar left Gergovia and faced an uprising in Gaul by the Aedui tribe. Caesar's plans to cross the Loire were disrupted, forcing him to head back to the province due to a shortage of food. The Bellovaci, who were already unhappy, began assembling an army in response to Aedui's revolt. Given the situation, Labienus changed his strategy and focused on returning his troops to Agendicum safely. He didn't desire to provoke the enemy or gain land; his priority was the protection of his army. The Bellovaci was putting pressure on one side, while Camulogenus' army was on the other. The troops were separated from the garrison by the great river, and Labienus realized that he had to rely on his own energy and skill to overcome these difficulties.

7:60

At dusk, he called a council of war, urging his troops to obey his commands with urgency. He gave a ship to each Roman knight and told them to silently drift down the river for four miles, waiting for him. Leaving behind five steady cohorts to guard the camp, he directed the remaining five to march with all their baggage in the middle of the night, causing great commotion. He collected small boats and ordered them to row loudly in the same direction. Afterward, he silently led three legions to the location where the ships were to be stationed.

7:61

He came and caught them off guard during a storm. The Romans swiftly moved across the river with the help of some knights. The enemy heard commotion in the Roman camp and thought they were outnumbered. They divided their forces and Labienus was able to take advantage of the situation.

7:62

At first light, our soldiers were ferried across and the enemy appeared
before us. Labienus rallied his men with tales of their past victories and
the memory of Caesar, under whose command they had always been
triumphant. He gave the signal to attack. The enemy fell quickly on the
right where the seventh legion stood, but the twelfth legion held strong
despite losing their front ranks. Camulogenus, the enemy general,
urged his troops on, but it was not enough. When the tribunes of the
seventh legion heard of the left wing's struggles, they attacked from the
rear and the enemy was surrounded. Yet, they fought on, refusing to
retreat until they were all slain, including Camulogenus. The few who
remained to guard the enemy camp were quickly overthrown. Our
cavalry pursued those who fled into the woods and mountains. After
the battle, Labienus returned to Agendicum to retrieve the army's
luggage before joining Caesar with all his forces.

7:63

The Aedui revolted and caused danger to the war effort. They sent
messengers everywhere to incite rebellion using influence, authority,
and money. They killed hostages too. They asked Vercingetorix to join
and lead them. Gaul convened a council in Bibracte, where they voted
unanimously for Vercingetorix to lead. The Remi, Lingones, and
Treviri were absent as they supported Rome alliance. The Aedui were
unhappy to lose their role, but they still joined the war and followed
Vercingetorix. Eporedirix and Viridomarus submitted reluctantly to
him.

7:64

He demanded hostages and set a specific deadline, called for cavalry to
prevent the Romans from obtaining resources, and promised dominion
and freedom for those who sacrificed their property. With ten
thousand infantry and eight hundred horse, he waged war against the
Allobroges, and sent other groups to destroy territories. He even used
secret messages to tempt the Allobroges with money and power.

7:65

No more than twenty-two cohorts were guarding against all threats. Lucius Caesar, the lieutenant, gathered them from across the province to face the enemy. The Helvii fought with their neighboring foes but lost, causing them to retreat to their towns and forts. The Allobroges defended their borders with serious attention, placing guards along the Rhine. Knowing his troops were lacking in cavalry, and with no support from Italy or the Province, Caesar seeks help from his former foes across the Rhine. He calls on the light-armed infantry skilled at fighting against the Germans and provides them with the best horses he could find, even taking them from the tribunes, veterans, and Roman knights.

7:66

Meanwhile, as these events unfold, the Arverni's troops and cavalry gather along with the others from Gaul. With Vercingetorix leading the way, they set up three camps about ten miles from the Romans. The council of cavalry commanders is called, and they are urged to attack the Romans whilst they are on the move. According to Vercingetorix, the moment for victory has come, and the enemy is retreating to the Province, leaving behind Gaul. While it will ensure immediate freedom, it will do little to promote peace and tranquillity in the future as the Romans will return with more substantial forces. The cavalry agrees to an oath in which they will only return once they have ridden through the enemy army twice.

7:67

The proposal was accepted by all, and they were required to take an oath. The next day, the cavalry was split into three sections, with two making movements on our flanks and another obstructing our march. When Caesar heard of this, he ordered his cavalry to divide and charge the enemy. The action unfolded in every direction. If our men were struggling, Caesar ordered the troops to move forward and support them, which slowed the enemy's pursuit and lifted our men's spirits. Eventually, the Germans on the right wing reached the top of the hill, drove the enemy out of position, and chased them down to the river where Vercingetorix and the infantry were based, killing many. Witnessing this, the remaining enemies fled in fear of being surrounded. A massacre ensued, and we caught three of the most prominent Aedui commanders: Cotus, Cavarillus, and Eporedirix.

7:68

Vercingetorix retreated his troops from the battle in the same order they had lined up, heading towards the town of Mandubii. Caesar chased after, leaving two legions to protect his luggage, slaughtering around 3,000 of the enemy, and setting up camp in Alesia the following day. Despite the hard work of drawing a line around the city, he pushed his men to continue as he saw that the enemy was fearful due to their cavalry being defeated.

7:69

The town sat atop a lofty hill and was well-defended. Two rivers flowed at its base, and the town was surrounded by hills of equal height. The Gauls filled the space under the wall and fortified their position with a trench and a six-foot stone wall. The Romans had begun a fortification circuit of eleven miles. The camp was strong, with twenty-three redoubts and vigilant guards stationed day and night to prevent surprise attacks.

7:70

Horses charging and hills breaking the plain, a fierce cavalry action
begins. Caesar sends Germans to assist our troops and lines up legions
to guard against surprise infantry attacks. The added legions boost our
men's courage, and we route the enemy, trapping them at the narrow
gates. Germans pursue them and a bloodbath ensues. Some desperate
souls try to climb the wall, but Caesar orders the legions forward.
Inside the fortifications, the Gauls panic and cry "to arms" while
Vercingetorix orders the gates closed, fearing an attack. The Germans
retreat, having killed many and taken horses.

7:71

Vercingetorix sends away all of his cavalry by night, urging them to
gather as many warriors as possible for the war. He reminds them of
his loyalty to their cause and pleads for them to not surrender him to
the enemy. With barely enough provisions to last 30 days, he tightly
rations their supplies. He takes control of all available resources and
issues severe punishments for disobedience. With these preparations,
he waits for reinforcements from Gaul to continue the fight.

7:72

On learning from deserters and captives, Caesar fortified his position
by digging a deep trench, with vertical sides extending outward from its
base, and situating his other defenses four hundred feet away from it.
This strategy prevented the enemy from launching a surprise attack,
while also guarding against weapons hurled against his men. Behind
two more trenches, he built a wall equipped with stakes protruding
from the battlements like deer antlers to dissuade scaling, and
surrounding the entire perimeter with turrets positioned every eighty
feet.

7:73

Necessary to get wood, corn, and build fortifications at the same time. Troops reduced in number from advancing and defending against Gauls. Caesar added more works for defense, using sharp stakes arranged in five rows and intersecting in a quincunx, likely to impale anyone who entered. They called them "cippi." Pits with tapering stakes were also dug in oblique rows, resembling a lily. Hooks on stakes planted in small intervals were called spurs.

7:74

He finished the job by leveling the terrain as best he could in the rough land, enclosing fourteen miles and building similar fortifications to protect against enemies. He made sure to separate these fortifications from the main ones so the guards wouldn't be surrounded, even by a large number of foes. To reduce the soldiers' risks when venturing out, he ordered the stockpiling of enough forage and corn to last for thirty days.

7:75

During the war at Alesia, the Gauls called upon their nobles to decide on who should bear arms. Vercingetorix suggested a fixed number should be selected from each state, a wise idea as it meant they could govern and feed their men. The Gauls demanded troops from numerous regions, such as the Aedui and their allies, the Bituriges, Senones, Pictones, and many more. The Bellovaci did not contribute their fighters, choosing to fight the Romans their way. However, they sent two thousand men to honor their bond with Commius.

7:76

Caesar had a loyal ally in Commius, who he rewarded with tax exemption and land. But the Gauls were determined to regain their freedom and honor in battle. They gathered a massive army of 240,000 infantry and 8,000 cavalry. The commanders, including Commius, gathered in Alesia to strategize with representatives from each state. They were confident in their numbers and abilities and expected the Romans to be no match for them, especially in the two-front battle inside and outside the town.

7:77

The blockaded at Alesia, out of corn and with no hope of aid, gathered to discuss their situation. Some suggested surrender, while others thought a sally was possible. But Critognatus, from the noble Arverni family, spoke with cruel conviction. He was not interested in those who suggested surrender, calling it disgraceful cowardice. Instead, he focused on those who wanted to fight. He believed true valor came from enduring hardship and those who willingly offered themselves to death were braver than those who didn't. He urged them not to think only of themselves, but to consider all of Gaul that they had stirred up to aid them. If they lost the battle, the rest of Gaul would be doomed to endless slavery. He reminded them of their loved ones, who had risked everything for their cause. He urged them to be like their ancestors, who survived on the corpses of their elderly during the war against the Cimbri and Teutones. And though he knew it was a cruel decision, he believed it was necessary to establish a precedent of such savagery that the Romans would be too scared to come back.

7:78

When discussions arose, they decided that those too old or ill to fight should leave the town. They would exhaust all options before seeking Critognatus' counsel. But if things became dire and allies were slow to help, they would rather execute that plan than surrender. The Mandubii, who welcomed them, were forced to abandon the town with their families. When they reached the Roman fortifications, they pleaded to be taken in as slaves and given food, but Caesar stationed guards on the rampart and denied them entry.

7:79

Commius and other leaders arrived at Alesia with their army, camping a mile away from our fortifications. The following day, they filled the plain and stationed their infantry on higher ground while Alesia watched from above. The besieged were overjoyed at the sight of the auxiliaries, readying themselves for battle. They set up hurdles and filled trenches, preparing for any eventuality.

7:80

Caesar's army lined up on either side of the fortifications, with each soldier knowing their post, awaiting the cavalry's attack. The Gauls embedded archers and light infantry among their cavalry to counter our forces, resulting in a few unexpected casualties. The Gauls' yells and shouts sustained their troops but neither side was victorious. As sunset approached, the Germans charged in a compact body, causing the Gauls to flee, and the archers were killed. Our soldiers also drove the retreating enemy to their camp. Alesia's reinforcements retreated back to town, looking dejected and doubtful of their success.

7:81

The Gauls waited for a day while making weapons and then snuck out of their camp at midnight, heading towards our fortifications. They shouted suddenly to warn those inside of their arrival and started attacking us with arrows, stones, and slings. Vercingetorix gave a signal to his troops and they came out from the town to fight. Our troops defended the fortifications as best they could, using slings, stakes, and bullets. It was too dark to see much, so both sides suffered many wounds. Marcus Antonius and Caius Trebonius, the lieutenants in charge, sent troops from other areas to help when they saw where our troops were struggling.

7:82

The Gauls attacked from afar with deadly force, but as they got closer, they fell victim to the spurs and darts of the ramparts. Eventually, they retreated, unable to break through. Meanwhile, those inside prepared to sally forth but were too late as their enemies had already retreated. Their mission remained unfulfilled.

7:83

The Gauls lost twice and sought advice from locals who knew the land. They found a hill north of our camp and positioned themselves there. The enemy chose 60,000 strong soldiers from the bravest states and attacked at noon. Vergasillaunus led the attack after hiding behind the mountain and letting his weary soldiers rest. Cavalry approached the fortifications while the rest of the army made a show in front of camp.

7:84

From the citadel of Alesia, Vercingetorix emerged with long hooks, pent-houses, and mural hooks. The battle ensued on all sides and every trick in the book was used. The Romans were stretched out, fighting with difficulty in every quarter. The cries of combatants behind them caused great fear in our men for they knew their safety depended on the valor of others. As always, distant troubles are the most threatening.

7:85

Caesar picked a spot with a view, able to monitor his troops and send help when needed. Both sides knew this was their best shot. The Gauls desperately trying to break through the lines, Romans ready to call it quits if they won. Big battle was up top, with Vergasillaunus there in charge. A little slope had a big impact. Some throwing stuff, others advancing with their testudo. New guys switching out the tired ones. The earth piled in front made a way up for Gauls, hiding Roman defenses. Our guys were out of weapons and energy, though.

7:86

Caesar saw the enemy movements and sent Labienus with six cohorts
to aid his soldiers. He told him to retreat if necessary, but not without
need. Meanwhile, Caesar rallied the rest of his troops and encouraged
them to push on. The battle was crucial, and victory hung on the
balance. The Gauls tried to attack from the steep slopes since they
couldn't breach the fortified walls. They used all their weapons, but the
defenders held their ground until they resorted to using hooks to tear
down the ramparts.

7:87

Caesar sends young Brutus with six cohorts, and later Caius Fabius
with seven more. As the fighting grows fiercer, he calls upon fresh
soldiers to join the fray. After repelling the enemy and renewing the
attack, he leads his men towards Labienus. He drafts four cohorts and
orders a cavalry attack from the outside. Unable to hold off the enemy,
Labienus sends word to Caesar. The great man races to the battlefield
to join the action.

7:88

As the sun rose, his arrival was announced by the color of his robe and
the troops of cavalry. The enemy spotted him too from their forts on
the lowlands, and charged into battle. A shout erupted, followed by
more and more until it echoed like thunder. Our troops fought fiercely,
abandoning their javelins for swords. Suddenly, the Gauls were
ambushed by our swift cavalry and other cohorts which charged at
them mercilessly. The Gauls fled and we chased them, killing many.
The Lemovices general, Sedulius was also slain and Arvernian,
Vergasillaunus was captured. Caesar gained 74 military standards as a
result of the battle, and few of the Gauls survived. The besieged in the
town saw the defeat of their army and retreated. A flight of the Gauls
from their camp ensued, and if not for the tiredness of our soldiers, we
could have destroyed all of them. After midnight, our cavalry attacked
again and the Gauls who survived the day, fled to different states.

7:89

Vercingetorix called together a council and said he fought for freedom, not himself. He offered himself to the Romans for death or alive. Caesar got their arms and leaders, seating himself before the camp. The Gallic chieftains were brought before him and they put down their weapons, surrendering Vercingetorix. Caesar hoped to gain the Aedui and Arverni's support and gave each soldier a captive as plunder.

7:90

He marched into the land of the Aedui and took it back. The Arveni sent embassadors who promised to obey him. Caesar asked for many hostages, then sent his legions to winter. He released twenty thousand prisoners to the Aedui and Arverni. He ordered Labienus to take two legions and cavalry to the Sequani, Fabius and Basilus with two legions to the Remi, Antistius Reginus to the Ambivareti, Sextius to the Bituriges, and Caninius Rebilus to the Ruteni, each with one legion. Cicero and Sulpicius were sent to Cabillo and Matisco to get supplies while Caesar stayed in Bibracte for the winter. The senate in Rome celebrated with a twenty-day supplication after hearing about Caesar's victory.

◆◆◆

GALLIC WARS BOOK 8 (51-50 B.C.E.)

In the final installment of the Gallic Wars, Book 8 chronicles the events of 51-50 BCE as Caesar's conquests in Gaul reach their conclusion. In this captivating account, the narrative shifts focus to the mop-up operations, as Caesar works to consolidate Roman control and quell any remaining pockets of resistance. As you embark on this last chapter, prepare to be engrossed by the strategic maneuvers, diplomatic efforts, and the enduring spirit of the Romans and the Gauls, as they navigate the tumultuous aftermath of a long and brutal conflict that forever transformed the face of Western civilization.

8:0

At your request, Balbus, I've taken on a challenging task, one I've refused before out of laziness. I've written my own version of Caesar's Commentaries on his Gaul wars, not as good as his, but a decent continuation. I've also finished what he left incomplete after the Alexandria campaign, up until his death. I didn't want to do this, not wanting to appear foolish and presumptuous for meddling with Caesar's work. His writing is peerless, elegant and meticulous, a perfect resource for historians. Even though we know he wrote with ease and speed, I can only marvel at his flawless technique. I wasn't there with him in Alexandria or Africa, and hearing about it after the fact isn't the same as experiencing it for oneself. I must admit that I'm not fit to be mentioned in the same breath as Caesar. Goodbye.

8:1

After Caesar had fought relentlessly during the last summer and wished to rest his soldiers in winter quarters, news arrived that hostile states were renewing their efforts. The Gauls knew they couldn't beat the Romans with one force, so they hoped to attack in different places. Caesar's army had no aid, time, or resources to fight them all off. No state should refuse any inconvenience to gain liberty, others could take advantage of later.

8:2

To prevent the Gauls from thinking he's weak, Caesar left his quarters with Marcus Antonius in command and rode out with just a few soldiers on the last day of December from Bibracte to meet up with his thirteenth and eleventh legions stationed near the Aedui's lands. He left a couple troops to guard his stuff and marched the rest into the rich Bituriges country. They had a lot of land and cities, and didn't care about one measly legion being in their territory. They were getting ready to fight.

8:3

Caesar showed up like an unwelcome guest, catching the locals off-guard while they were working the land. They didn't have time to flee to the safety of their towns, since Caesar had ordered his men to avoid burning them down. Instead, he scooped up thousands of them, and even those who managed to get away found no protection in the neighboring regions. Caesar was too quick for them. Through his proactive approach, he managed to keep his allies in check, while also scaring off anyone who might've thought of challenging his power. But eventually, when the Bituriges realized he wasn't as ruthless as they feared, they came around and accepted his offer of friendship.

8:4

Caesar pledges to reward his soldiers with two hundred sestertii each for their hard work and endurance during the harsh winter, treacherous roads, and biting cold, promising them money instead of loot. He orders his legions back to their quarters after forty days and returns to Bibracte to serve justice. However, when the Bituriges plead for Caesar's aid against the aggressive Carnutes, he quickly mobilizes the fourteenth and sixth legion, stationed on the Saone for corn supplies, with only eighteen days in winter quarters, intent on pursuing the Carnutes.

8:5

When enemy heard we approach, they fled. Houses they left empty, hastily raised just to survive winter. We rested at Genabum to avoid vicious storms, put troops in Gauls' homes and makeshift thatched tents. Horse and auxiliaries sent to enemy's reported positions, returned with loot. The Carnutes, beaten by the winter and fear, run and hide among neighbors after losing theirs.

8:6

Caesar, satisfied with scattering enemies and avoiding summer warfare, stationed Caius Trebonius in Genabum with two legions. With frequent embassies from the Remi, he learned that the Bellovaci and neighboring states were preparing to invade Remi's patron state, Suessiones. To protect allies and his own reputation, Caesar ordered the 11th legion out of quarters and instructed Caius Fabius to march with his two legions to Suessiones' territory. He also requested a legion from Trebonius. Caesar shifted the burden of the expedition to each legion without ceasing his own efforts.

8:7

Caesar gathered his troops and marched towards the Bellovaci, camping in their lands. He sent out horse troops to capture prisoners and learn the enemy's plan. They reported that most people had fled and the Bellovaci were gathering with other tribes in a camp surrounded by a dangerous morass. They moved their baggage to remote woods and several nobles managed the war, but the people followed Correus, who hated the Romans the most. Comius left to seek aid from the neighboring Germans. The Bellovaci planned to fight Caesar with three legions, but if he came with more, they would stay in their position and ambush the Romans.

8:8

When Caesar learned the truth from several sources and saw the wise plans, he knew that the enemy had to be provoked into a fight. His three veteran legions, seventh, eighth, and ninth, were in good shape. The eleventh legion was made up of young and talented fighters with only eight campaigns under their belts, still lacking the reputation of their veteran comrades. Caesar addressed his soldiers in council to encourage them. He devised a strategy to deceive the enemy by hiding some of his legions behind the baggage while the seventh, eighth, and ninth legions marched forward. By adopting this formation, Caesar could show the enemy only as many troops as they would wish to face. The army was almost in a square and reached the enemy sooner than expected.

146

8:9

The Gauls were reported to Caesar as being bold, but when they saw the legions advancing with a precise formation, they didn't engage in battle. They simply positioned themselves on a high ground near their camp, perhaps to keep an eye on us. Although Caesar wanted to fight, the enemy's vast numbers surprised him. So, we camped opposite them with a deep valley separating us. Caesar ordered us to construct a formidable camp, complete with a 12-foot rampart, breastworks, and two 15-foot trenches with vertical sides. Additionally, three-story turrets with connected galleries were built and protected by small parapets made of osiers. Two rows of soldiers were tasked to repel the enemy with their darts, with those higher up being able to throw further with more daring. And those on the rampart were shielded from falling darts by the galleries. The entrance was secured by high gates and turrets.

8:10

Caesar built a fort with two purposes: to appear afraid and to boost confidence in the barbarians - if his camp was ever attacked, his works would secure it with a small force. Skirmishes were frequent across the marsh with few sallying out from both camps. Sometimes, our allies pursued the enemy and sometimes the enemy beat them back. Our foragers were often surrounded by the enemy but we only lost cattle and servants. Comius returned with a few German cavalry and the barbarians were elated by their arrival.

8:11

Caesar watched his enemy holed up in their secure camp, surrounded by marshes and ready for a fight. His army wasn't strong enough for an assault, nor to enclose the camp with lines. He had a plan. Caesar asked Trebonius to get the thirteenth legion from winter quarters amid the Bituriges under Titus Sextius, an officer in his army, and then come to him with three legions as soon as possible. He sent Remi cavalry, Lingones, and other countries to protect his foraging and support against any surprise attacks.

8:12

For days, the Bellovaci observed our horse and knew their daily path.
They chose a spot covered in the woods for their ambush, and decoyed
our soldiers into it. The Remi fell into this trap as it was their turn to
lead the duty. They saw the enemy cavalry's weakness, and attacked
them with fervor, but they were overwhelmed and surrounded by the
enemy's foot. Disorder prevailed, and they had to retreat faster than a
cavalry would usually do. Vertiscus, the governor of the Remi, and
their general, fought alongside his soldiers despite his old age. He fell in
battle, and the barbarians rejoiced in their victory. We learned to be
more vigilant and cautious from this defeat, and to never underestimate
our enemy.

8:13

Skirmishes every day near two camps, fighting at the ford and pass of
the morass. Germans crossed marsh and killed men from far away,
scared them so much they all fled. The whole army confused, hard to
tell if they were happy or sad.

8:14

After a few days in the same spot, the Bellovaci guards heard Caius
Trebonius and his legions were getting closer. They were anxious about
a potential siege, like what happened in Alesia. So, they quickly sent
away the elderly, sick, and any unarmed folks along with their stuff.
The Gauls were always accompanied by lots of wagons, causing chaos
before they could set off. When daylight came, they pulled out their
troops before their camp to prevent the Romans from pursuing them
before their baggage was far away. Caesar knew attacking them head-
on was risky, considering the steep hill they stood upon, and staying
too far away could lead to danger. But noticing a deep marsh dividing
their camps, he built a bridge and led his army across, soon reaching
the top of the hill's plain. The plain was protected on each side by steep
inclines, so he positioned his troops for fighting and headed to the
furthest hill. From there, they launched an attack with their weapons
into the thick of the enemy.

8:15

The Gauls, confident in their position, remained in order of battle, unwilling to divide their forces. Caesar kept his legions ready for battle and fortified his camp. The Bellovaci could not wait any longer without provisions and devised a plan to protect their retreat. They piled bundles of straw and sticks in front of their line, lit them on fire at dusk, and fled in the cover of the flames.

8:16

Caesar couldn't see the enemy leaving due to the fire, but thought they might use it as cover to escape. He sent his legions to advance and some horse to chase them, but was careful of an ambush. The horse couldn't make it through the flames, so the enemy fled without harm. They set up camp and attacked Rome's foragers with ambushes.

8:17

Caesar found out that the general of the Bellovaci, Correus, planned to ambush the Romans while they searched for food. Caesar sent more legions than he usually did, along with cavalry and light infantry, to protect the foragers. He led the charge towards the Bellovaci as fast as possible.

8:18

In ambush, the Gauls waited on level land no more than a mile wide, surrounded on all sides by thick wood or deep river. Our men, knowing the enemy's plan, marched with confidence, ready to fight with legions at their back. As Correus saw a chance to strike, he attacked with a small party. Our soldiers stood firm, avoiding the usual mistake of huddling together under surprise attacks from the horse.

8:19

Our men fought smart, taking turns to avoid being surrounded, while
some of the enemy broke out from the woods. The battle raged on
with great vigor, and our horse began to lose ground to the enemy
foot. But our light infantry arrived in time, fighting bravely and turning
the tide of the battle. Even though the enemy ambushed us, we
sustained no loss and eventually became superior. As the legions
approached, our men fought even harder, not wanting to share the
glory of victory. The enemy lost heart and tried to escape, but they
were trapped in the same labyrinth they planned to entrap us in. They
lost the battle and fled in fear, some seeking refuge in the woods or
river, but they were pursued and killed by our men. Correus, still
undefeated, refused to accept defeat and kept fighting until he was shot
down by our victorious men.

8:20

Caesar arrived right after the battle and figured the enemy would be
down enough to abandon their camp, even though the river blocked
his path. His army marched over and advanced, but the Bellovaci and
others found out about their loss from a few wounded men who
escaped and returned. They learned everything turned out bad, Correus
was dead and the best of their fighters were gone. They thought the
Romans were attacking them, so they quickly called a council and sent
out embassadors and hostages to Caesar.

8:21

Comius the Atrebatian fled to the Germans after everyone approved
the proposal. The rest sent ambassadors to Caesar, asking him to be
satisfied with the punishment already dealt to their enemy. They
believed that if Caesar had the chance to punish them before the battle,
he would not have done so. The cavalry had already defeated the
Bellovaci and killed many of their best soldiers. Only a few men
survived to tell the tale of their defeat. The Bellovaci did gain
something from the battle, though. They killed Correus, who rebelled
against the state and caused the people to act against the senate.

8:22

Caesar told the embassadors making the request that the Bellovaci had fought a war with other Gallic states last year and were the most obstinate in their pursuit. He knew that people easily blamed the dead for their crimes, but no one person could start a war without the consent of the nobles, and against the wishes of the senate and virtuous men. Although he was content with their punishment, he knew they brought it upon themselves.

8:23

The night after the ambassadors came back with Caesar's answer and prepared the hostages. Other ambassadors came from nearby states, waiting for the outcome of the war with Bellovaci. They took Caesar's orders and gave hostages, except Comius, who didn't trust anyone with his safety. Labienus found out the year before that Comius was plotting against Caesar and sent Quadratus to kill him during a conference. Comius got wounded, but survived. From then onward, he swore never to come near a Roman again.

8:24

Caesar, having conquered all the tough nations, saw that there were none left to challenge him. Some were running away to avoid getting captured, while others had risen in arms. So, he split his army into different parts. He kept Marcus Antonius the quaestor with the eleventh legion with him, and dispatched Caius Fabius with twenty-five cohorts into the remotest part of Gaul. As he did not believe that Caius Caninius Rebilus, who had control over that area, was strong enough to protect it with two legions, he ordered Titus Labienus to be with him. He sent the twelfth legion, which had been with him in winter quarters, to Hither Gaul to defend the Roman colonies, and prevent any loss by the inroads of barbarians who caused destruction to Tergestines the year before. He himself marched to empty Ambiorix's country. Although he scared the latter and made him flee, he despaired of being able to control him. He believed it most consistent with his honor to destroy the country's inhabitants, cattle, and buildings in case any of his countrymen survived, they would hate him for the calamities he had brought on them, and he would be prevented from returning to his state.

8:25

He dispatched armies to conquer Ambiorix's lands, destroying it with violence and pillage. Many were captured, many were killed. Labienus was then sent with two legions to fight against the Treviri, a people akin to the savage Germans due to their proximity to the German border. They were never loyal, except when Caesar's armies were near.

8:26

Caius Caninius, a lieutenant, received intel from Duracius that the enemy was in the Pictones' country, so he marched towards Limonum. Upon his approach, some prisoners disclosed that Duracius was captured by Dumnacus and that Limonum was under siege. Despite his weak legions, Caninius refused to face Dumnacus and instead chose to camp in a secure spot. Dumnacus, upon hearing of Caninius's move, attacked the Roman camp, but after several failures, he returned to besieging Limonum.

8:27

Caius Fabius brings states to allegiance, confirms submission by taking hostages. Caninius informs Fabius of Pictones' proceedings. Fabius goes to assist Duracius. Dumnacus, fearing Roman army and town's people, retreats with all his forces. Fabius crosses Loire to pursue Dumnacus. Horse attacks Dumnacus's rear on march, slays many, takes rich booty. Horse returns to camp.

8:28

Fabius sent his horse to engage the enemy and delay their march. General Varus, a skillful and spirited leader, fought with our men, positioning some troops and battling fiercely against the enemy's cavalry. The fight was hotly contested, as our men, fueled by a desire for victory, fought valiantly against the foot. The enemy thought they had the upper hand, but our cavalry proved them wrong.

8:29

The fight raged on fiercely with Dumnacus leading his army to alternate foot and horse. Suddenly, the legions appeared in close order, startling the barbarian horse and terrifying the foot. They broke through the line of baggage and fled in disarray with a loud shout. Our horse, who had fought them fiercely, pursued and slaughtered them, killing over twelve thousand men and taking their entire baggage train.

8:30

After losing the battle, they found out that Drapes, a Senonian who had gathered all sorts of men and women seeking freedom, including the exiled, robbers, and slaves, and had taken Roman supplies, was heading to the province with only five thousand men. Luterius, a Cadurcian, had joined him. Caninius chased after them with two legions to avoid shame or harm to the province at the hands of these desperate men.

8:31

Fabius marched with the army to Carnutes and other states. He knew
they had been auxiliaries for Dumnacus in the previous battle. Fabius
believed they would be more obedient after their losses. If given time,
they might follow Dumnacus again. Fabius was fortunate to regain
control over the states quickly. The Carnutes submitted and gave
hostages, even though they had never before asked for peace. The
other states near the ocean, called Armoricae, followed the lead of the
Carnutes and obeyed Fabius immediately. Dumnacus was expelled
from his territories and forced to flee to the most remote part of Gaul.

8:32

Drapes and Luterius, aware of Caninius' approaching legions and their
own inability to escape the province unscathed, decide to settle in the
territory of the Cadurci. Luterius, once a respected member of this
tribe, uses his influence to rally his and Drapes' followers and take the
fortified town of Uxellodunum.

8:33

Caninius marched quickly to the village, he saw that it was well-
defended by rocky terrain that would make it hard for soldiers to climb
even without opposition. He also noticed that the villagers had valuable
possessions and wouldn't be able to escape from our troops. Caninius
then split his army into three groups and set up camps on high ground,
planning to gradually surround the town as his soldiers could handle it.

8:34

When the townsmen got wind of his plan, memories of the distress at
Alesia filled them with fear of a siege. Luterius, who had witnessed the
calamity, advised his people to stock up on corn. So, they decided to
leave some of their troops behind and set out to gather corn with their
light troops. Drapes and Luterius won the support of their peers and
set off from the town, leaving two thousand men to guard it. They
spent a few days in the country of the Cadurci, sometimes taking corn
from them and sometimes facing attacks on their small forts at night.
Caninius avoided drawing his works around the town entirely in order
to avoid leaving them unprotected or making his garrisons too weak.

8:35

Drapes and Luterius stocked up on corn, planning to gradually
transport it into town from their location ten miles away. They each
took on their designated roles: Drapes stayed behind to guard the army,
while Luterius escorted the provisions into the town. Luterius, with
guards stationed along the way and utilizing forest paths, set out at
night. But our camp's sentinels caught wind of their movements, and
Caninius and his cohorts quickly attacked at dawn. The convoy fled in
panic, and the escort was met with relentless force. None were spared.
Luterius managed to escape with a handful of followers, and he never
returned to the camp.

8:36

Caninius was told by some prisoners that the enemy forces were
camped nearby with Drapes. He saw an opportunity to attack,
believing that the defeat of one leader would scare the others. He sent
his cavalry and German foot to the enemy's camp, while he took one
legion without baggage. Scouts told him the enemy was in a low camp
near a river, so he marched up with his legion. The battle started when
the German horse attacked. Our men then took the higher ground and
attacked from all sides, killing or capturing them all. Drapes was taken
prisoner.

8:37

Caninius completed the job easily, with barely a scratch on his men. He then went back to besieging the town, tearing down the opposition outside the walls. This let him finish his defensive positions and surround the enemy on all sides. Later, Caius Fabius arrived to assist and focus on one side of the siege.

8:38

Caesar left Caius Antonius with fifteen cohorts among the Belgae to prevent future plans. He traveled to other states, gathered many hostages, and eased their fears with kind words. When he arrived at the Carnutes, he demanded that Guturvatus, who started the rebellion, be punished. Although Guturvatus was afraid of his own people, he was soon found and punished by Caesar's soldiers. Despite his natural compassion, Caesar had to punish Guturvatus for the soldiers' sake. He was whipped to death and his head was cut off.

8:39

Caesar received letters from Caninius regarding the unwavering rebellion of the town's inhabitants and the fate of Drapes and Luterius. Though he felt their resistance was insignificant, Caesar feared that other Gaul states may follow their lead, resulting in a challenging summer for the Romans. To prevent this, he decided to discipline the rebellious town harshly. He left a lieutenant with two legions to follow him while he rode with his cavalry to Caninius as quickly as possible.

8:40

Arrived at Uxellodunum, finding it surrounded, and with no way out, Caesar decided to cut off their water supply. The only river nearby ran too low for diversion and was surrounded by difficult terrain. Caesar stationed his archers and slingers, and positioned engines to prevent the townsmen from accessing the water. They were forced to gather water from one location, allowing Caesar to tighten his siege.

8:41

Near the town's walls, a spring flowed out spilling waters over nearly
three hundred feet without any river. Others hoped to cut off the
besieged from the water, but Caesar saw the danger. Across from the
spring, they began to move the vineae toward the mountain while
constantly fighting. The locals ran down from high ground with no risk
to themselves, wounding many of our men. However, the men
continued forward, overcoming the situation without fear. They also
worked on their mines and moved the crates and vineae to the
fountain's source. A mound of sixty feet rose up, and on it stood a
turret of ten stories to rise above the top of the spring. When the
engines began to shoot, the locals could not get any water without
taking risks. There men, cattle, and working cattle all died of thirst due
to lack of water.

8:42

The townfolk were spooked and prepared for attack. They stuffed
barrels with oily tallow, pitch, and dry wood. These barrels were set
ablaze and hurled towards us. As they did this, they valiantly fought to
keep us from stopping the inferno. The blaze quickly spread
throughout our fortifications, being fueled by everything that went
tumbling down the slope. Our troops, despite their challenging
surroundings, remained calm and level-headed. They fought on while
perched atop a high point, with our army watching closely. A
tremendous roar rose up from both sides of the battle, making every
warrior stand tall and face the enemy and flames head-on, showing
their valor for all to see.

8:43

Caesar saw his wounded men and ordered the cohorts to ascend the mountain and shout as if they were attacking the walls. This fearful commotion made the besieged call off their troops and abandon the walls. Our men got the chance to extinguish the fires and cut off communication without risking a battle. The townsmen kept resisting, even after losing many forces to drought. But eventually, our mines cut across the veins of the spring, causing their source to dry up. This left them in despair, imagining it was the will of the gods. Finally, forced by necessity, they surrendered.

8:44

Caesar knew that his mercy was widely known, and he didn't want to be seen as cruel. He realized that if rebellions popped up everywhere, his problems would never end. So he decided to make an example of those who rebelled by cutting off their hands. Though he spared their lives, their punishment was clear. Drapes, captured by Caninius, died after refusing food for several days, either out of indignation or fear of a harsher punishment. Luterius, who had escaped the battle and was captured by Epasnactus, was handed over to Caesar by his friend without hesitation. Epasnactus recognized the power of Caesar and knew he couldn't hide for long.

8:45

Labienus fought well on horseback, slaying both Treviri and German soldiers. He captured the leaders, including Surus, an Aeduan known for his bravery and noble lineage, who had not given up the fight until then.

8:46

Upon hearing of his successful conquests in Gaul and realizing that Aquitania had not been personally conquered, Julius Caesar set out with two legions to achieve victory over the Aquitanians. He accomplished this with his usual efficiency and fortune, as all the states of Aquitania sent ambassadors to deliver hostages. After his triumph, Caesar dispatched four legions throughout Gaul to maintain order and peace. He then settled public disputes, rewarded the most deserving, and determined the state of the republic after the recent revolt in Gaul.

8:47

He finished his business and went back to his soldiers in Belgae where he spent winter in Nemetocenna. He found out that Comius, the Atrebatian, fought with his cavalry. When Antonius settled into winter quarters and the Atrebates remained loyal, Comius, who always stood with his countrymen in times of trouble, moved to advise and lead his people in war. After his state surrendered to the Romans, Comius and his supporters relied on looting with their cavalry, stole from the roads, and ambushed the convoys that brought food to the Roman camps.

8:48

Volusenus, Antonius' commander of horse, was sent after the enemy's cavalry. He had a strong hatred for Comius and was eager to follow orders to ambush them. After several successful skirmishes, a particularly violent one led to Volusenus being wounded when he recklessly pursued Comius. Our troops initially faltered but rallied when they saw their commander hurt. Many of the enemy were wounded, trampled or captured, but Comius managed to flee. Volusenus was carried back to camp with severe wounds. Comius, having lost most of his followers or having satisfied his hatred, offered hostages to Antonius, requesting to not be brought before any Romans. Antonius agreed, seeing it as a reasonable request. Nothing noteworthy happened the following year, but for those curious, Caesar's army was in Gaul at the time.

8:49

Caesar, in the Belgae countryside during winter, only cared about
keeping the states amicable towards him and avoiding any chances for
rebellion. He loathed the idea of leaving only to engage in a new war,
leaving his army behind to finish what the Gauls would eagerly take up.
By showing due respect to the states, giving generous gifts to the
notable individuals, not adding unnecessary weight to their current
obligations, and softening the possessive terms, he smoothly kept Gaul,
already exhausted from constant defeats, in line.

8:50

When his army moved out of winter quarters, Caesar went to Italy,
taking his time to visit free towns and colonies. He was there to
support his treasurer, Marcus Antonius, who was running for
priesthood. Some people, who rejected Antonius, wanted to undermine
Caesar's influence when he left office. Although he heard that Antonius
had been elected augur, Caesar still felt obligated to thank the towns
and colonies for supporting Antonius and to plead his case for the
upcoming consulate. His rivals boasted that Caesar's friends would be
stripped of their honor and dignity, and part of this was seen when
Sergius Galba, who had more votes and interest, was unfairly denied
the appointment of consul because of his connection to Caesar.

8:51

When Caesar showed up, the towns and colonies were really happy to
see him. They hadn't seen him since he beat up all of united Gaul. They
did a lot of stuff to make everything look good for him, like decorating
the gates and roads. People and their kids went out to greet him too.
Everybody sacrificed animals all over the place. They even put on
parties at the markets and temples because they were so excited. Rich
people made things real fancy, while poor people were just really
enthusiastic.

8:52

Caesar left Cisalpine Gaul swiftly and reviewed his legions in the Treviri territories. He made Labienus the governor of Cisalpine Gaul to gain his support for the consulate. He took journeys for the health of his men, ignoring rumors of Labienus betraying him and Senate's attempt to take away his army. Curio, a tribune, proposed Caesar and Pompey should both resign and disband their armies, but the consuls and Pompey's friends stopped it.

8:53

The senate spoke as one and proved their consistency; last year they defied the laws of Pompey and Crassus to undermine Caesar's authority, but when Marcellus sought to raise envy against Caesar, the senate turned the other way. The move did not break Caesar's opponents, but it taught them to widen their alliances to pressure the senate to heed their wishes.

8:54

The senate said Pompey and Caesar must send one legion each for the Parthian war. But Pompey gave Caesar his own legion, which he took from Caesar's province. Caesar knew it was a trick, so he returned the legion to Pompey and gave his own 15th legion instead. Then he sent his 13th legion to Italy instead. He put his troops in winter quarters, and sent Trebonius and Fabius with four legions each to the Belgae and Aedui, respectively. Caesar knew that by keeping these two powerful tribes under his control, he could keep the rest of Gaul safe.

8:55

Caesar headed to Italy where he learned two legions he sent home should have gone to Parthian war but were with Pompey, thanks to Caius Marcellus. Caesar knew war loomed but hoped for a peaceful resolution.

✦✦✦

Civil Wars Book 1 (50 B.C.E.)

As the narrative transitions from the conquests of Gaul to the tumultuous events of the Civil Wars, Book 1 plunges readers into the heart of the escalating conflict between Julius Caesar and his rivals in Rome, led by Pompey the Great. Set in 50 BCE, this gripping account lays the foundation for a monumental struggle that would not only shape the destiny of the Roman Republic but also determine the fate of its key players. Embark on this riveting journey, as the stage is set for a titanic clash of political ambitions, military prowess, and the unyielding determination of some of history's most legendary figures.

Vossius said the ones who don't believe Caesar wrote the
Commentaries on the Civil War are fools. Even without Suetonius'
proof, the way it's written would convince anyone Caesar wrote it. The
beginning of the Commentaries is missing, and it seems like Caesar
didn't start it so abruptly. That's why Plutarch, Appian, and Dion's facts
were necessary to fill in the gaps. Caesar wanted the consulate and to
extend his command of the province, but Lentulus and Marcellus
didn't want it to happen. Marcellus was a real jerk, arresting the
principal man of Caesar's recently planned colony of Novumcomum
and sending him to make complaints. Curio went to Caesar and
informed him of the efforts made by his enemies to crush him. Caesar
thought he should pay attention to the republic's tranquility, so he
asked for two legions and some provinces instead. Caesar then wrote a
letter to the Senate asking for favor and stating he would disband his
army if they did too. Curio was scared the consuls would suppress the
letter, so he kept it until a Senate meeting with the tribunes of the
commons.

1:1

Caesar's letter arrived. The consuls resisted its reading, but after much
tribune intervention, the letter was allowed to be read in the senate. No
questions were asked on it. The consuls instead asked about the state's
regulation. Lentulus promised loyalty to the senate, but warned against
courting Caesar's favor. Scipio echoed this sentiment, pledging support
for the republic if the senate acted with conviction.

1:2

Scipio spoke in the senate, with Pompey near, and it sounded like
Pompey's words. Those who spoke more moderately, like Marcellus
and Calidius, were met with harsh rebukes. Lentulus refused Calidius's
proposal, and most of the senate reluctantly adopted Scipio's idea that
Caesar should disband his army. Antonius and Cassius tried to
intervene, but violent opinions prevailed among Caesar's enemies.

1:3

After the senate disbanded for the night, Pompey gathered his own people and rallied them for the next day's vote. He praised the eager and criticized the cautious, turning them against Caesar. Across the city, Pompey's supporters and former soldiers flocked to his side in search of rewards. In the senate house, Caesar's enemies crowded around, intimidating the uncertain and silencing those who spoke out. Some suggested sending messengers to Caesar, like Piso and Roscius, or even a commission to inform him of the senate's desires.

1:4

Scipio, Cato, and the consul rejected all proposals while stirring up opposition against Caesar. Cato was driven by an old grudge and envy after a defeat. Lentulus was tempted by the promise of wealth and power while Scipio desired a province and armies to share with Pompey, his ally. Pompey himself, urged on by Caesar's enemies, had severed ties with him and sought reconciliation with their common enemies. Meanwhile, he was eager for war after incurring disgrace for boosting his own power by redirecting two legions from their expedition through Asia and Syria.

1:5

Everything was done quick and messy. No time for Caesar's relations to tell him what's going on. No liberty for the tribunes of the people to protect themselves. They couldn't even use their authority to help. But on the seventh day, they needed to think about their own safety, something they don't usually care for or fear. Then, the senate had to use their extreme and final decree, which they only used when the city was in danger or they had given up on public safety. The first five days they could meet, they passed tough and hurtful decrees against Caesar's government and the tribunes of the people. The tribunes escaped and went to Caesar, who was waiting in Ravenna, hoping to find a peaceful solution with his enemies.

1:6

Outside the city the senate is called, with Pompey repeating his
previous declarations through Scipio. He tells them of his ten legions,
the disaffection of Caesar's soldiers, and the inability to persuade them
to defend him. The senate makes motions on various subjects,
including levies throughout Italy, granting money to Pompey, and
honoring king Juba. However, Marcellus denies this motion and Philip
stops the appointment of Sylla. The provinces are decreed to private
citizens, praetors are appointed, and levies are made throughout Italy.
The consuls depart and private citizens have lictors, unlike previous
times. Italy is in unrest with forced arms and money taken from
municipal towns and temples. All sense of what is holy is lost.

1:7

Caesar got word of these things and spoke to his soldiers. He reminded
them of his enemies' wrongs against him and how Pompey, who he
always supported, had been turned against him by envy. He
complained about how the intercession of the tribunes had been
suppressed, despite it being a power they had before. Caesar urged his
soldiers to defend his honor against his enemies who sought to slander
him. The soldiers of the thirteenth legion pledged to protect their
general and the tribunes from harm.

1:8

Caesar learned about his soldiers and met with the fleeing tribunes. He
called upon his legions and ordered them to follow him. Young Lucius
Caesar, whose father was a lieutenant-general, arrived and delivered
private commands from Pompey. Pompey wanted to explain himself to
Caesar and make it clear that his actions were for the republic, not to
offend Caesar. Caesar should prioritize the good of the state over his
own desires and not harm the republic in his pursuit of revenge. The
praetor Roscius also spoke with Caesar, relaying the same message
from Pompey.

1:9

Caesar wanted to tell Pompey his thoughts since he had people who could share them. He hoped that they could settle their dispute and free Italy from fear. His honor was essential to him, and he was upset that people believed his enemies' lies about him. Even though he lost his command for six months and was forced to return to the city, he still submitted to it for the republic's sake. He asked the Senate to resign from their armies, but they refused. Everyone in Italy was in arms, and he feared all of it was leading to his ruin. He was willing to do anything for the republic, from going to Pompey's province to putting down their weapons. If Pompey and Caesar could meet, maybe they could settle their conflict.

1:10

Roscius and Lucius Caesar got the message and headed to Capua to meet the consuls and Pompey. They spoke about Caesar's conditions, and after some thought, the consuls and Pompey sent written proposals to Caesar. Their offer was simple: leave Ariminum, disband the army, and return to Gaul. If Caesar agreed, Pompey promised to go to Spain. But until Caesar gave assurance that he would keep his word, the consuls and Pompey would continue their levies.

1:11

Not fair, Pompey wants Caesar to leave Ariminum and give up his army while keeping his own province and troops. He said he'll go to his province, but won't say when. No promise of meeting for peace talks. Caesar sent Antonius with soldiers to Arretium and stayed in Ariminum to recruit more. He also stationed a cohort each in Pisaurus, Fanum, and Ancona.

1:12

Meanwhile, Caesar got word that Thermus had Iguvium fortified with
five cohorts, but the people were on his side. So, he sent Curio with
three cohorts from Ariminum and Pisaurus to take the town. Thermus,
doubting the loyalty of the townspeople, fled and his soldiers also
deserted him. Curio and the townspeople reclaimed Iguvium. Caesar
heard of this and, trusting in the loyalty of the other towns, took all the
cohorts of the thirteenth legion from the garrison and headed for
Auximum where Attius had brought his cohorts and raised new levies.

1:13

The senate of Auximum went together to Attius Varus upon hearing of
Caesar's arrival. They claimed it was not up to them to decide, but they
could not tolerate Caius Caesar being excluded from their town and
walls. Varus, frightened by their warning, retreated with his garrison.
When the battle commenced, Varus was abandoned by his troops, with
only a few switching sides to join Caesar. Lucius Pupius, the chief
centurion, was taken by Caesar as a prisoner. Caesar, impressed by the
soldiers of Attius, released Pupius, thanked the people of Auximum,
and promised to show his gratitude.

1:14

Upon hearing news of Caesar's approach, Lentulus the consul retreated
from Rome and the rest of the magistrates followed suit. The panic
spread throughout the city as rumors of Caesar's cavalry at the gates
circulated. Pompey had already left Rome for Apulia where he had
arranged the legions. The levies within the city were halted, and citizens
sought refuge in Capua. Lentulus attempted to raise levies but was
warned by friends of potential backlash. He distributed the gladiators
among the slaves of Campania for protection.

1:15

Caesar advanced through Picenum with the aid of friendly governors
and embassadors from the town of Cingulum. Lentulus Spinther
occupied Asculum, but fled upon hearing of Caesar's approach. He was
abandoned by some of his men and later met with Vibullius Rufus,
who dismissed him and gathered more cohorts for Pompey's army.
Together, they marched to Corfinium to join forces with Domitius
Aenobarbus and his troops from neighboring states.

1:16

Caesar took back Asculum and drove out Lentulus. He ordered his
men to find the deserters and do a muster. After getting some corn, he
marched to Corfinium. The enemy sent five cohorts to break down the
bridge, but Caesar's army beat them out of there quickly. The enemy
retreated into the town while Caesar and his legions encamped outside.

1:17

Domitius, upon seeing the danger, sent messengers who knew the land
well, promised them a big reward, to go to Apulia and plead with
Pompey to help him. If he didn't help, Caesar could be trapped and
starved of necessities. Domitius encouraged his soldiers, set up
weapons on the walls, and gave each man a specific place to guard. He
then promised the soldiers land as a reward, four acres for every regular
soldier and more for the high-ranking ones.

1:18

Caesar learned that Sulmo's people were willing to follow him but
Quintus Lucretius and Attius stood in their way. To take control,
Caesar dispatched Marcus Antonius with cohorts. The town welcomed
Antonius and handed over Lucretius and Attius. He added the cohorts
and prepared for the arrival of the rest of his forces. Caesar built
another camp for the incoming troops and fortified it before the
messengers from Pompey returned.

1:19

After reading Pompey's letter, Domitius kept the truth hidden and told his council that Pompey would come to their aid soon. He advised them to stay strong and prepare for the defense. But Domitius's face and actions showed fear and confusion, and he had secret meetings with his friends to plan his escape, which was impossible due to the blockade around the town. Pompey had already stated that Domitius had acted without his consent, and there was no more concealing the truth.

1:20

Word spread of Domitius's plan, causing the soldiers in Corfinium to rise in rebellion. In a meeting with their leaders, they realized they were trapped and that their general had deserted them. The Marsians disagreed on how to proceed, resulting in a violent clash. But eventually, they learned of Domitius's treachery, and united to confront him. They then offered to surrender to Caesar and turn over Domitius.

1:21

On hearing this, Caesar knew he had to control the town and his soldiers quickly to prevent any unwanted influence. But he couldn't risk plundering the town and disturbing the peace, so he told his men to be alert and secure the gates and walls. They formed a circle around the fortification, keeping a close eye on any possible threats. Nobody slept that night, too excited about what would happen next - whether it be the fate of the Corfinians, Domitius, Lentulus or anyone else.

1:22

In the fourth watch, Lentulus Spinther requested to speak with Caesar, escorted out of town by Domitius' soldiers. In peril, he begged for his life and recalled their past friendship, the grace Caesar had shown him. Caesar cut him off, explaining he had left his province to defend against enemies, fight for the people's freedom and bring justice. Lentulus, emboldened, asked to return to town, hoping his safety would inspire others. Caesar granted his request and Lentulus left.

1:23

At dawn, Caesar gathered senators, soldiers, knights, and children before him. He protected them from the insolent soldiers, reminding them of the ungrateful return for his kindness, then released them all unharmed. The public treasury returned sixty sestertia to Domitius, showing fairness in matters of money. Domitius's soldiers swore loyalty to Caesar as they marched, and he moved on to Apulia through the Marrucinians, Frentanians, and Larinates. Caesar stayed seven days before Corfinium, performing the regular march.

1:24

Pompey heard about what happened at Corfinium, so he marched from Luceria to Canusium, and then to Brundusium. He told all the new soldiers to join him, even those who were slaves. He gave them weapons and horses, and they became about three hundred strong. Lucius, the praetor, ran away from Alba with six cohorts, and Rutilus, Lupus, the praetor, fled from Tarracina with three cohorts. They saw Caesar's cavalry from far away, commanded by Bivius Curius, and they abandoned their praetor and joined Curius. During the rest of Caesar's march, other cohorts joined his army, some even joining his cavalry. Cneius Magius, from Cremona, Pompey's chief engineer, got caught on the road and was taken to Caesar. Caesar sent him back to Pompey with this message: "We haven't talked yet, so it's important for the commonwealth's safety that we meet. It's better to argue face-to-face than through someone else."

1:25

With his message delivered, Caesar marched with his six legions to Brundusium. The consuls had left with a large part of the army, but Pompey remained with twenty cohorts. Caesar was unsure if Pompey stayed to control the Adriatic or if he simply lacked ships. To prevent Pompey from accessing the harbor, Caesar built a mole of earth on each side of the narrowest point and placed double floats before them, secured with four anchors at each corner. He added more floats, covered them with earth, and constructed a parapet of wicker work for defense. Turrets were placed on every fourth one to defend against possible attacks.

To counter Caesar's plans, Pompey took giant merchant ships from Brundusium harbor, building turrets three stories high on them. Furnished with loads of weapons, he tried to break through Caesar's works. Every day there were skirmishes with slings and arrows. Caesar carried on as if he wouldn't let peace slip away. Even though he sent Magius to Pompey with a message, and Magius never came back, he still hoped for peace. Caesar sent another friend, Caninius Rebilus, to talk to Scribonius Libo, who was a good friend of Caesar. He wanted Libo to make peace for Caesar but, above all, Caesar wanted to talk to Pompey. Caesar thought if he spoke with Pompey, they would put an end to the fighting on equal terms. When Libo talked with Pompey, he returned with the answer that no deal could be made without the consuls. Caesar then gave up his efforts to make peace and prepared for war.

1:27

Caesar worked for nine days on his battle plans and the ships that brought his army to Dyrrachium were sent back. Pompey, either scared of Caesar's progress or planning to leave Italy all along, got ready to go when the ships arrived. He blocked the gates, streets, and avenues with walls and trenches, and sharp stakes. Pompey ordered his soldiers to sneak on board, and left a few light-armed men on the wall and turrets. He planned to call them off with a signal and leave them row-galleys.

1:28

The folks of Brundusium were pissed off by the rudeness of Pompey's soldiers and Pompey's disrespect towards them. So, they supported Caesar's gang. When they found out that Pompey had left and his soldiers were fooling around, they signaled from the rooftops. Caesar got wind of their plan and told his men to arm themselves and get ready to fight. Pompey left in the evening. The soldiers on the wall were called back and ran to the ships. Caesar's soldiers reached the walls using ladders, but the locals warned them about the traps and trenches. So, they stopped and took a long way around, and captured two of Pompey's ships that hit Caesar's barriers.

1:29

Caesar liked the idea of gathering ships and chasing Pompey across the sea to hasten the war's end, but he feared the lengthy delay it required since Pompey already took all the ships. Caesar's only option was to wait for a fleet to arrive from far-off lands, which seemed tiresome and inconvenient due to the season. He didn't want his army and the two Spains, one loyal to Pompey, to become more powerful and take over while he waited, nor did he want Gaul and Italy to be subdued without him.

1:30

He gave up chasing Pompey, choosing instead to head to Spain. He ordered folks in charge of free towns to get him ships and lead them to Brundusium. His lieutenant went to Sardinia with a legion, while his propraetor went to Sicily with three. Once they took Sicily, they headed straight to Africa. The guys in charge when he got there were scared and fled. Cato fixed ships and gathered Roman citizens. He was pissed at Pompey for not being ready for this unnecessary war. He voiced his complaints, then ran away from his province.

1:31

Valerius arrived in Sardinia and Curio in Sicily to no one in charge. Tubero also found the governor missing in Africa. Attius Varus had run off with his cohorts and seized the land. He had even raised two legions. Varus knew the people and the land well because he had been the governor a few years before. When Tubero arrived in Utica, Varus blocked him from entering and wouldn't allow his son to set foot on land due to illness. He forced them to leave the place by sea.

1:32

Caesar finished his business and left the soldiers to rest in nearby towns while he went to Rome. He reminded the senate of his enemies' injustice, saying he wanted no more than what every citizen had a right to. Despite Cato's tiresome speeches, a bill was passed allowing him to stand for consulate, even in the consulship of Pompey, who could have stopped it but didn't. Caesar spoke of his own patience and suggested the senate manage the republic with him. If they refused, he would handle it alone. He proposed sending deputies to Pompey, brushing off Pompey's assertion that authority was only for those to whom embassadors were sent, saying such thoughts were those of weak-minded people. Caesar aimed to excel in both glory and justice.

1:33

The senate agreed on envoys, but none were brave enough to fulfill the task. Each person, haunted by their own fears, refused the office. Pompey had proclaimed in the senate that he would hold in equal esteem those who remained in Rome and those in Caesar's camp when he left the city. Hence, three days were spent in arguments and apologies. Furthermore, Caesar's enemies bribed Lucius Metellus, one of the tribunes, to obstruct Caesar's intentions and hinder any other proposals he made. After days of fruitless attempts, Caesar discovered Metellus's intention and left the city to save time. He travelled to Transalpine Gaul without achieving his desired result.

1:34

Arriving there, he learned that Vibullius Rufus, taken by him in Corfinium, was sent by Pompey to Spain. Also, Domitius went to seize Massilia with seven row-galleys he manned with his slaves and colonists. Young noble men of Massilia had been sent ahead of him after Pompey urged them not to forget Caesar's former favors. Hearing this, the Massilians shut their gates and called for help from the Albici. They stocked up on corn, opened armories, and repaired their defenses.

1:35

Caesar called for fifteen important people from Massilia to meet with him. He spoke to them about how they should follow the example of Italy rather than obey one man's will. Caesar used logical arguments to convince them to see reason. The delegates reported what Caesar said to their people and the state answered back that they didn't have enough knowledge or judgment to decide which side was better. They received equal benefits from both Pompey and Caesar, and so they would neither help nor harm them.

1:36

While the treaty advanced, Domitius showed up in Massilia with his fleet, took governorship, and was given full control of the war efforts. He sent the fleet everywhere and captured any merchant ship in sight, bringing them all to the harbor. The nails, timber, and rigging from these ships were used to improve their own vessels. They put groceries from the captured ships in the public stores and kept the rest for the city attack. As revenge, Caesar approached with three legions to besiege Massilia. He constructed turrets and vineae to attack the city and constructed twelve ships surrounding Arelas. Being built and equipped within 30 days, they arrived in Massilia under Decimus Brutus' command; Caius Trebonius was left as his lieutenant for city investment.

1:37

As he readied his men, Caesar sent Lieutenant Caius Fabius with three legions to Spain. Their task: to seize the passes of the Pyrenees from Afranius, a lieutenant of Pompey. Fabius moved quickly, displacing Afranius' detachment and catching up with his army. The other legions, far away, were to follow as soon as possible.

1:38

When Vibullius Rufus arrived in Spain as per Pompey's orders, Afranius and Petreius, his lieutenants, shared their territories. Petreius had to pass through the Vettones and merge with Afranius, while Varro defended Further Spain. Some new troops were requested from Lusitania and other barbarous neighboring nations. Once the reinforcements arrived, Petreius proceeded to Afranius and they decided to fight near Herba due to its strategic location.

1:39

Afranius had three legions and Petreius had two. Eighty cohorts were raised in Hither and Further Spain, with different shields for each province. Five thousand horse were raised in both provinces. Caesar brought his legions, six thousand auxiliary foot, and three thousand horse from his previous wars, all consisting of the most noble and valiant men from each state, including the Aquitani and mountaineers from Gaul. Pompey was on his way to Spain through Mauritania with his legions. Caesar borrowed money from tribunes and centurions to distribute among his soldiers, gaining their loyalty and affection.

1:40

Fabius talked to the neighboring states by letters and messengers. He made two bridges over the Segre River, four miles from each other. He sent his foragers over the bridges because there was no more forage on his side. Pompey's generals did the same thing. The cavalry had skirmishes with each other. Suddenly the bridge broke under the weight of the cattle and water. The horse got stuck and could not go back to the main army. Petreius and Afranius knew about it, and Afranius used his bridge to march against Fabius's two legions. Lucius Plancus led the legions and drew up his army with two fronts so that the horse couldn't surround them. Even though outnumbered, Plancus fought with the legions and horse. The battle began when the horse charged, and both sides saw two legions' colors. Caius Fabius sent them over the far bridge to help his men, as he suspected the enemy's plan. The battle ended when the legions arrived, and each general went back to their camp.

1:41

Caesar arrived at camp in two days with nine hundred horse for his guard. He swiftly repaired the broken bridge and left six cohorts to protect bridges, camps, and baggage. The next day, he led his forces in three lines towards Ilerda and halted near Afranius' camp, offering him a fair battle. Afranius refused and posted his forces on a hill near his camp. Caesar then encamped, a short distance from the foot of the mountain. To avoid any unexpected attack from the enemy, he ordered his soldiers to draw a trench instead of a wall on the front opposite the enemy. The first and second lines remained armed while the third line completed the work in secret. Afranius only noticed the fortification when it was already complete.

1:42

At night, Caesar brought his legions into a trench and rested them under arms the next night. The following day, with materials needing to be brought from a far distance, he assigned each legion one side of the camp to fortify and ordered trenches of the same size to be cut. Afranius and Petreius challenged Caesar to battle, drawing out their forces to the mountain's foot; yet he did not get disturbed, relying on the protection of three legions and the strength of the fosse. They stayed for a short time, not advancing too far, before returning to their camp. The third day Caesar fortified his camp and ordered his other cohorts to be removed to it——a focus on the task at hand.

1:43

Between Ilerda and the next hill where Afranius and Petreius were, a plain of three hundred paces stretched. In the middle was a raised eminence, and Caesar aimed to seize it and prevent the enemy from reaching the town and bridge. From the camp, he led three legions to take the eminence, but the cohorts on guard for Afranius raced to occupy it too. Our men were repulsed, forced to retreat and regroup with the legions' standards.

1:44

The soldiers fought by charging forth audaciously and seizing posts, not paying mind to strict ranks and fighting in small groups. If things got tough, they didn't mind retreating and surrendering the post, as it was the way of the Lusitanians and other uncivilized tribes. This style of fighting scared our men, who were unaccustomed to it. They feared being surrounded from all sides by individual soldiers who ran forward, and thus believed they should maintain their ranks and not abandon their posts without just cause. So, when the enemy's advanced guard fell back, the stationed legion on that side also retreated to the next hill.

1:45

Caesar rallied his army after a surprise attack, leading the ninth legion to counter the enemy's advance. The legion pursued too eagerly, pushed into unfavorable terrain at the foot of a steep mountain where they were outnumbered and surrounded. Despite being at a severe disadvantage, our troops fought with valor and perseverance, enduring heavy casualties as fresh cohorts from the enemy's larger force were continuously deployed to replace exhausted fighters. In order to support our troops, Caesar was forced to send his own cohorts to that position as reinforcements.

1:46

For five hours straight, our men bravely fought with depleted weapons against a stronger foe. When they had no more javelins to throw, they unsheathed their swords and charged the enemy up the hill. They killed a few and forced the rest to flee. Fearful cohorts retreated to the wall and some ran into the town. Our cavalry on either side of the battle joined the struggle and rode between the two armies, securing our retreat. The battle had its twists; we lost seventy of our own, including Quintus Fulgenius, who was promoted for his valor. Six hundred were wounded. Afranius's party lost over two hundred men, including Titus Caecilius and four centurions.

1:47

On this day, two sides clashed and each thought they won. Despite
being considered weaker, Afranius's soldiers stood their ground and
repelled our initial attack. But our men fought for five grueling hours,
charging up the hill and forcing the enemy to retreat to the town. The
enemy held the hill with reinforced fortifications and a garrison.

1:48

With hardly a moment to catch their breath, disaster struck Caesar and
his army. A raging storm unleashed its fury, causing floods of epic
proportions that swept away the bridges recently built by Fabius. The
camp, situated between two rivers, was now cut off from the outside
world, with no means of foraging or replenishing their supplies. The
already scarce corn was now nearly ripe, and the states were drained of
every available resource by Afranius prior to Caesar's arrival. Even the
cattle, usually a fallback for times like these, had been taken far away
for safety. To make matters worse, enemy troops were lurking in the
area, making it impossible for Caesar's men to venture out in search of
food or forage.

1:49

Afranius had everything his army needed - plenty of corn, ample
forage, and access to it all through the Ilerda bridge. Caesar couldn't
touch the resources beyond the bridge, making Afranius even better
supplied.

1:50

The floods kept on coming for days. Caesar tried to fix the bridges, but
the water was too high. Cohorts placed along the banks made it
impossible to finish the repairs. They had a good position to stop the
repairs because they could throw their darts from different parts of the
bank, and the river's nature and high water made it difficult to
complete the work and avoid the darts at the same time.

1:51

Afranius heard that Caesar's huge convoy had stopped at the river. Gaul's horse and Rutheni's archers, along with six thousand others, including senators' sons and Caesar's subordinates, had arrived. They traveled without any concern, as there was no order or discipline. Afranius attacked at night, starting with his cavalry and three legions, but the Gallic horse gave him a tough fight. They retreated when the legions arrived, and our men took advantage of the delay to retreat to higher grounds, avoiding further casualties. Only a handful of servants, bow-men, and horses were lost that day.

1:52

The cost of food went up, a disaster that comes with times of scarcity and the fear of future need. Soldiers grew weak from lack of grain, and things only got worse each day. Fortune turned, and our men struggled to get by without necessities, while the enemy had everything they needed and an advantage. Caesar asked his allies for cows, and he sent non-combatants to faraway lands. He did everything he could to fix the shortage.

1:53

Afranius, Petreius, and their pals sent detailed news to Rome, inflating the situation to make it seem like the war was nearly over. When Rome got wind of this, folks rushed to Afranius' house to offer praise and celebration. Some even left Italy entirely to be the first to tell Cneius Pompey, while others wanted to avoid being seen as latecomers.

1:54

Caesar's plan was ruined, and the passes became impassable due to mounted soldiers of Afranius. Bridges to cross the river were also unavailable. Caesar knew how to build boats from his experience in Britain before. His soldiers used light timber for the keels and ribs, while the rest was created from wickerwork and hides. They worked hard and made them in a night. These boats were drawn down the river, in wagons, for twenty-two miles, and soldiers were taken across the river. They captured a hill quickly that was close to the bank, fortifying it unnoticed. He moved his troops and built a bridge on both sides over the next two days. This saved Caesar's convoy and those who went out to forage. He started the preparations to transport provisions.

1:55

On the same day, he led his horses across the river and surprised the foragers, taking a great number of cattle and prisoners. When the enemy sent reinforcements, our men split in two and one group protected the spoils, while the other fought off the foe. They isolated and surrounded a cohort that had strayed, put them to death, and returned with a hefty bounty over the bridge to the camp.

1:56

As Ilerda witnessed the ongoing affairs, Domitius' advice was heeded by the Massilians who readied seventeen ships of war, eleven of which were decked. Additional smaller vessels were added to invoke fear in our fleet by sheer numbers, and were manned with archers and Albici. Domitius claimed certain ships for his personal use, which were manned with colonists and shepherds. Fully equipped and with great audacity, he advanced towards our ships, under the command of Decimus Brutus, strategically located on an island across from Massilia.

1:57

Brutus had fewer ships, but Caesar chose the bravest men from his legions to lead the fleet. They came prepared with hooks, harpoons, and an arsenal of weapons. When they learned of the enemy's approach, they engaged the Massilians with great courage. Both sides fought hard, with the Albici showing their strength from their upbringing on the highlands. They had recently made promises to the Massilians, and their shepherds were eager to fight for their freedom.

1:58

The Massilians had swift ships and skilled pilots. They were able to escape our grasp and tried to surround us whenever they could. But they also tried to attack single ships with multiple vessels and remove our oars. Our men were not as experienced and were slowed down by our heavy vessels. When we had a chance to engage closely, we fought hard and took down nine of their ships, sinking some and capturing others.

1:59

When the news of Caesar's victory at Ilerda arrived, the completed bridge was a symbol of the changing fortunes. The enemy, no longer bold and free, held back and retreated, foraging close to camp or avoiding patrols altogether. When threatened, they fled, even leaving their goods behind. As a last resort, they chose to forage at night, contrary to all custom.

1:60

The Oscenses and Calagurritani offered to submit to Caesar. Tarraconenses, Jacetani, Ausetani, and Illurgavonenses followed. Caesar demanded they provide him with corn, to which they agreed. One cohort of the Illurgavonenses, aware of their state's plan, joined Caesar with their colors. The addition of five powerful states, completion of the bridge and availability of corn led to a change in affairs. Distant states revolted from Afranius and teamed up with Caesar after rumors of Pompey's arrival faded.

1:61

Caesar dug deep, drawing off a part of the river Segre, and created a convenient ford. His enemies, Afranius and Petreius, feared being cut off from necessary supplies and decided to leave their posts, taking the war to Celtiberia. They sought aid from the barbarians and prepared for a winter war. They constructed a bridge from boats and fortified their camp with a high rampart.

1:62

Scouts gave notice, Caesar toiled day and night, soldiers fatigued, river drained, horses able to cross with difficulty, foot soldiers slowed by deep water and swift current. News arrived of bridge near completion over Ebro and ford discovered in Segre.

1:63

The enemy grew impatient and quickened their pace, leaving only two cohorts behind while they crossed the Segre with their full force to join their legions. Caesar had limited options, as he couldn't take his cavalry over the bridge without taking a long detour. Instead, he sent his horse to cross the ford, surprising Afranius and Petreius in the third watch. They found themselves surrounded by Caesar's cavalry, slowing their march.

1:64

At first light, the soldiers at Caesar's camp saw they were attacked by
our horsemen from the rear. The last line sometimes broke and halted,
and sometimes engaged in a fight where our men were defeated and
chased by their cohorts. The soldiers felt disappointed that they had let
the enemy escape and prolonged the war. They begged their leaders to
tell Caesar they were willing to work hard and risk their lives, even
crossing the river where the horsemen had gone. Though Caesar
hesitated to expose his army to the large river, he agreed to try it. He
chose the stronger soldiers and left the weaker ones to guard the camp
with one legion. He led his army across the river using a great number
of horses as support. Some of them got carried away by the current,
but not a single one died. Once they were on the other side, he
organized them into three battalions, and by the ninth hour, they
caught up with their enemies who had started earlier.

1:65

Afranius and Petreius were scared shitless when they spotted Caesar's
army from a distance. They stopped on a hill and got ready for battle.
Caesar was smart and let his tired soldiers rest on the plain before
going after the enemy. He caught up with them and forced them to set
up camp early because there were mountains ahead. The enemy
planned to use the narrow roads behind the mountains to cross the
Ebro without getting attacked, but they were too tired to do it that day.
Caesar camped on the next hill, ready for anything.

1:66

At midnight, some of the opposing soldiers were caught fetching water
and told Caesar that their generals were quietly withdrawing troops
from the camp. Caesar then signaled to pack up and raise the military
shout. The enemy halted in fear of engaging in battle under their
baggage or being stuck in narrow roads by Caesar's horse. The
following day, both camps sent out small parties to reconnoiter the
country and reported that there was a level road for five miles followed
by a rough and mountainous area, with whoever triumphed in the
defiles preventing the other from moving forward.

1:67

Afranius and Petreius debated in the council on when to march. Most suggested going at night to sneak through the defiles undetected, but some argued that Caesar's cavalry was patrolling all night and that battles at night are riskier due to soldiers losing courage. They decided to go by day instead for the sake of duty, shame, and keeping the soldiers in line, even though there may be losses. The next day, at dawn, they set out.

1:68

Caesar saw the land and before the sky turned light, he led his army on a winding path, without any set road towards the Ebro and Octogesa. The enemy's camp blocked the path and his soldiers crossed harsh valleys. The cliffs were sharp and obstructed their march, so they had to pass their weapons from one person to another, and had to make their way unarmed. They helped each other climb up the rocks. Yet, no one complained about the tiredness, thinking that their hardship would be over if they were able to prevent the enemy from reaching the Ebro and their supplies.

1:69

Afranius's soldiers started off leaving their camp with high spirits, mocking our shortage of necessary subsistence for the escape to Ilerda. Their generals thought it was a smart move to stay within the campsite. They noticed we didn't carry any wagons or baggage, so they were sure that our endurance was limited. When they realized we were heading towards the right, and our van had already passed their line of the camp, they immediately recognized the need to march and stop us. They raised the call of arms, and all except a few, who remained to watch the camp, began the trek toward Ebro.

1:70

The battle came down to speed; whoever claimed the defile first would also conquer the mountains. Caesar's troops faced challenging roads, but their cavalry slowed Afranius's march. Afranius's men could avoid danger if they took the mountains, but they couldn't save their possessions or cohorts left behind in camp. Caesar arrived first, positioning his army behind ample rocks, ready to fight. Afranius took a pause on a hill, noticing his rear under attack from Caesar's cavalry. He dispatched Spanish light infantry to the highest mountain to secure it for his forces to cross, but they were quickly spotted and attacked by Caesar's horse, leading to their inevitable defeat.

1:71

Caesar saw a chance to win if he attacked now. His army surrounded the enemy, and they appeared fearful. His men urged him to start the battle. Afranius would come down eventually because of the lack of water. No need to hesitate.

1:72

Caesar hoped to end the affair without a fight, cutting off the enemy's supplies to avoid risking his soldiers' lives. He felt compassion for the citizens he foresaw would suffer, and preferred gaining his aim without harm to anyone. His decision was not popular, and the soldiers said they wouldn't engage even if Caesar wanted to. Despite this, he persisted and moved his camp closer to the enemy, fortifying it as best he could.

1:73

The next day, the enemy generals worried about losing supplies and access to the Ebro. They debated whether to head back to Ilerda or march to Tarraco. As they talked, news arrived that our cavalry had attacked their watering parties. They quickly sent out horse and foot soldiers, mixed with some elite troops, to build a rampart from their camp to the water. Petreius and Afranius oversaw the construction personally.

1:74

The soldiers had some time to talk amongst themselves without any officers around. A bunch of them came out and asked each other if they knew anyone in our camp. Then they thanked us for not killing them when we had the chance before, and started asking about our general and if they could trust him. They said they were sorry they didn't join us earlier, and that they felt bad for fighting against their own family. After some talking, they asked for their guys, Petreius and Afranius, to not be killed for betraying their own people. We said okay, and they promised to take their flags down and send some of their guys to talk peace with Caesar. Some of their people even came to our side to say hi. Everyone was happy and congratulating themselves on not having to fight. Caesar got a lot of love for not being a total jerk before.

1:75

Afranius heard the news and left his work, resolved to face whatever may come with composure. Petreius also prepared, arming his servants and a few soldiers, and attacked our men, killing as many as he could. However, our men fought back, wrapping their arms in cloaks and defending themselves with swords, ultimately retreating to safety under the protection of the cohorts on guard.

1:76

Petreius, once finished, toured the troops, calling them by name, and begged them not to hand over him and Pompey to their adversaries. They hurried to the leader's tent and pledged not to betray the army or take action that wasn't in their best interests. Petreius followed the oath and compelled Afranius to do the same. The other officers swore too, and the soldiers took the same oath. They ordered anyone with Caesar's soldiers to come forward and executed them in front of the praetorium. Fear, fierce discipline, and a stern vow stopped any hope of surrender, restoring the soldiers' morale and returning the war's course to its previous state.

1:77

Caesar searched the enemies' soldiers thoroughly and ordered them to leave his camp after they arrived for a meeting. But the tribunes and centurions chose to stay, and he treated them kindly. He even made some centurions higher-ranked and honored the Roman knights as tribunes.

1:78

Afranius's men struggled to find food and water. The legionaries had enough corn, thanks to the beef brought from Ilerda. The Spanish and auxiliary forces had no provisions, and their bodies couldn't bear the weight of carrying them. Every day, more of them defected to Caesar. Their situation was tough, but returning to Ilerda to plan for the future seemed like the best option. Tarraco was too far away and too many variables could change. Caesar sent his cavalry to hassle their rear, and he followed with his legions. Our horses kept them engaged at every opportunity.

1:79

Their way of battle was simple: light cohorts covered their backs and fought on level ground, where they could easily stand their ground. If they had to climb a mountain, the advanced guards protected those who followed them. But when they got to a valley or hill, and couldn't keep up with the advanced men, our horse took advantage of the situation and attacked them from higher ground. Then they were in danger, and their only way out was to stop the legions, push our horse back, and quickly run down to the valley. They did not get any help from their own horse, which was so intimidated that they had to protect them themselves. And no one could leave the line during their march without getting caught by Caesar's horse.

1:80

Skirmishes were fought slowly and with many stops to help the rear. The enemy took post on a mountain, entrenched themselves and did not remove their baggage. When they saw Caesar's camp, they rushed out at noon and hoped to delay Caesar with his horse. Caesar saw this and followed them with the remaining legions, leaving a few cohorts to guard his baggage. The horse charged the rear so hard that they almost fled and some were killed. Caesar's army was close and danger loomed.

1:81

Caesar and his men were forced to camp on unfavorable ground without water due to lack of options. Caesar did not attack the enemy, instead choosing to wait and observe. The enemy spent the night extending their camp and fortifying their position. The following day, they continued to do so but found themselves further from water. Caesar wanted to weaken them until they surrendered, so he focused on building a wall and trench to prevent a surprise attack. The enemy, running low on provisions, killed their baggage cattle before marching forward.

1:82

They spent two days on this work and its deliberations. By the third day, Caesar had made significant progress. They interrupted him on the third day by placing their legions in battle order outside their camp. Caesar had to prepare his army and cavalry to avoid losing face. But, he was against fighting because of the close proximity of the two camps. Since he was expecting a quick retreat in case of defeat, he decided to resist the enemy only if they attacked first.

1:83

Afranius had five lines, auxiliaries in the third, reserves. Caesar had three lines, four cohorts from each legion in the first. The slingers and archers in the middle, cavalry flanked. Both armies waited, Caesar not wanting to fight, Afranius wanting to stop Caesar. The next day, Caesar worked while the enemy tried to cross the river. Caesar sent Germans and horses to guard the banks.

1:84

They were surrounded, had no food or water for four days, and begged for a meeting in private. Caesar refused but agreed to a public meeting with Afranius. Caesar took Afranius's son as a hostage. Afranius spoke in front of both armies saying they had done their duty to Pompey and suffered enough. They were now like caged animals, unable to get water or even leave. They admitted defeat and asked for mercy. Afranius spoke humbly and submissively.

1:85

Caesar spoke firmly, reminding them that they had deviated from the laws of conference and truce, and had put to death unarmed and innocent people who were deceived by a conference. He pointed out that they must now face the consequences of their obstinacy and arrogance, which had led to this moment of surrender. He made it clear that he did not seek to increase his power, but simply desired the disbandment of their armies. He warned them of the measures that had been taken against him, the alteration of the laws of the magistrates, and the establishment of a new sort of government to keep him under check. He urged them to leave the provinces and disband their army so that he would not have to face them again. He said, "If this was complied with, he would injure no person; that these were the last and only conditions of peace."

1:86

Afranius's soldiers were happy to receive a dismissal without asking for it, which they showed by their joyful signs. They demanded an immediate release from their position on the rampart, as they could not be certain of their fate if it was delayed. After some discussion, those who had belongings in Spain were dismissed right away, and the rest at the river Var. Caesar promised not to harm them and not to force anyone to pledge allegiance to him.

1:87

Caesar said he'd give them corn until they reached the river Var, and give back whatever his soldiers took from them during the war. The soldiers got paid in money for those things. Afranius' soldiers let Caesar solve their problems. When the legions wanted pay and almost revolted, Afranius and Petreius said it wasn't time yet and asked Caesar to decide. A third of the army left soon after. Caesar ordered two legions to go ahead and the rest to follow the enemy, and Quintus Fufius Kalenus was in charge. They marched to the river Var and disbanded.

CIVIL WARS BOOK 2 (49 B.C.E.)

As the dramatic narrative of the Civil Wars unfolds in Book 2, the year 49 BCE brings the simmering tensions between Julius Caesar and Pompey the Great to a boiling point. In this enthralling account, readers are swept into the whirlwind of war, as Caesar makes the fateful decision to cross the Rubicon, setting the stage for a series of confrontations that would forever change the course of Roman history. Prepare to be captivated by the intricate strategies, daring gambits, and unyielding determination displayed by both sides, as the epic struggle for power and dominance rages on in this pivotal chapter of the Civil Wars.

2:1

As things unfolded in Spain, Caesar's lieutenant, Caius Trebonius, dug
in to conquer Massilia. He ordered the construction of vineae, turrets,
and a mound on two sides of the town - one facing the harbor and
docks, the other blocking off the passage into Gaul and Spain. Massilia
sat by the sea on nearly all sides, with just one avenue for attack by
land. But even that stretch, which led to the fortress, was tough due to
the steep valley and rough terrain. To achieve his goal, Trebonius
brought in loads of carriages, men, hurdles, and building materials from
the entire Province. In the end, he managed to erect an impressive
mound towering eighty feet high.

2:2

In the town, they had gathered a great amount of weapons and war
materials, enough to overpower any hurdle barriers. Huge iron-tipped
poles, launched from their powerful engines, would pierce through
four rows of hurdles. The vineae were then covered with thick beams
to withstand the attack. A sixty-foot testudo was used to level the
ground and protect from enemy fire and stones. However, the height
of the walls and towers and numerous engines slowed down our
progress. Frequent Albici sallies, throwing fire on our structures, did
little damage as our men quickly repelled and beat them back into the
town.

2:3

Lucius Nasidius, sent by Pompey, arrived unexpectedly in Messana
with sixteen ships, some with brass beaks. The nobles and senate fled,
scared by his sudden appearance, and he made off with one of their
ships. Once he joined his fleet, he sailed to Massilia and prompted
Domitius and the Massilians to fight Brutus's fleet with his added help.

2:4

The Massilians fixed their old ships with skill and speed, filling them
with seamen, archers, and engines. With renewed confidence and aided
by the prayers of their people, they set sail to join Lucius Nasidius. The
Massilians took the right, Nasidius the left.

2:5

Brutus went to the same spot, with more boats added to his fleet, taken from the Massilians - six boats that had all the necessary equipment following the last battle. He encouraged his troops to not fear a defeated people whom they had beaten previously. From Trebonius's camp and the higher grounds around, you could see everything that happened in the city. Everyone was asking the gods for victory. Every person there believed that their future depended on what happened that day. The younger and most respected people went to the boats so that if they lost, there would be nothing left for them to try. If they won, they could hope to save the city.

2:6

The Massilians fought with valor as though it was their last defense, knowing that if their city was taken, they would all face the same fate. The ships were slyly maneuvering with the help of skillful pilots, and when ours were distressed, the Massilians quickly came to their aid. The Albici joined in without hesitation and did not fall short in their bravery. However, our men were caught off guard by sudden dart attacks from the smaller ships. Two of their three-decked galleys targeted Decimus Brutus' ship, but he swiftly outsmarted them, causing them to collide and eventually be sunk by our fleet.

2:7

Nasidius's ships bailed on the fight without hesitation - no familial urging or love of country could sway them to risk it all. In the end, all of their ships remained intact, while the Massilians lost five ships and had four taken. The survivors made a beeline for Spain, save for one who was sent to Massilia to deliver the grim news. The people of the city were wrecked when they heard what had happened, as if they'd been overrun by invaders. Nevertheless, the Massilians gritted their teeth and got straight to work fortifying their city, without rest.

2:8

The soldiers on the right watched the enemy sally forth and thought a brick turret below the wall would be good protection. They built it small at first, to guard against surprise attacks. They hid there and defended themselves against stronger forces, and also attacked from there. It was 30 feet on each side and had 5-foot walls. Through experience and cleverness, they raised it to the standard height of turrets.

2:9

They built the turret with care and cunning, making sure that no part of it would be vulnerable to the enemy's fire. They laid the flooring on the walls, covering the ends of the joists with small bricks, and built up from there, using beams and joists to support the structure. Three mats of cable ropes, each the length of the turret walls and four feet broad, were hung around it on the sides facing the enemy. This they knew from experience was the only defense that could not be pierced by darts or engines. Gradually, using screws and mats, they raised the tower higher and higher, building each story securely and without danger. They left loop-holes for their engines in the walls where they thought best. Through their careful planning and execution, they raised the tower to six stories high, impervious to their enemy's attacks.

2:10

Confident in their ability to shield the nearby works, they built a timber musculus, sixty feet in length and two feet square. First, two even beams were laid on the ground four feet apart and small pillars were fastened to them, joined together by a gentle slope with timber laid on top to support the roof. They added beams two feet square, fixed with iron plates and nails. For the upper covering, they used laths to hold tiles and mortar to the structure and prevent fire from causing damage. Hides and mattresses were placed to avoid water and protect against stones and flames. The soldiers finished the work and stealthily moved it forward with the use of naval machinery, rolling it up to touch the enemy's turret.

2:11

The folks in the town were scared when they saw what was happening. They used big rocks and threw them at the enemy but it didn't work. Then they tried setting barrels on fire and rolling them towards the enemy, but they just rolled off. Our soldiers were undercover and used crowbars to remove the lowest stones of the enemy's turret. We defended ourselves with darts from our engines, and the enemy couldn't get a chance to attack our walls. Finally, we managed to pick away some stones from the enemy's turret, and it fell down suddenly.

2:12

The enemy, distressed by the unexpected fall of the tower, awed by the gods, and fearing their city's plunder, fled unarmed from their gates, hands outstretched in supplication. The war ceased as soldiers abandoned battle to hear their desperate pleas. The enemy fell to their knees before commanders and the army, begging them to wait for Caesar's arrival. They knew their city was conquered, and no defense remained. They warned of the soldiers' inevitable plunder and destruction should they be denied. Arguments were delivered with mournful pathos, for these were a learned people.

2:13

The lieutenants showed mercy and withdrew the soldiers from attack, leaving only sentinels. A temporary truce was established while everyone waited for Caesar's arrival. Both sides ceased all hostilities, as if the battle was already over. Trebonius had strict orders from Caesar not to take the town by force, for fear that the soldiers, angered by the inhabitants' revolt and contempt, would massacre all grown adults as they had threatened to do. It was difficult to restrain the soldiers from entering the town, and they were frustrated with Trebonius for stopping them.

2:14

The foe had no honor and waited for a chance to deceive. Days later, when our men let their guard down, resting or scattered about the walls, the enemy struck. They set fire to our defenses and in the chaos of the flames, our weapons and towers were lost. We fought back but were no match for their arrows and engines. The enemy tried again the next day but this time we were prepared. We fought bravely and forced them to retreat, without reaching their goal.

2:15

Trebonius worked with great vigor to repair the destruction caused, and the soldiers were motivated to help as they were angered that their efforts had been in vain. They were mocked for their bravery due to the truce being broken. Timber was scarce, but they constructed a new kind of mound using two walls of six-feet-thick brick and timber floors just as wide as the mound. They added pillars and beams when needed and covered it all in mortar and hurdles. The soldiers worked tirelessly and safely under the cover they built until the job was done with gates in the wall for sallying forth.

2:16

The enemy found that their defenses were no match for the speedy and skillful repairs made by our soldiers. We had surrounded their town with walls and turrets, leaving them nowhere to hide. Their weapons and tactics were useless against our brave men. Surrender was their only option.

2:17

In Further Spain, Marcus Varro was unsure of Pompey's success during the disturbances. He spoke favorably of Caesar despite being Pompey's lieutenant. Varro knew his duty and the province's disposition toward Caesar. He didn't take sides, but when he learned of Caesar's difficulties at Massilia and Ilerda, he changed his tune and followed the tide of fortune.

2:18

He raised troops and gathered supplies. He sent corn to friends and allies. He had ships built and guarded precious goods. He spoke harshly of Caesar and demanded tribute. He punished those who spoke out against him. He prepared for war in an island. Caesar would not leave a war unfinished.

2:19

Two legions under Quintus Cassius head to Further Spain. Caesar takes 600 horse, moves fast, and calls on magistrates and nobility to appear in Corduba. The proclamation is heard throughout the province and all states send their senate. The senate in Corduba takes action and guards the town, holding two cohorts for defense. Meanwhile, Carmona's people force three cohorts out of town and shut the gates.

2:20

Varro wanted to reach Gades quickly to avoid getting stopped on the way or while crossing to the island. The people in Gades liked Caesar so much that they wrote him a letter before Varro got far, saying they had teamed up with a tribune to kick out Gallonius and hold the city and island for Caesar. Hearing this, one of Varro's legions, Vernacula, took the colors from Varro's camp and went to Hispalis without causing trouble. The citizens there were totally cool with it and even offered to host them. Varro tried to go to Italica, but the gates were closed. Finally, he sent word to Caesar saying he was willing to hand over his legion, which he did when he got to Corduba. Then he gave Caesar all the money, corn, and ships he had, and that was that.

2:21

Caesar gave a speech in Corduba, thanking everyone: the Romans for keeping the town, Spaniards for driving out the garrison, Gaditani for defeating his enemies and securing their freedom, and the guards for their valor. He also remitted the citizens' tax and restored goods to those who spoke freely. After staying two days, he sailed to Gades and had stolen treasures returned to the temple. He left Cassius in charge, gave honors to some states, and journeyed to Narbo and Massilia. There, he learned of his nomination as dictator by Lepidus' law.

2:22

The Massilians, beaten, sick, and starving, surrendered without deceit. Their walls had crumbled, their food was old and damaged, and no aid could reach them. But Lucius Domitius had left just in time, sneaking out on a small ship with a brisk wind at his back while others pursued him. The Massilians followed orders, giving up their weapons, machines, ships, and treasure. But Caesar, respecting their age and renown, spared them. He left two legions behind and took the rest to Italy as he went back to Rome.

2:23

At the same time, Caius Curio crossed the sea from Sicily to Africa. He had little respect for the forces of Publius Attius Varus and brought only two of the four legions given to him by Caesar, along with five hundred horsemen. They arrived at Aquilaria after a two-day journey, where there was a convenient harbor enclosed by two projecting promontories. Lucius Caesar, who was waiting with ten ships, became scared after seeing Curio's fleet and fled on his covered galley to Adrumetum leaving his vessel on the nearest shore. Caius Considius Longus guarded Adrumetum with one legion, while the rest of Caesar's fleet also went to Adrumetum after Lucius Caesar's flight. Marcus Rufus pursued Lucius Caesar with twelve ships and brought back a ship left on the shore. Finally, he returned with his fleet to Curio.

2:24

Curio led Marcus and his army to Utica by fleet, leaving Caius Caninius Rebilus with the legions at the river Bagrada after advancing for two days. He rode ahead solo to scope out the Cornelian camp, a desirable location for camping due to its straight ridge that jutted into the sea, steep and rough on both sides with a gentle slope opposite of Utica. Utica was only a mile away in a straight line, but a spring on the way caused the sea to overflow and form a large marsh- a troublesome obstacle that required a lengthy six-mile detour to avoid.

2:25

Curio surveyed the terrain and spotted Varus's well-defended camp, fortified by the town and a nearby theater. He saw that the roads were busy with carriages and cattle, so he sent his cavalry to snatch some loot. Meanwhile, Varus had dispatched 600 Numidian horse and 400 foot soldiers, allies of king Juba, to guard the convoy. The Numidians put up a fight, but in the end, they were stymied and retreated. With reinforcements, Curio ordered all anchored merchant ships near Utica to leave or face the consequences. Within moments, all two hundred ships had set sail for the Cornelian camp, providing the army with much-needed supplies.

2:26

Curio returned to his camp at Bragada, greeted by a chorus from his army who hailed him as imperator. From there, he marched his troops to Utica and set up camp, hastily finishing the works before receiving warning that King Juba's forces were on their way. The sight of a cloud of dust on the horizon heralded their arrival, but Curio was taken aback by their sudden assault. Ordering his horse to hold them off, he quickly rallied his legions and prepared for battle. The disordered mass of Juba's forces proved no match for the disciplined Roman army, who slaughtered many of their infantry while the surviving horsemen fled to safety in the city.

2:27

Two Marsian centurions and twenty-two of their men deserted from Curio's camp to join Attius Varus. They claimed that the whole army was disaffected to Curio and suggested a meeting between the two armies. Varus, convinced by their words, led his troops out of the camp the next day. Curio followed suit, and they faced each other with only a small valley between them.

2:28

In Varus's army was a man, Sextus Quintilius Varus, who had been in Corfinium. Caesar gave him his freedom and he moved to Africa. Curio brought over the legions that Caesar had recently acquired under his command at Corfinium, so the soldiers and officers were mostly the same, save a handful of centurions. Quintilius saw this as an opportunity to address the soldiers and plead with them not to turn against those who had fought alongside them and shared their hardships, nor to fight for those who had insulted them. He promised to reward those who followed him and Attius. But Curio's army didn't respond to the speech, and both sides returned to their respective camps.

2:29

Fear spread fast in Curio's camp, fueled by rumors and individual opinions. Some said it was a civil war, that men had the right to choose which side to take. These sentiments came from soldiers who had recently joined Caesar's army after being offered a deal to switch sides. Harsh words were spoken but not by all, and some soldiers were not pleased. Others added more to the mix, trying to prove their loyalty.

2:30

Curio called a council to discuss the welfare of all. Some thought it best to attack Varus's camp to avoid idleness, while others advised withdrawing to the Cornelian camp for safety and time to think. Each man spoke his mind.

2:31

Curio criticized both ideas, claiming that one lacked courage and the other was too foolhardy. He questioned the reliability of storming a heavily fortified camp and the usefulness of abandoning the assault after suffering great losses. Curio believed that success was essential to gaining the respect and loyalty of the army, and that fleeing the camp would lead to universal despair and mistrust. He argued that doubts about the army's loyalty should be kept hidden, and desertion in any form should be avoided. Curio rejected the suggestion to attack at midnight, as such a cowardly scheme could only thrive in darkness. He advocated for a more cautious approach before forming his own opinion on the matter.

2:32

He dismissed the council and gathered the soldiers. Caesar wanted them to remember how they aided him in Corfinium and how he trusted them to protect Rome and Italy. He reminded them of how they supported him before, and the importance of being loyal in the future. The soldiers shouldn't be deceived by those who want them to change sides. They should remain loyal and fight alongside Caesar until the end. He reminded them of their history and successes, and the importance of following through with the goals they had set out to achieve. Loyal soldiers deserved respect, for they fought hard with courage and determination.

2:33

The soldiers, affected by the speech, tried to interrupt him. They appeared to bear with excessive anguish the suspicion of treachery. As he left, they unanimously beseeched him to be brave and engage the enemy to test their courage. Curio determined to risk a battle with general consent, changing the wishes and opinions of all. The next day, he led his forces and ranged them for battle, and Varus drew his men out for a chance to tamper or fight.

2:34

There was a valley between the two armies, not too deep, but with a steep ascent. They waited for the enemy to try and cross so they could engage with the advantage of the ground. On the left wing, the cavalry of Publius Attius mixed with light-armed infantry were seen coming down into the valley. Our cavalry and two cohorts of the Marrucini charged against the enemy's horse who fled back to their own friends. The light-infantry was left alone and was surrounded and taken down by our men. Varus's whole army saw the chaos and were frightened. Rebilus, a lieutenant of Caesar, shouted, "You see the enemy are daunted, Curio! Why do you hesitate to take advantage of the opportunity?" Curio merely replied that the soldiers should remember their commitments to him from the day before and then led them into battle. The valley was so steep that the soldiers in the front needed assistance from those behind. The minds of Attius's soldiers were filled with fear and they never thought to fight us. Before we could even throw a dart or get close to them, Varus's whole army turned and retreated to their camp.

2:35

A soldier, Fabius, in Curio's army shouted out to Varus by name, mistaking him for one of his own men. When Varus stopped and asked who he was, Fabius swung his sword at him, narrowly missing his target. Fabius was quickly surrounded and killed by enemy soldiers, as panic and chaos ensued. Although Curio's troops were close to taking the enemy's camp, they lacked the means to storm it. The enemy retreated to the safety of the town, and Varus wisely followed suit under the cover of darkness, leaving behind a few tents as decoys.

2:36

The following day, Curio aimed to besiege Utica by drawing lines around the town. The folks within were inexperienced in war, having lived in peace for too long. Some were Uticans, grateful to Caesar for his kindness, while others were a mix of Roman people with differing opinions. Fear from past battles lingered, causing them to openly consider surrender and persuade Attius not to ruin them all with his stubbornness. In the midst of this, messengers arrived from King Juba with news that he was marching towards them with substantial forces, offering hope and relief to the disheartened citizens.

2:37

Curio received the same intelligence but couldn't believe it at first as he was confident in his own luck. Caesar's success in Spain was announced in Africa, which made Curio even more confident. However, when he learned that the king's forces were only twenty miles away from his camp, he left and fortified the Cornelian camp. Curio also ordered his legions and cavalry to come from Sicily. His camp was in a strong position close to the sea with plenty of water, salt, and resources like timber and corn. So, Curio decided to wait for his forces and prolong the war with the agreement of his troops.

2:38

The plan was set and approved, then deserters arrived with information that Juba was gone and Sabura was drawing near. Curio, young and confident, sent his cavalry to attack Sabura's camp that night. They succeeded in surprising the enemy, who were encamped without order, and managed to kill several and take prisoners. However, they did not realize that Juba was not far behind.

Curio set out in the dark with most of his troops, leaving just five cohorts to guard the camp. After marching six miles, he encountered some men on horseback who had news of what had gone down at Bagrada. They told him that Sabura was in command. Curio heard enough and didn't ask any further questions. He just turned around to his troops and said, "Boys, don't you see that what these prisoners have said tallies with what our deserters have told us? The king's not there, he's sent a small force that was no match for these few horse. Let's go now and take our spoils and glory. We'll figure out how to reward you later." The horsemen had done well to defeat such a large number of Numidians, and they bragged about their accomplishments. They brought back lots of loot and showed off the prisoners and horses they'd nabbed. Curio was spurred on by his men's enthusiasm and led the horsemen towards Bagrada, hoping to catch the enemy off guard. But the horses were tired from the previous night's exertions, and they couldn't keep up with him. That didn't stop Curio from pressing on, though.

2:40

Juba was told of the nighttime battle by Sabura and quickly sent two thousand Spanish and Gallic horse to reinforce his infantry. He himself followed with the remaining forces and forty elephants, suspecting Curio would be close behind. Sabura ordered his army to retreat as if in fear, ready to attack when necessary. Curio, seeing this, thought the enemy was retreating and foolishly led his army down from the hills to the open plain.

2:41

He marched forward for sixteen miles until his men were exhausted
and had to stop. Sabura rallied his army, but only used infantry as a
display. Meanwhile, Curio encouraged his soldiers to rely on their
bravery in battle. Despite their weariness, the soldiers and horses
fought with great courage, but their numbers were few. They forced
the enemy to retreat but were unable to pursue them far due to
exhaustion. The enemy's cavalry soon surrounded them on both sides,
making it unsafe to either maintain or leave their positions. As the
men's strength began to fail due to fatigue and injuries, they became
desperate and resigned themselves to their impending deaths.

2:42

When Curio saw that his words and pleas meant nothing to his
panicked comrades, he knew their only chance was to reach the nearest
hills. But horses under Sabura's orders took control of the area, leaving
our men hopeless and some were killed trying to escape. Cneius
Domitius and a few soldiers encouraged Curio to run to his own camp,
promising to stay with him. But Curio, ashamed to face Caesar after
losing his army, fought until his death. Only a handful of soldiers who
had stayed behind survived after seeing the defeat from afar.

2:43

The soldiers met their fate without exception. Marcus Rufus, the
Quaestor who remained at the camp, reassured his men while they
pleaded to escape to Sicily. He agreed and instructed the shipmasters to
bring the boats to shore in the evening. Nevertheless, fear plagued the
troops: some claimed to spot the dust from the armies of Juba or
Varus, but there was no truth to their claims. Others were fearful that
the enemy fleet would soon attack. Chaos and panic ensued, leading to
a desperate grab for safety. The heavier ships sank in the overload of
people, delaying the escape of the rest. Only a few small fishing boats
followed orders and escaped on time.

Aged and weary soldiers, either by influence or compassion, were taken
in Sicily. The others sent their centurions as messengers to Varus and
gave themselves up at night. Juba saw their cohorts the next day and
claimed them as his own, ordering many to be killed. Varus couldn't
protest as he didn't want to lose face. Juba rode in on a horse,
accompanied by Senators, and within a few days, he arranged
everything in Utica as he pleased. In a few more days, he returned
home with all his forces.

CIVIL WARS BOOK 3 (48-47 B.C.E.)

In Civil Wars Book 3, the narrative reaches a fever pitch as the events of 48-47 BCE unveil the decisive confrontations between Julius Caesar and Pompey the Great. In this gripping account, readers witness the culmination of a struggle that would dictate the future of the Roman Republic and its key players. As the war intensifies, Caesar's military genius and unrelenting determination are put to the test in legendary battles such as Pharsalus. Embark on this enthralling journey, as the stage is set for a climactic showdown, with power, ambition, and the fate of Rome hanging in the balance.

Julius Caesar wrote of the Civil Wars with a terse style, using short sentences to tell a story of power, betrayal, and violence. His third book details the battles and political intrigue of the year 48-47 B.C.E., when factions vied for control of Rome. Caesar's writing captures the intensity and immediacy of the time, as armies clashed and men fought for their lives. In Hemingway's style, the prose becomes even sharper, with spare language conveying the brutality of war and the complex motivations of its players.

3:1

Julius Caesar, a dictator, made himself consul alongside Publius
Servilius. The laws allowed him to do so. In this year, Italy was facing a
credit crisis and debts could not be paid. To resolve this, Caesar
appointed arbitrators to assess the worth of the debtors' properties
before the war and hand them over to the creditors as payment. This
was a clever way to prevent the abolition of debt, which usually
happens during times of civil war. He also restored some people who
were previously convicted of bribery, after consulting the people.
These people had offered their services to Caesar at the beginning of
the civil war, and he valued them for it. Caesar wanted the people, not
himself, to be the judges of their restoration to their former condition.

3:2

He accomplished much in eleven days, including celebrating the Latin
festival, elections, and resigning the dictatorship. Then, he headed to
Brundusium where he expected to meet twelve legions and all his
cavalry. However, he had only enough ships for fifteen thousand
soldiers and five hundred horses. Caesar wished to end the war
immediately but the lack of ships prevented that. Additionally, the
soldiers who embarked were fewer because some died in previous wars
and the journey took a toll on their health.

3:3

Pompey got a year off to gather forces without fighting or serving any
opponents. He pulled together a sizeable fleet from various places,
such as Corcyra, Athens, and Egypt. Pompey ordered the building of
many additional ships. He demanded that Asia, Syria, and other
provinces give him a large sum of money. He also made the
governments of those provinces under his rule give him a significant
amount of money.

3:4

He gathered nine Roman legions, five from Italy that he brought along, a veteran legion from Sicily, one from Crete and Macedonia of discharged veterans, two from Asia, recruited by Lentulus' enterprise. He mixed soldiers from Thessaly, Boeotia, Achaia, and Epirus with his legions as reserves. He counted on two legions from Syria with Scipio along with three thousand archers, six cohorts of slingers, two thousand mercenaries, and seven thousand horsemen from Crete, Lacedaemon, Pontus, Syria and other regions. He acquired six hundred horsemen from Gaul with Deiotarus, five hundred from Cappadocia with Ariobarzanes, and the same number from Thrace with Cotus's help. Two hundred soldiers of great courage arrived from Macedonia, commanded by Rascipolis, and five hundred Gauls and Germans. Gabinius's troops from Alexandria also arrived with eight hundred slaves raised by Pompey, the son. Tarcundarius, Castor, and Donilaus gave three hundred from Gallograecia, and Comagenus Antiochus sent two hundred soldiers from Syria, most of them archers. He also gathered troops from Macedonians, Thessalians, and other nations, completing the previously mentioned number.

3:5

He hoarded vast amounts of corn from lands such as Thessaly, Asia, Egypt, Crete, and Cyrene. He intended to bunker down at Dyrrachium and Apollonia during the winter to impede Caesar's sea passage. To achieve this, he placed his fleet along the coastline. Pompey the Younger led the Egyptian fleet, Decimus Laelius and Caius Triarius led the Asian fleet, Caius Cassius led the Syrian fleet, Caius Marcellus and Caius Coponius led the Rhodian fleet, while Scribonius Libo and Marcus Octavius led the Liburnian and Achaian fleets. However, Marcus Bibulus was the overall commanding officer of the maritime department and held the highest authority.

3:6

Caesar talked to the soldiers in Brundusium. He said they should leave
their stuff and slaves to get on the boat faster. He told the soldiers they
could get everything they need in victory, but not to expect it before
then. They agreed with him. On the fourth of January, Caesar sailed
out with seven legions. The next day, he found land near dangerous
rocks. He landed at a place called Pharsalus without losing any boats.

3:7

Lucretius Vespillo and Minutius Rufus were stationed at Oricum with
18 Asiatic ships delegated by Decimus Laelius. Marcus Bibulus was
stationed at Corcyra with 110 ships, but lacked the courage to venture
out of the harbor. Caesar only had a convoy of 12 ships, with just 4
having decks. Bibulus' fleet was in disarray and his sailors were
dispersed. Caesar was spotted on the continent before any news of his
arrival had even spread to the area.

3:8

Caesar landed his men and sent ships back to Brundusium that same
night to get the rest of the troops. Lieutenant Fufius Kalenus was in
charge and needed to move quickly. The ships left too late and didn't
use the night wind, so they were caught on their way back. Bibulus in
Corcyra knew Caesar was close, and hoped to capture some of their
ships. When he found them empty, he burned them all, along with the
sailors and masters, hoping to scare others. Bibulus filled the shores
from Salona to Oricum with fleets and guarded them carefully, waiting
for Caesar.

The Liburnian fleet departed and Marcus Octavius sailed with his ships from Illyricum to Salona. He riled up the Dalmatians and other barbarians to draw Caesar's connection with Issa away. Unable to convince Salona's council with promises or threats, he decided to storm the town. Salona was well-fortified on a hill and Roman citizens built wooden towers to secure it. When they couldn't resist and were weakened, they freed their mature slaves and turned women's hair into ropes for engines. Octavius surrounded the town with five encampments and began to besiege them. After facing hardships, they asked Caesar for corn. When they got a chance, they attacked Octavius's camps with their wives, children, and freed slaves. They beat them all, killed many soldiers, and chased Octavius away. Winter was near and Octavius left to Pompey at Dyrrachium, realizing he couldn't capture the town after sustaining such losses.

Vibullius Rufus, an officer of Pompey's, was caught twice by Caesar at Corfinium and in Spain. Caesar believed he could influence Pompey by sending Rufus with proposals. In summary, Caesar urged them to end their hostility, as both incurred significant loss, Italy, Sicily, Cardinia, and the two Spains, and one hundred and thirty cohorts of Roman citizens, all gone. They should show mercy to themselves and the republic, and be careful with their future. The peace agreement must be presented to the Roman senate and people, and both should take an oath in public assembly to disband their armies within three days. To prove his good intentions, Caesar would even dismiss his garrisons.

Vibullius got orders from Caesar and had to tell Pompey about it. He rode day and night, changing horses often, to tell Pompey that Caesar was coming with his army. Pompey was traveling to his winter quarters when he heard the news. He hurried to Apollonia to stop Caesar from taking control of the maritime states. But Caesar got to Oricum before Pompey and the governor tried to fight him off. The Greek people in the town didn't want to fight against Caesar and opened the gates for him. Caesar spared the governor's life.

3:12

Caesar swiftly marched to Apollonia after conquering Oricum. The governor, Staberius, tried to defend the citadel with water and hostages, but the town refused to close its gates to the consul. Caesar knew their loyalty and escaped undetected. The people of Apollonia welcomed Caesar and even neighboring states followed their lead to submit to his authority.

3:13

Pompey got wind of what happened at Oricum and Apollonia, and rushed to Dyrrachium without stopping. When word got out that Caesar was coming, Pompey's army freaked out - they were exhausted and disoriented from the non-stop marching. The army was in such a panic that many of them deserted their posts, giving the impression of an all-out retreat. Finally, once they got to Dyrrachium, Labienus swore to never abandon Pompey, followed by the other officers and soldiers who also took the same oath. In response, Caesar didn't hurry to Dyrrachium since Pompey already had it under control. Instead, he camped out by the river Apsus in Apollonia, making sure that he protected the people who supported him. He decided to stay put until his other legions arrived from Italy, and winter there in the tents. Pompey followed suit and filed up his troops on the other side of the river Apsus.

3:14

Kalenus followed Caesar's orders and got the legions and cavalry onto ships at Brundusium. But, they had only a few vessels. Kalenus then set sail, but Caesar sent word that the enemy fleet occupied all the ports and the entire shore. Kalenus turned back and withdrew all the vessels. One ship, a private vessel with no troops, ignored Kalenus and continued to Oricum, where Bibulus captured and killed all onboard, including slaves and children. This event proved crucial for the safety of the entire army, relying on time and luck.

3:15

Bibulus blocked Caesar's sea access from Oricum, but Caesar's land parties controlled the shore, leaving Bibulus without wood, water, or anchorage near the land. Struggling with scarcity, Bibulus had to transport supplies from Corcyra and even catch dew from hides during storms. Despite these hardships, they persisted with no complaints, believing it necessary to maintain the blockade. Eventually, Bibulus and Libo appealed to Caesar for a discussion of important matters. They requested a truce, which Caesar desired, hoping for some advantage from Bibulus's proposals.

3:16

Caesar left one legion to get food while he went to Buthrotum. Acilius and Marcus sent letters to Caesar about Libo's and Bibulus's demands. Caesar then returned to Oricum and met with Libo at a conference. Libo apologized for Bibulus's absence, and said that Pompey wanted them to reconcile and stop fighting. Libo said they couldn't negotiate anything on this subject because they had given up control of the war to Pompey. They would send Caesar's demands to Pompey, who would make the final decision by their persuasion. Libo spoke of the cause of the war and his own forces.

3:17

Caesar said nothing to their proposal, which was not worth remembering. He demanded the ability to send envoys to Pompey without harm and asked them to either agree or take his envoys to Pompey themselves. The war was at a stalemate, and both sides were blocking each other's resources. Caesar proposed that the blockade on the seas be lifted in exchange for lifting the restrictions on land and fresh water. However, they did not accept Caesar's terms and instead referred everything to Pompey. They only cared about a truce, not peace. Caesar saw through their deceit and knew they wanted to avoid danger. He decided to continue with the war.

3:18

Bibulus got sick from the cold and couldn't land or leave. He died, and the commanders did their own thing. Vibullius tried to talk to Pompey, but he shut him down. Pompey didn't want people thinking he owed Caesar anything. Caesar found out later and still tried for peace.

3:19

Pompey and Caesar's armies were separated only by the Apsus River. The soldiers spoke to each other without throwing weapons. Caesar sent his lieutenant, Publius Vatinius, to propose peace. Vatinius spoke humbly and asked whether citizens could send deputies to negotiate peace. Varro agreed to meet for a conference the next day, and a fixed time was set for the meeting. However, Labienus interrupted the conversation with thrown darts. Several were wounded, including centurions and privates. Labienus declared they couldn't have peace until they had Caesar's head.

3:20

In Rome, the praetor Marcus Caelius Rufus took up the cause of debtors. He set up his tribunal next to the bench of Caius Trebonius, the city praetor, and promised relief to anyone who appealed to him regarding debts made by Caesar's appointed arbitration. However, Trebonius's fair judgments and kindness meant that no one dared to appeal. Caelius grew harsher and enacted a law that debts should be paid off in six equal payments of six months each, without interest.

3:21

Servilius and the magistrates opposed him. He failed to accomplish
what he wanted, so he gave two new acts to the people. One forgave
the rent on houses, the other allowed insolvency. After this, the people
turned violent and attacked Caius Trebonius, injuring many and driving
him away. The senate got word of this and Caelius was removed from
power. The consul then stopped him from addressing the people.
Outraged at the humiliation, he pretended he would go to Caesar but
instead contacted Milo, a murderer, and formed an alliance. They
immediately began to execute their plan but their scheme was
discovered, and the town of Capua was shut, so he changed his route.

3:22

Milo sent letters to free towns, claiming that he acted under Pompey's
orders delivered by Bibulus. He tried to win over debtors but failed. So
he freed some slaves and attacked Cosa in Thurinum. A stone, thrown
by Quintus Pedius' legion, hit him, and he died. Caelius acted like he
was going to Caesar but went to Thurii instead, where he offered
money to Caesar's horse and was executed. Italy could finally rest after
all the commotion.

3:23

Libo sailed from Oricum with fifty ships, took an island by
Brundusium and seized some of our transports. He instilled terror in
our men by landing archers and soldiers in the night, beating our horse
guard, and gaining the advantage. He wrote Pompey that he could
prevent Caesar from receiving his auxiliaries with his own fleet, and
recommended the repair of their ships.

3:24

Antonius, with his brave troops, hid on long-boats and attacked the
enemy with surprise. They overwhelmed Libo's ships, taking one and
causing them to retreat. The enemy's thirst worsened as they were
unable to get water, and they ultimately lifted the blockade in
frustration.

3:25

Winter was almost over and Caesar's soldiers and ships didn't show up from Brundusium. He thought he missed some chances, even though the winds were on his side. He had to trust them. Pompey's fleet was guarding the coast and getting more confident every day. They got letters from Pompey scolding them for not stopping Caesar before and expected to stop him now. Caesar was worried, so he ordered his officers to set sail as soon as the winds were right, even if they had to go to Apollonia and ground their ships. The enemy's fleet wouldn't follow them there, as they were too scared to go too far from the harbor.

3:26

His officers, emboldened by the guidance of Marcus Antonius and Fusius Kalenus, and cheered on by the soldiers, set sail with a southerly breeze, passing by Apollonia and Dyrrachium. When Quintus Coponius of the Rhodian fleet pursued them, the wind shifted and saved them. Despite the storm's fury, the officers persevered and the ship was carried beyond Dyrrachium until they reached the port of Nymphaeum. But as soon as they safely anchored, the south wind miraculously changed direction to the south-west.

3:27

Fortune turned quickly. Once we feared for ourselves, but then we found safety in a secure harbor, while our enemies who threatened us were left uneasy. The storm protected us and wrecked the Rhodian fleet. Sixteen ships, without exception, were lost, and many seamen and soldiers met their end against the rocks. Our men took some as prisoners, but Caesar spared their lives and sent them home.

3:28

Two ships, out of sync with the rest, dropped anchor near Lissus in the dark of night, unaware of where their fleet went. Otacilius Crassus, in command of Pompey's squadron, dispatched barges to seize them. He also offered to spare their lives if they surrendered. One boat held over 200 fresh-faced recruits; the other, less than 200 seasoned veterans. The recruits, overwhelmed by the enemy's armada, surrendered timidly after Crassus guaranteed their safety. The oath-sworn officer, however, treacherously ordered their crucifixions right before their colleague's eyes. The veterans suffered through bitter tempests, the sickening seas, and the water pump: Still, believing in their valor, played out the night by bargaining to surrender until they demanded the helm and deliberately steered their vessel aground at dawn. There, they found a sheltered site on the shore and waited until Crassus' troops, four hundred horsemen and rebels, appeared at daybreak. However, the veterans fought fiercely, killing several attackers and returning to their own ranks without casualties.

3:29

Romans at Lissus gave aide to Antony and he sent most ships back, leaving the pontons there in case Pompey mobilized his army to invade Italy. Antony informed Caesar of his landing and troop count with haste.

3:30

Caesar and Pompey got word of the ships passing by Apollonia and Dyrrachium. They both headed out to find them, but didn't know where they were. Once they found out, Caesar went to join with Antonius while Pompey tried to attack Antonius's army from an ambush. They both set out from their winter camps along the river Apsus that day, Caesar during the day and Pompey in secret during the night. Finding a ford was harder for Caesar and easier for Pompey, who marched quickly and forcefully towards Antonius. Pompey found a good place to set up his army and kept them hidden. When Antonius heard of this, he sent word to Caesar and waited one day. The next day, when Caesar arrived, Pompey left his place and went to Asparagium and set up his army there.

3:31

At that time, Scipio took losses near mount Amanus, but claimed the title of imperator and demanded heavy sums from states and princes. He made tax-gatherers pay two years' rent, lend money for the next year, and provide horses. He left behind the Parthians, who had recently killed Marcus Crassus, and went to the province amid anxiety about the Parthian war. The soldiers vowed to fight against an enemy but not a countryman or consul. Scipio retreated to Pergamus for winter with his legions and gave wealthy cities gifts, letting them plunder to win their loyalty.

3:32

At that time, the province was forced to pay up the money demanded with great force. The avarice of Caesar led him to invent fresh ways to raise funds by imposing new levies. Every slave and child became subject to a tax, along with columns, doors, corn, soldiers, sailors, arms, engines and carriages. Officers were appointed to collect money not just in cities, but in villages and forts too. The most inhumane officers were considered the best men and citizens. The province was inundated with officers and tax collectors. The amount collected was doubled in two years, with exorbitant interest imposed. The debt of the province kept increasing, but taxes continued to be imposed on Roman citizens, corporations, and states as loans. In fact, taxes for the next year were demanded upfront as a loan from the collectors on their first appointment.

3:33

Scipio took money out of the temple of Diana in Ephesus. He got a letter from Pompey saying Caesar crossed the sea with his legions. Scipio quickly prepared to leave for Macedonia and saved the money at Ephesus.

3:34

Caesar met Antonius's army and withdrew his own from Oricum,
which was watching the coast. He tested the provinces' inclinations and
decided to advance further into the country. When Thessaly and
Aetolia sent ambassadors offering to obey him if he sent a garrison to
protect them, he sent Lucius Cassius Longinus and Caius Calvisius
Sabinus to those regions, respectively, along with provisions for their
young soldiers and horse parties. Two legions went to Macedonia,
ordered by Caesar with crucial provisions for an important political
figure in the Free region.

3:35

Calvisius arrived in Aetolia and took control of the land by defeating
the enemy in Calydon and Naupactus, and gaining favor. Cassius led
his legion to Thessaly where the citizens were divided over their loyalty.
Hegasaretus was for Pompey, while Petreius and his friends stood for
Caesar.

3:36

Domitius arrived in Macedonia and embassies awaited him. News came
that Scipio approached with legions, causing rumors. Scipio quickly
marched against Domitius and wheeled toward Cassius Longinus in
Thessaly. To speed his march, Scipio left baggage behind and ordered a
fort built. As Cotus's cavalry attacked Cassius's camp, Cassius fled and
Scipio pursued. Dispatches from Favonius revealed that Domitius
marched against him, so Scipio changed route and came to Favonius
just in time. Domitius's vigilance saved Cassius, and Scipio's haste
saved Favonius.

3:37

Scipio waited two days by the river Haliacmon, then led his army
across at dawn and encamped. Domitius wanted a battle, but there was
a plain between them. He stationed his men in front of Scipio's camp,
but Scipio wouldn't leave his trench. When Scipio saw our troops were
eager to fight, he retreated across the river at night. Later, his horse
ambushed our foraging party, but we fought them off with few losses.

3:38

Domitius feigned scarcity of corn to entice Scipio into battle, moving his army three miles away and concealing them. Scipio sent cavalry and light infantry to explore, but our ambush was discovered when their horses sparked suspicion. Our men captured two troops, including Marcus Opimius, and killed or took the others prisoner.

3:39

Caesar withdrew his troops from the ports, leaving three cohorts at Oricum to guard the town and watch over the warships he brought from Italy. Acilius, as lieutenant-general, oversaw this charge and commanded the town. He secured the ships in the harbor, anchored a vessel at the entrance to block it, and stationed soldiers in a turret facing the port to keep guard from sudden attacks.

3:40

Pompey's son, Cneius, found out about the enemy's plan and set out to attack. He used ships with high turrets and fresh troops to overpower our men. Cneius attacked the town on all sides, using ladders and his fleet to divide the enemy's force. Our men were overwhelmed by fatigue and darts. Cneius took the ship and a natural mole to form an island. He attacked ships of war and carried off four of them, while setting the rest on fire. Leaving Laelius to hinder provisions, Cneius went to Lissus where he attacked thirty merchantmen and set them on fire. He also tried to storm Lissus but failed after a vigorous defense by the Roman citizens and soldiers.

3:41

Caesar heard Pompey was at Asparagium. He set out with his army and took the capital of the Parthinians. He reached Pompey in Macedonia three days later and offered him battle. Pompey stayed within his trenches, so Caesar led his army back to camp. The next day, he went on a long circuit through a narrow road to Dyrrachium. Pompey didn't know Caesar's design and followed. Caesar encouraged his troops and arrived at Dyrrachium early in the morning, while Pompey's army was still far away.

3:42

Pompey trapped in Petra, cut off from Dyrrachium, so he fortified his position and gathered supplies. Caesar realized the war would drag on, had no hope for his own convoys, and sent Canuleius to secure corn from far-off Epirus. With little luck there, he searched nearby for supplies, but the pickings were slim. Pompey had already raided and taken all the grain from the Parthini.

3:43

Upon hearing of these events, Caesar took appropriate measures in accordance with the terrain. He seized the high, jagged hills around Pompey's encampments, establishing fortified guards atop them. These fortresses became the foundation for an encompassing line of defense, drawn from fort to fort with careful consideration of the landscape. Caesar's aims were twofold: to secure a steady supply of food and provisions from all directions, despite their meager stores, and to prevent Pompey from success in foraging with his powerful cavalry. By surrounding the enemy, Caesar also hoped to damage his reputation, which he knew rested heavily upon foreign opinions. When news of the blockade spread, it would become clear that Pompey was too scared to risk confrontation with Caesar.

3:44

Pompey won't leave the sea and Dyrrachium, where his gear and supplies are, so he can't stop Caesar's work without fighting. So, he takes all the hills he can and divides Caesar's forces. He raises twenty-four forts and forages within fifteen miles, leaving fields for the cattle. He builds a wall within our wall to prevent us from surrounding them. And when Caesar tries to take any place, Pompey sends slingers and archers to wound our men with arrows. We all make coverings of hair cloths, tarpaulins, or raw hides to defend ourselves.

3:45

They fought hard in taking the posts - Caesar wanted to keep Pompey trapped in a small area, while Pompey aimed to occupy as many hills as possible. They clashed many times. In one skirmish, Caesar's ninth legion secured a spot and began fortifying it. Pompey then took a hill opposite to it and tried to stop Caesar's men. They were hurt from every side, so Caesar decided they should retreat. They went down a cliff, but the enemy followed them, thinking they were afraid. Pompey boasted that he wasn't a good general if Caesar's troops retreated without any significant losses.

3:46

Caesar, wary of his soldiers' withdrawal, instructed his men to erect barriers and a trench for protection against the enemy. He stationed slingers to cover our retreat. As Pompey's men advanced, they destroyed the barriers and continued their pursuit. Afraid that such a display would be seen as defeat and cause greater losses, Caesar rallied his men into a sudden charge, pushing the enemy back. Though impeded by obstacles, our men retreated without harm, taking new hills and reinforcing their position.

3:47

Warfare was different than ever before, for Caesar besieged an entrenched enemy, not waiting for weakness nor defeat, and with inferior numbers. He surrounded them sound and unhurt, with abundant provisions arriving daily by ship, and favorable winds at every turn. Meanwhile, his own men suffered, with no corn to be found, but they endured with the strength of past victories in Spain and over mighty nations. Barley, pulse, and cattle were held in high regard, and Caesar's soldiers refused none.

3:48

Troops of Valerius found a root named chara. Mixed it in milk, gave them strength. Made it into bread. Pompey's soldiers, mocking our men for hunger, received loaves of it, crushing their spirits.

3:49

The corn was ripening and the soldiers took solace in the hope of abundance. They swore they'd rather eat bark than let Pompey escape, though they were told he and his men fared poorly. They were confined to narrow spaces with the stench of dead bodies and a great need for water. Caesar had rerouted and dammed the streams, leaving them with the daunting task of finding marshy land and digging wells in addition to their daily work. However, Caesar's army had plenty of water, good health, and provisions other than corn. The ripening grain offered a glimmer of hope for better times ahead.

3:50

In this different battle, novel strategies were created by the leaders. Pompey's soldiers, detecting our cohorts on duty by our nighttime fires, ambushed them with arrows and then vanished. Against this, we learned to build fires in one spot and stand guard somewhere else. Experience taught us well.

3:51

Publius Sylla brought two legions to aid Caesar's cohort, easily repelling Pompey's forces. Although the Pompeians were positioned on disadvantageous ground, they feared pursuit from Caesar's men if they attempted to retreat down the steep hill before sunset. Pompey instead fortified an eminence out of range of our engines, effectively keeping all his forces there. Some think a vigorous pursuit could have ended the war that day, but Sylla, acting as a lieutenant-general, was content with saving Caesar's camp and men.

3:52

There were fights in two more spots, while Pompey besieged numerous forts all at once to split our troops up. Volcatius Tullus held back a legion and three cohorts in one spot, and chased them away. In another, the Germans surged over our barriers, killed some foes, and then made it back to our camp.

3:53

In a single day, six battles were fought, three each in Dyrrachium and at the fortifications. The count of those who fell on Pompey's side, including volunteer veterans and centurions like Valerius, son of Lucius Flaccus, former praetor of Asia, was around two thousand. Meanwhile, our losses were minimal, with just twenty missing in action. But the soldiers in the fort didn't escape unscathed - not one was without injury, with four centurions even losing their eyes. The soldiers brought evidence of their ordeal, presenting Caesar with over thirty thousand arrows and a shield belonging to centurion Scaeva, sporting an impressive two hundred and thirty holes. Caesar rewarded Scaeva with two hundred thousand pieces of copper money, promoting him from eighth to first centurion. Scaeva's efforts saved the fort, and he was later given double pay, corn, clothing, and other military honors as a token of appreciation.

3:54

Pompey added to his defenses by night and built high turrets the next day. He faced one side of his camp with mantelets and blocked all gates to avoid pursuit. At midnight, he led his army away in silence and retreated to his old fortifications five days later.

3:55

Aetolia, Acarnania, and Amphilochis fell to Cassius Longinus and Calvisius Sabinus. Caesar saw an opportunity to advance and take Achaia, so he sent Fufius with cohorts led by Quintus Sabinus and Cassius. Rutilius Lupus, in charge of Achaia for Pompey, built up defenses at the Isthmus to halt Fufius. Kalenus claimed Delphi, Thebes, and Orchomenus by peaceful means, while others were conquered through force or diplomacy. Fusius was at the forefront of these endeavors.

3:56

Caesar challenged Pompey to battle each day, positioning his troops just out of reach of enemy fire. Pompey, concerned for his image, responded by keeping his army close to their protective ramparts during battle.

3:57

As things were happening in Achaia and Dyrrachium, Caesar sent his pal Clodius to Scipio in Macedonia. They were good buddies and Pompey introduced Clodius to Caesar. The letters Caesar gave Clodius explained that he made a go at peace but the fault was on those who messed up the negotiations. Now Scipio has the authority to make the right choices and even force Pompey if he's still erring, because he has his own army. If Scipio can make it happen, all will owe him for a peaceful Italy, provinces, and empire. Clodius delivered the message, which was okayed at first, but then Scipio got chewed out by Favonius and things went unraveled. Clodius returned with bad news.

3:58

To trap Pompey's horse in Dyrrachium, Caesar built strong forts at the narrow passes. Pompey soon realized his cavalry was of no use and shipped them back to camp. With little food for his horses, Pompey had to resort to feeding them leaves and roots. When the meager supply ran out, he planned to travel to Corcyra and Acarnania for more food. But when even the trees were bare, Pompey had to consider a sally.

3:59

Two Allobrogian brothers, Roscillus and Aegus, were cavalry men under Caesar's command. Sons of Abducillus, their father held power in their home state for many years. These brothers were men of courage and had served Caesar well in the wars in Gaul. Acknowledging their valor, Caesar entrusted them with positions of power in their own country, while also placing them in the senate at an early age. Not only did he grant them lands confiscated from the enemy, but also rewarded them with wealth. Their bravery earned them the respect of Caesar and the entire army. However, their foolish and barbaric attitude led them to abuse their power, display arrogance, and cheat their fellow cavalry men. As a result, their men complained about their treatment to Caesar, citing false reports and stealing of funds.

3:60

Caesar knew it was not the right time to confront them, so he let their faults slide, despite exploiting their armies. He told them to expect future results based on his past actions, hoping it would correct their behavior. The rebuke backfired, and their reputation in the army plummeted. They sensed this, and their guilt caused them shame. They feared a future trial, and decided to leave and join Pompey. They then attempted an assassination to justify their betrayal, but failed. So they bought horses and fled with their followers, hoping to make amends.

3:61

They were noble and learned, with a big retinue and cattle, and Caesar valued them. Pompey flaunted them around his works, as it was a new occurrence. No soldier had deserted Caesar to Pompey, until they did. But mostly, the deserters were from the soldiers levied in Epirus and Aetolia, or in the areas Caesar controlled. These brothers knew of the shortcomings of our works and gave Pompey a detailed account of everything.

3:62

Pompey heard the news and planned to attack. He told his soldiers to cover their helmets in ozier and gather fascines. They set out in small boats and row galleys at night with light infantry and archers, and headed toward Caesar's camp. Pompey sent sixty cohorts from the greater camp and outposts to the same spot, along with ships he had prepared. Lentulus Marcellinus was stationed there with the ninth legion, but as he wasn't well, Fulvius Costhumus came to help him command.

3:63

Facing the enemy, there was a fifteen-foot ditch and a ten-foot-high rampart with a ten-foot-wide top. Six hundred feet from there, a rampart faced the other way with lower works. Caesar had built a double rampart, fearing that his men might be surrounded by sea, but he had not finished the seventeen-mile extent of the lines. Pompey knew this and attacked at daybreak, taking our men by surprise. They cast darts on the front rampart and filled the ditches with fascines. They attacked with scaling ladders and weapons of all sorts. The coverings of oziers on their helmets protected them from the stones our soldiers used. Our men struggled to resist, and Pompey's soldiers attacked from the back, where the work was unfinished. Our men were beaten and forced to flee.

3:64

Marcellinus heard of the chaos and sent some cohorts to help. But they saw their comrades running and got scared, causing even more fear and danger. The fleeing soldiers made it impossible to retreat. In the midst of it all, the eagle-bearer, badly wounded, spotted our cavalry and pleaded with them to protect the eagle, which he had guarded for years. All the centurions of the first cohorts were killed, except for the leader, but at least the eagle was saved.

3:65

The Pompeians advanced, causing terror among our cohorts, but Marcus Antonius and twelve cohorts arrived to halt their progress. Caesar, notified by smoke signals, joined the fight and saw that Pompey had taken the coast and was free to forage. With his plans foiled, Caesar ordered a strong encampment near Pompey.

3:66

Caesar's scouts saw one or two legions that seemed like cohorts heading to the old camp behind the wood. The situation was this: a while ago, Caesar's ninth legion was trying to enclose a group of Pompey's troops, so Caesar's folks set up camp there. The camp was close to the woods and about four hundred paces from the sea. But later, Caesar shifted his approach and moved the camp a bit further away. After a few days, Pompey moved in, added more defense and left the inner rampart standing, planning to keep several legions there. That way, the smaller camp, enclosed by a bigger one, acted as a fort and citadel. He also dug an intrenchment from the camp's left angle to the river about four hundred paces away so his soldiers could fetch water with ease and safety. But he changed his plans and left. The camp stayed there for many days, all the works and defenses intact.

3:67

From Caesar's scouts came word that a legion's standard was here. Higher forts confirmed it. A half mile from Pompey's camp. Caesar needed to surprise them and make up for the day's loss. Leaving two cohorts behind to fake an entrenched position, with thirty-three others including the battered ninth legion, he approached. Two lines deep. It worked. He caught Pompey off-guard and the attackers forced their way in. A short battle at the barricades, but our men were victorious. Pulcio, who helped Caius Antonius's betrayal, put up a good fight. But our men succeeded. Both the larger and smaller camps were taken, and the legion inside suffered heavy losses.

3:68

Fortune, an enigmatic force in war, caused a great turning point due to a small mistake. Caesar's cohorts on the right, unaware of their location, mistakenly followed a wall from the camp towards the river, thinking it to be a gate. They soon realized it led to the river and crossed over the wall, unchallenged. The cavalry soon followed.

3:69

While Pompey's army advanced towards Caesar's, the cavalry and men in the camp became alarmed. The right wing tried to flee the way they entered, jumping into a 10-foot trench and trampling on each other; the left wing worried about being trapped and also retreated. Chaos ensued as Caesar grabbed colors and tried to stop running men, but nobody would turn and they all fled.

3:70

Amidst calamity, a stroke of luck saved our army. Pompey, suspicious of an ambush, held back and his horses were slowed by Caesar's soldiers guarding the passes and gates. This delay, caused by a minor obstacle, proved crucial for both sides. Caesar's victory march was halted by the rampart between the camp and river, while the enemy's pursuit was slowed, thus saving our army.

3:71

Caesar lost nine hundred and sixty men and some distinguished knights in two battles today. Many of them died without even a scratch, trampled to death by their own frightened comrades. Pompey was given the title of Imperator after the fight, but he didn't wear the laurel wreath that came with it. Labienus, the deserter who wanted to impress Pompey, ordered all the prisoners to be slain in front of the army, asking them if it was customary for veterans to run away.

3:72

Pompey's party felt invincible after their triumph, disregarding tactical disadvantages and dangers that led to our defeat. They failed to acknowledge that victory was not won through regular battle, and our loss was greater due to limited space and numerical disadvantage. They didn't consider the unpredictability of war, the impact of misconceptions, panic, or poor leadership on a battle's outcome. Believing themselves unbeatable, they boasted their win to the world.

3:73

Caesar, dissatisfied with his initial strategy, altered his entire plan of operations. He called in all of his outposts, ceased the siege, and gathered his forces together. He spoke to his troops, urging them not to be disheartened by recent setbacks but to recall their many triumphant battles. They had much to be grateful for in the favor of Fate. With Her help, they had taken over Italy without bloodshed, conquered both Spains, subdued neighboring states rich in food, and successfully navigated through blockaded enemy fleets. If success was not guaranteed, then it must be earned through hard work. Any losses should be viewed as caprices of Fate rather than his own errors. He had chosen a safe battleground and overpowered the enemy when met with resistance. Regardless of why the victory had been interrupted, they must now use all their strength to recover their losses. In doing so, they could turn misfortune into opportunity as they did at Gergovia. Those too afraid to fight would be the first to accept battle.

3:74

He finished talking and demoted some flagbearers. The whole army was sad about their loss and wanted to make up for it, so they gave themselves harder work as punishment. They were also eager to fight the enemy, making the top officers think they should keep their positions and fight. But Caesar didn't trust them yet and thought they needed time to feel better. He left his post and worried about running out of food.

3:75

Without delay, he tended to the sick and wounded and then sent his baggage ahead quietly to Apollonia, accompanied by one legion. Keeping only two legions at his camp, he led the rest of his army out before dawn through various gates, maintaining military protocol by signaling their departure in a timely manner. Caesar himself followed behind, out of sight from the camp. Learning of Caesar's plan, Pompey mobilized his own forces, aiming to catch them off guard as they moved with their baggage. The cavalry skirmished at the Genusus river, but Caesar's light troops and horsemen defeated them without suffering any losses.

3:76

Caesar marched his army as he planned, crossed the Genusus river, and set up camp near Asparagium. His soldiers stayed close to the trenches and the horse returned through the Decuman gate. Pompey did the same, taking his post in his old camp. The soldiers had nothing to do, so some collected wood and forage and others went back to their tents to collect their belongings. Caesar saw this coming and gave the signal to march. He doubled that day's march and went eight miles beyond Pompey's camp, who couldn't follow because his troops were too spread out.

3:77

The next day, Caesar sent his gear ahead at night and left himself after the fourth watch. He did this to be ready if sudden fighting happened. He kept doing this for days, so his army could cross deep rivers and tricky roads without trouble. Pompey tried to catch up, but after four days, he quit and chose another route.

3:78

Caesar went to Apollonia to tend his wounded, pay his soldiers, confirm friendships, and leave garrisons. He wasted no time and raced to join Domitius, fearing he would be caught off guard by Pompey. Caesar's strategy was simple: lure Pompey away from the sea, force him into battle, or march to Italy to join forces with Domitius. Caesar sent messengers to Domitius, stationed soldiers at various towns, and set off through Epirus and Acarnania. Pompey guessed Caesar's plan and raced to Scipio. If Caesar headed that way, Pompey would assist; otherwise, he would attack Domitius with his entire army.

3:79

They all learned to move quickly, to help friends and surprise enemies. Caesar ended up in Apollonia and not on the direct path. Pompey went through Candavia, the short road to Macedonia. Caesar didn't know that Domitius had left Scipio's camp for provisions, which took him to Heraclea Sentica, a city subject to Candavia. Caesar was unaware of this. Pompey sent out letters to provinces and states that exaggerated the facts about the action at Dyrrachium. People started to believe that Caesar had fled and lost almost all his forces. This made the roads dangerous, which made it impossible for Caesar's messengers to reach Domitius. However, the Allobroges, who were with Aegus and Roscillus, and had deserted to Pompey, met a scouting party of Domitius. They told them everything and revealed that Caesar had left and Pompey had arrived. Domitius, who was close by, avoided danger and met Caesar at Aeginium, just before Thessaly.

3:80

Caesar combined the armies and marched toward Gomphi, the first
town of Thessaly on the way from Epirus. The Thessalians had offered
him their support, but fearing his misfortunes, Androsthenes shut the
gates and called for help from Scipio and Pompey. Caesar prepared for
a sudden attack and urged his soldiers to take advantage of the
opportunity before reinforcements arrived. The soldiers, filled with
unusual ardor, stormed the town and took it before sunset. Caesar
allowed the army to loot the town and then promptly moved on to
Metropolis, faster than any news of their victory could reach.

3:81

Metropolis people heard rumors, locked gates, and manned walls. But
when they learned about Gomphi's downfall from some prisoners, they
opened their gates. Caesar saved them, so most Thessaly states, except
Larissa, let Caesar in. Caesar chose a spot to wait for Pompey and make
it his center of war operations, with easy access to ripe corn.

3:82

Pompey arrived in Thessaly a few days later, speaking to the joined
army and encouraging Scipio's soldiers to earn a portion of the rewards
and spoils of the battle. All of Pompey's forces were grouped together
in one camp and he shared his rewards with Scipio, earning a pavilion
and trumpet ceremony. With the two robust armies united, their
previous aspirations were confirmed, and their hope for victory was
amplified. The delay in their return to Italy was inconvenient and
whenever Pompey acted cautiously, they said it was a minor matter. In
their council, there was a lively debate about rewards, priesthoods,
allocations of properties, and the praetorship candidacy of Lucius
Hirtius. His friends urged Pompey to fulfill his promise and not to
seem deceitful, whilst others argued that all should be treated equally.

3:83

Domitius, Scipio, and Lentulus Spinther bickered daily about Caesar's priesthood with vulgar insults. Lentulus, emphasizing his age, Domitius, boasting his power, and Scipio, assuming his alliance with Pompey mattered. Attius Rufus accused Lucius Afranius of betraying the army in Spain, and Lucius Domitius wished for all senators to pass judgment on those who didn't aid them in their military efforts. Pompey's army spoke only of their rewards and vengeance, not the strategy to defeat their enemies.

3:84

Corn supplied, soldiers rested. Sufficient time passed since Dyrrachium. Caesar tested his troops to see if Pompey wanted to fight. Soldiers led out of camp, set up in battle formation. First on home ground, then advanced to Pompey's camp, inspiring fresh courage. Youngest, most active chosen for cavalry, practiced to create experience. A thousand of his cavalry could stand against seven thousand of Pompey's. Successful cavalry action resulted in killing an Allobrogian deserter and several others.

3:85

Pompey's army was encamped atop a hill, awaiting Caesar to make a misstep. Caesar, unable to provoke an attack, chose to constantly move his troops, hoping to tire out his opponent and provoke a battle. As they prepared to march, Pompey's army unexpectedly advanced from their trenches, giving Caesar a chance for fair combat. Determined to seize the opportunity, Caesar rallied his soldiers and led them into battle.

3:86

Pompey, urged by his friends, planned to fight Caesar. He spoke in council about his strategy to defeat Caesar's army, promising something almost unbelievable. The cavalries were to attack Caesar's right flank and surround his army, creating chaos and victory without much effort. With higher numbers in cavalry, victory was certain. Pompey encouraged them to be ready for battle and not let their reputation fail.

3:87

Labienus spoke with disdain for Caesar's army and praise for Pompey's strategy. He belittled the soldiers and their abilities, claiming that he knew firsthand of their losses and shortcomings. Labienus then vowed to never return to camp unless victorious and inspired the others to do the same. Pompey and the rest took the oath without hesitation. The council ended on a high note, optimistic about their chances of success with such experienced leaders at the helm.

3:88

Caesar neared Pompey's camp and saw the army's formation. The left wing held the two legions given by Caesar to comply with the Senate's decree, one named first and the other third. Pompey led this wing, while Scipio had command of the center with the Syrian legions. On the right were the steadiest troops, the Cilician legion, along with Spanish cohorts brought over by Afranius. The remaining cohorts were dispersed amongst the center and wing, totaling forty-five thousand men, with two volunteer cohorts and seven others protecting the camp and forts. The cavalry, archers, and slingers secured the left wing by a river with steep banks.

3:89

Caesar, true to his usual tactics, positioned the tenth legion on the right and the depleted ninth on the left, almost merging them together for support. With a force of twenty-two thousand men, eighty cohorts were arranged on the field, with two left to protect the camp. Antonius took the left, P. Sulla the right, and Cn. Domitius the center, while Caesar stood opposite Pompey. Caesar was also wary of Pompey's cavalry flanking his right, and swiftly formed a fourth line of a single cohort from each of the third line's legions to counter them. He instructed them on the importance of their bravery in securing victory that day and commanded the entire army not to charge until his signal.

3:90

As he rallied his troops to the fight, following military tradition, he reminded them of the benefits he had bestowed upon them. He made it clear that he sought peace, even going as far as seeking talks with Labienus through Vatinius and negotiating with Scipio through Claudius. He recounted his efforts to gain permission from Libo to send envoys and pledged that he always sought to avoid casualties and did not want to lose the republic's armies. With his soldiers eagerly waiting for the signal, he gave it by trumpet and launched into battle.

3:91

In Caesar's army, there was a brave volunteer. Crastinus was his name, a former centurion of the tenth legion. He led the charge with a bold declaration, "Follow me, my brothers, and fight for our general with all we've got. Today is our final battle, and we will earn our liberty with a victory." Turning to Caesar, he promised to do his duty even if it meant his life. With that, he charged forward, followed by a select group of warriors, straight into battle.

3:92

The space between the lines was enough for the armies to meet. Pompey ordered his soldiers to wait, hoping Caesar's soldiers would tire from running so far. He thought they would be easier to defeat if they were exhausted and disorganized. But Pompey's plan was flawed. All men have a natural desire to fight and should be encouraged to do so. Our ancestors knew this, and that's why they sounded the trumpets and raised a great shout.

3:93

Our men charged forward with their javelins at the ready, but halted midway when they saw that Pompey's men did not advance. They conserved their strength and resumed their charge, throwing their javelins and drawing their swords as ordered by Caesar. Every man knew his place, and Pompey's army stood their ground and launched their own javelins. Pompey's cavalry charged our own, and our cavalry gave way. Caesar gave the signal to his fourth line, and they charged forward with such ferocity that Pompey's cavalry fled to the mountains, leaving the archers and slingers to be cut down without protection. Our cohorts wheeled about and attacked Pompey's left wing, and advanced upon them from the rear.

3:94

As Caesar commanded his third line to advance, fresh troops rallied to support the battle-weary soldiers. They flanked Pompey's army and attacked their rear, causing them to flee in defeat. Caesar was correct in his prediction that victory would belong to the six cohorts he placed as a fourth line to oppose the horse. These soldiers routed the cavalry, slaughtered the archers and slingers, and surrounded Pompey's left wing. Pompey, seeing his defeat, abandoned the field and retreated to his camp. He ordered his centurions to defend the praetorian gate, while he visited other guards to encourage them. Desperately waiting for the outcome of the battle, Pompey retreated to his tent.

3:95

Caesar chased the Pompeians to their entrenched camp, urging his men to seize the opportunity and attack. Though exhausted in the scorching heat after fighting until midday, his soldiers obeyed without complaint. The Thracians and foreign auxiliaries defended the camp with great spirit, while others who sought refuge there were more concerned with fleeing than fighting. Overwhelmed by our barrage of arrows, the troops on the battlements fled to the mountains under the guidance of their leaders, leaving the camp defenseless.

3:96

In Pompey's camp, luxuries abound as tables are set with plenty of plate, tents shaded by ivy, and fresh sods underfoot. It was clear they were confident in victory, indulging in pleasures while mocking Caesar's army lacking even the basics. When our men breached their trenches, Pompey quickly shed his general's uniform and rode away with a few troops to Larissa, then on to the seaside, where he boarded a small ship with only thirty horse. He lamented being deceived by those he trusted for victory.

3:97

Caesar took over Pompey's camp and urged his soldiers to focus on winning the war rather than looting. He drew lines around the mountain, and the Pompeians retreated toward Larissa. Caesar split his troops and intercepted the enemy, despite their exhaustion. He cut off their access to water and forced a negotiation. Some senators escaped, but the battle was won.

3:98

At dawn, Caesar directed the mountaintop guard to abandon their high posts and descend to the plain to disarm. They obeyed, prostrating themselves and imploring mercy with outstretched arms and tears. Caesar consoled them, spoke of his own leniency, and granted them forgiveness, commanding his troops to harm neither them nor their possessions. Satisfied, Caesar then summoned his base legions to rendezvous with him and sent those with him to rest at camp, before making his way to Larissa before day's end.

3:99

In that scrap, only around 200 privates were AWOL, but Julius Caesar lost about 30 valiant officers, including Crastinus who fought bravely and died from a sword wound to the mouth. Caesar respected him greatly and deemed him worthy of praise. Pompey's army suffered a loss of 15,000 and over 24,000 men were taken captive, including cohorts in the forts who surrendered to Sylla. About 180 standards of colors and nine eagles were captured by Caesar. Lucius Domitius, weak from exhaustion, was offed by a horse while trying to escape from the camp and into the mountains.

3:100

Decimus Laelius sailed into Brundusium with his fleet and took an island near the harbor, just as Libo had done before. Governor Valinius attempted to lure Laelius's fleet with a few small boats, but only managed to capture a few vessels. He also positioned his horses along the shore to prevent enemy access to fresh water. Laelius, however, had prepared well and brought his own water supply from Corcyra and Dyrrachium. He was determined to stay put until he heard news of the battle in Thessaly, despite the risk of losing his ships and lack of necessities.

3:101

Around the same time, Cassius sailed into Sicily with a bunch of ships containing Syrians, Phoenicians, and Sicilians. Caesar's fleet was split in two, with Publius Sulpicius leading one group near the straits of Vibo and Pomponius leading the other in Messana. Cassius reached Messana before Pomponius knew he was coming. Cassius used the high winds to his advantage, and without any guards or order on Pomponius's fleet, Cassius filled some ships with flammable materials and sent them towards the fleet, causing all thirty-five ships to catch fire, including twenty armed ones. This scared Messana so much that even with a legion in guard, the city would have been doomed if not for horsemen bringing news of Caesar's victory. Cassius went on to attack the next fleet at Vibo, and again, he sent some flaming ships into the port causing five ships to turn to ash. The wind, however, spread the fire and the veterans on guard were too ashamed to have their ships burn, so they took over and attacked Cassius's ships, capturing two five-banked galleys, one of which Cassius was on. The news of Thessaly's fight even convinced Pompeians that Caesar's victory was no lie, and Cassius left the coast with his fleet soon after.

3:102

Caesar wanted to forget about business and track Pompey wherever he went, so Pompey wouldn't have time to prepare new forces and start the war again. Caesar rode every day as far as his cavalry could go and ordered one legion to follow him. Pompey made an announcement in Amphipolis saying that young men, Greek and Roman, should take the military oath. It's hard to tell if it was to hide his plan or to get new soldiers for Macedonia. Pompey gathered his friends and money and then he left from there when he heard Caesar was coming. He stopped in Mitylene for two days, got some more galleys for his fleet, and then went to Cilicia and Cyprus. People in Antioch and Roman citizens didn't let Lucius Lentulus, Publius Lentulus, and many others in. All these people followed Pompey, but they had to leave due to Caesar's arrival.

3:103

Pompey heard of the events and changed his plans. He took money from the revenue farmers, and borrowed more from friends. He brought brass and 2,000 armed men, including slaves and merchants chosen by his friends, and sailed to Pelusium. King Ptolemy, busy fighting his sister Cleopatra, was also there with a sizable army. Pompey asked to seek refuge in Alexandria under Ptolemy's protection, due to the past relationship between his father and Ptolemy. But Pompey's deputies went beyond their brief, urging Ptolemy's troops to be kind to Pompey even in his dire situation. Some of Pompey's soldiers were already in Ptolemy's army, having been left there by Gabinius after the war.

3:104

The king's pals, ruling the kingdom for the young chap, learned what was happening. They said it was because of fear, worrying that Pompey might take over Alexandria and Egypt by corrupting the king's troops. Or, maybe they just didn't like him anymore, because friends can become foes when times get rough. In front of other folk, they gave his messengers a nice answer, telling him to come see the king. But, on the sly, they planned against him. They sent Achillas, the guy who commands the king's guards and is pretty brave, along with a military dude named Lucius Septimius, to take him out. Being talked to kindly and fooled by his familiarity with Septimius, as the guy led a squad under him in a fight with pirates long ago, he took a small boat with a few helpers and came aboard. That's when Achillas and Septimius killed him. The king ordered Lucius Lentulus to be caught and offed in jail too.

3:105

When Caesar got to Asia, he found out that Titus Ampius had tried to swipe the cash from the temple of Diana at Ephesus. Ampius had called all the senators in the province to witness the sum, but Caesar swooped in just in time and Ampius bolted. So, twice Caesar rescued the money at Ephesus. At Elis in the Minerva temple, it was noted that on the same day Caesar won his battle, Victory's statue faced the temple entrance. At Antioch in Syria, the citizens heard trumpets and army shouting, making them arm themselves and head to the walls. The same thing occurred at Ptolemais, Pergamus, and Tralles- at Tralles was a Victory temple with a statue of Caesar that had a palm tree sprout up above it.

3:106

Caesar, delayed in Asia, set out for Alexandria with a weak force, two legions and a handful of ships. Though disabled soldiers could not follow, he relied on his own reputation. Upon landing, he learned Pompey died and a crowd gathered, angered by the fasces before him. Disturbances continued, and many of his soldiers died in the city.

3:107

He saw what was happening and called for more soldiers from Asia, plucked from Pompey's old ranks. But the winds were against him, keeping him stuck in Alexandria. He knew it was a matter for the Roman people, especially since he had made a deal with Ptolemy before. So he ordered the battling siblings, Ptolemy and Cleopatra, to put down their swords and present their cases to him, the consul, for a fair judgment.

3:108

Pothinus, the young tutor, complained to his friends about the king being summoned to plead his cause. He secretly called the army to Alexandria, and made Achillas commander. Ptolemy's will declared his eldest son and daughter as heirs, and the Roman people were urged to fulfill his wishes. One copy of the will was sent to Rome but was kept with Pompey, while another remained sealed in Alexandria.

3:109

As Caesar weighed in on the royal disputes, news arrived suddenly that the king's troops and cavalry were heading to Alexandria. With a weaker army, Caesar opted to stay put in the town and gather intel on Achillas's plans. The king dispatched his trusted friends, Dioscorides and Serapion, as envoys to Achillas, but they were executed without hesitation. Seeing opportunity in the king's name, Caesar safeguarded his person to maintain political sway and paint the war as an act of reckless rebels, not the king's doing.

3:110

Achillas had a force of twenty thousand soldiers, including Gabinius's men, who had lost their discipline and Roman identity in Alexandria. There were also convicts, highwaymen, and freebooters, as well as soldiers recruited from runaway slaves. These soldiers had gained military experience by engaging in numerous battles in Alexandria, including the restoration of Ptolemy the father and the killing of two of Bibulus's sons. They were experienced and dangerous soldiers.

3:111

Achillas, confident in his troops and disregarding Caesar's outnumbered soldiers, took Alexandria except for the area Caesar occupied. He tried to overpower the palace, but Caesar's cohorts in the streets pushed back. Meanwhile, they fought fiercely at the port since the enemy split their forces and aimed to capture the warships. With fifty vessels sent to Pompey's aid and twenty-two guarding the port, Caesar's opponents could control the sea and stop his supplies. Each side fought with all they had since the outcome decided their fate. Eventually, Caesar won and burned the ships, unable to defend them all. He then sent troops to Pharos with his remaining ships.

3:112

The Pharos, a tall tower on an island, built with incredible skill, is named after the island it stands on. It lies opposite Alexandria, connected by a narrow causeway and a bridge. The island harbors some Egyptian houses and a large village. Ships that mistakenly enter the coast are plundered by Egyptians like pirates. No vessel can enter without consent from the Pharos' masters. Caesar fears this and lands soldiers to seize the Pharos during the enemy's engagement, gaining access to supplies. In the rest of town, they fight equally due to narrow passages, but Caesar fortifies important posts. The king's palace quarter becomes Caesar's rampart. Ptolemy's younger daughter escapes the palace to Achillas, quarreling over command and increasing soldier presents. Regent Pothinus sends encouraging messengers, but Caesar puts him to death, leading to the start of the Alexandrian war.

♦♦♦

ALEXANDRIAN WAR

As readers delve into the captivating narrative of the Alexandrian War, they are transported to the aftermath of Caesar's victory over Pompey, where new challenges await in Egypt. This engrossing account brings to life the intrigue, power struggles, and military exploits that defined Caesar's campaign in the land of the Nile. Embark on this thrilling journey, as Caesar navigates the complexities of Egyptian politics, forges alliances with enigmatic figures such as Cleopatra, and engages in fierce battles against formidable adversaries, all in pursuit of securing Rome's interests and expanding its sphere of influence.

1

At the start of the war in Alexandria, Caesar sought out his fleet from Rhodes, Syria, and Cilicia. He called for archers from Crete and cavalry from Malchus, king of the Nabatheans. Military engines were prepared, and corn was brought along with dispatched forces to assist. Each day, he fortified his defenses with new works, adding strength to the weaker parts of the town using testudos and mantelets. Openings were created within the walls for the battering-rams to play, and they extended the fortifications over the ruined or taken territories. Alexandria was safe from fire, the houses were all built without wooden joists and were vaulted and roofed with tile or pavement. Caesar's ultimate goal was to enclose the smallest part of the town with works, and separate it from the rest towards the south with a marsh, using one general and council to lead the army as the city was divided into two parts. This strategy ensured he could provide support to his troops, and have quick access to water and forage that he was ill-prepared for. The marsh, however, resulted in plentiful water and forage, which served to replenish his army.

2

Alexandrians not idle, sent deputies to gather troops, made weapons in many workshops, enlisted all able slaves, and guarded city with walls and towers. Kept veteran cohorts in squares to act fast. City well-prepared.

3

The town was full of riches and art, supplying all the elements necessary for craftsmanship. The locals were sharp and inventive, copying our every move to the point that we seemed to be following them. They invented whole new creations and both defended their own works and attacked ours. Their leaders were convinced that the Romans were gradually trying to take over Egypt, as evidenced by Gabinius and Pompey's recent visits and Caesar's current encampment. They knew they had to act fast, lest Egypt become a mere Roman province. With the stormy season upon us, Caesar was stuck and could not receive any further supplies.

4

There came a time when the veteran army's leader, Achillas, and the youngest daughter of King Ptolemy, Arsinoe, began to contend for power. With the help of her governor, the eunuch Ganymed, Arsinoe was able to overcome Achillas and take control. She made Ganymed the army's commander, who then increased the troops' rewards and dutifully fulfilled his obligations.

5

In Alexandria, the ground beneath is hollow due to aqueducts from the Nile supplying water to private homes. The waters settle in cisterns and become crystal clear, a choice of the master and his family, as the Nile's waters can cause illness due to their thickness. The common folk, unfortunately, have no choice but to use the muddy Nile water, as there are no springs in the city. The river runs through the section of Alexandria controlled by its people. This realization sparks Ganymed's concern that our troops may lose access to water, as they rely on the aqueducts and private cisterns for their supply.

6

He started a arduous task, blocking all the channels that supplied his own reservoirs and using machines to extract vast amounts of seawater to pour continuously into the canals of Caesar's district. The nearby houses' tanks soon tasted more salty than usual, perplexing the inhabitants who could not comprehend the origin of the anomaly. They were skeptical of their senses until those who resided a little further away testified that their water remained unchanged. This prompted them to compare and test their tanks, and the discrepancy was easily discovered. However, shortly thereafter, the water in the closest homes became unusable, and the water downstream steadily grew more contaminated and brackish.

7

With this circumstance laying all doubt to rest, the troops were seized by a terror that made them think they had no other choices left. Some grumbled about Caesar's tardiness, wishing that he had ordered them to their ships at once. Others were afraid of an even greater misfortune, as they could not hide their plan to retreat from their enemies who were so close by. It was also impossible to embark in front of a relentless pursuer. Many of the townsmen were in Caesar's quarter, and he did not force them to leave their homes. They claimed to be in his favor and to have left their follow-citizens' camp. But offering a defense of these Alexandrians' integrity or strategy would be fruitless labor since those who know the character and mentality of the people know that they are the best traitors in the world.

8

Caesar spoke to his men to ease their worries, saying that fresh water could be found by digging wells and if not, they could go to Paraetonium or the island for water by ship. He urged them not to retreat, for it would be difficult to defend themselves without the advantage of their works. He warned that the Alexandrians were quick and familiar with the area, and would take the advantageous posts if given the chance. Victory, he said, was their only hope for safety.

9

By reassuring his men with a speech, he commanded the centurions to focus on the digging of wells day and night. They worked vigorously and found fresh water in the first night. This frustrated the mighty projects of the Alexandrians. In two days, Pompey's veteran legion arrived on the African coast with arms and provisions. Hindered by the easterly winds, they gave notice of their lack of water to Caesar through a dispatch sloop.

10

Caesar boarded a ship in the harbor to determine the wisest course of action. He left the land forces behind to defend the works. When he arrived at Chersonesus, he sent sailors to fetch water. Some of these sailors were caught by the enemy's horse, revealing Caesar's presence on board without any soldiers. The Egyptians saw this as an opportunity and manned their ships to meet Caesar on his return. However, he declined to fight as he had no soldiers and it was getting late in the day. He knew the darkness would benefit his opponents who were familiar with the coast, and he couldn't inspire his men effectively in the darkness. Therefore, Caesar drew his ships to the shore where he hoped the enemy would not follow.

11

One galley of Rhodes was left alone in Caesar's right army amidst the others. Their enemies noticed this and came forward with mighty ships and open barks to attack. Caesar had to go to their rescue, not wanting to witness the loss of one of his own ships. Though he believed the galley deserved its fate had he left it to perish, the Rhodians showed great courage and fought hard to not be deemed responsible for any damage to the fleet. They won the battle completely, taking one ship and sinking another, alongside killing all the crew aboard. If the night had not intervened, Caesar would have gained control of the entire enemy fleet. Caesar, making use of the chaos, took the transports and lead the victorious fleet to Alexandria once the winds became calmer.

12

The Alexandrians, downcast at their loss, retreated to their rooftops and barricaded their streets in fear of a land assault from our fleet. However, after a confident assurance from Ganymed, they regained hope and began repairing their damaged vessels, determined to increase their fleet's strength. Despite losing over a hundred ships, their desire to control the sea persisted, knowing that it would hinder Caesar's reinforcements. As seasoned mariners, they returned to their rightful domain, eager to regain the advantages they once possessed with their small fleet. They worked tirelessly to restore their naval superiority.

13

Ships lined the Nile's mouths, awaiting customs gathering. Old vessels were refurbished from the king's private arsenals, and oars were scrounged from public buildings. With the city's abundance and their ingenious minds, they were able to meet their needs with ease. Their focus was on the present and the port, not the long voyage ahead. Before long, they had amassed twenty-two quadriremes, five quinqueremes, and several smaller barks, ready for battle. On the other side, Caesar had Rhodian, Pontian, Lycian, and Asian galleys, and though outmatched in size, he trusted his soldiers and forged ahead.

14

With both sides confident in their own strength, Caesar sailed around Pharos and formed a battle line against the enemy. The Rhodian galleys were placed on the right wing and those of Pontus on the left. A space of four hundred paces was left between them for extending and maneuvering the vessels. The rest of the fleet was kept in reserve, with each ship assigned to give aid to the appointed vessel. The Alexandrians, with their fleet and smaller vessels carrying fire and combustibles, tried to intimidate us. Between the fleets were narrow channels, making it difficult to retreat or maneuver a ship in case of misfortune.

15

Euphranor led the Rhodian fleet. They were brave men who deserved to be among our own. He became admiral due to his courage and experience. He saw Caesar's fear of engaging before the whole fleet could arrive. Euphranor promised to fight until the fleet cleared the shallows, so they could not triumph in sight. Caesar agreed and praised him. The battle began with four Rhodian ships attacked by the Alexandrians. The Rhodians fought with skill and courage, not letting any enemies break their oars. The rest of the fleet arrived, and the fight became a test of valor. Everyone in Alexandria prayed for victory from the highest points they could reach.

16

The battle was imbalanced, as a loss would mean we had no land or sea resources. Even if we won, the future was uncertain. The Alexandrians had everything to gain and still had a chance at good fortune if they lost. The safety of all lay in the hands of a few brave souls. Caesar reminded his troops of this daily before the fight. Each man urged his comrades to fight for the common interest. They fought with unwavering courage, unfazed by the cunning of the skilled Egyptian sailors or the size of their fleet. We captured a quinquereme and a bireme, with no loss on our side. The rest fled to the town, hiding under forts and moles to avoid us.

17

To take away the enemy's future resources, Caesar decided he must become the master of the mole and island. His plan was to defend himself in both the city and island, and he hoped to achieve this by putting ten cohorts of light-armed infantry, along with some of the strongest Gallic cavalry into boats and small vessels. He then sent them to attack the island, while simultaneously attacking with his fleet, promising great rewards to those who could claim victory first. Although the enemy fiercely resisted at first, our men eventually gained control of the island by relentlessly pushing forward, and as a result, the Pharians retreated. The rest of the enemy left their ships and moved into the safety of the town to protect their homes.

18

They did not last there for long. Although their buildings resembled those of Alexandria and their towers were high enough to form a wall, our men were ill-equipped to breach them. Lacking ladders, fascines, and assault weapons, fear clouded our men's judgment and weakened their strength. Even those who stood against us on even ground faltered in the face of a few fallen comrades and scattered in panic. They dared not confront us on the thirty-foot high ground, and instead flung themselves into the sea in an effort to gain the town, over eight hundred paces away. Many lost their lives, but six hundred were captured.

19

Caesar relinquished the loot to his soldiers and instructed the destruction of the houses. He strengthened the castle at the end of the bridge, nearer to the island, and assigned a troop to secure it. The Pharians had abandoned this, but the other was held by the Alexandrians and was stronger. Taking possession of these two forts would provide Caesar with control over the harbor and ward off any potential attacks. By using arrows and machines, Caesar had already managed to force the garrison to evacuate the premises and retreat towards the city. He had also landed three cohorts, the maximum the site could hold. The remaining troops remained stationed in their ships. Caesar then ordered the construction of a fortification on the bridge, to be used against any enemy incursions, block any access for boats through the arch, and prevent piracy. When one of these plans was put into action, the ships were entirely locked, and the other was started. At that moment, the Alexandrians left the town in droves and took up position in an open place opposite our trench near the head of the bridge. They also left some vessels at the mole to attempt to set fire to our larger ships. Our soldiers fought on the bridge and the mole, while the Alexandrians fought from the area across the bridge and their ships.

20

Whilst Caesar was occupied with his troops, a multitude of rowers and sailors abandoned their vessels and rushed towards the mole, some out of curiosity and some to participate in the skirmish. Initially, they used stones and slings to expel the enemy's vessels, and their javelins proved even more effective. Nonetheless, when a few Alexandrians were able to land and attack them from the flank, the indisciplined sailors fled in haste. Witnessing this triumph, the Alexandrians disembarked in sizable numbers and launched a vigorous offensive against our men, who by now had been thrown into disarray. The remaining soldiers in the galleys, comprehending the gravity of the situation, raised the ladders and pushed off from the coast so that the enemy could not oust them from their ship. The soldiers belonging to the three cohorts, who had been responsible for guarding the bridgehead of the mole, were astounded by the confusion they saw around them, as well as by the chants emanating from their own side, and the slaughtering of their comrades by the Alexandrians. Additionally, they were unable to withstand the relentless barrage of darts raining down on them, and they feared the possibility that if their ships left, they would be encircled, and their escape plan would be foiled. Consequently, they abandoned the fortifications they had constructed on the bridge and rapidly scampered towards the galleys. Some individuals boarded the nearest vessels, which were then swamped and sunk, while others who attempted to resist the enemy and were unsure which path to take, were torn apart by the Alexandrians. A handful who were more fortunate reached the ships that were safely anchored, and a few with large bucklers put up a fierce fight and managed to swim to the nearby vessels.

21

Caesar tried to rally his soldiers and defend the works, but they all gave way. He retreated to his galley with his men, but it became crowded and impossible to operate. He anticipated what was to come and jumped into the sea, swimming to distant ships to send help to his men. Although he managed to save a small number, all those aboard his ship went down with it. The Alexandrians took control of the fort, clearing the port and allowing for free navigation. In all, around 400 soldiers and sailors perished.

22

The loss did not discourage our men. On the contrary, it stirred them up, and they launched frequent attacks on the enemy, destroying their works and thwarting their advances. They were eager to engage in combat, exceeding even Caesar's commands. Their determination to fight was so great that Caesar had to hold them back instead of urging them forward.

23

The Alexandrians, upon realizing that victory buoyed the Romans and defeat spurred them on further, saw no other option for themselves. They either heeded the advice of their friends in Caesar's camp or acted on their own plan, and covertly sent envoys to Caesar with a request to release their king so he could return to his people. The people were tired of being ruled by a woman under an unstable and barbaric regime, and sought the king's leadership. They were prepared to follow his orders, and if they could win Caesar's protection and alliance, they were confident they could overcome any obstacle.

24

Caesar knew the people were fake and deceitful, not speaking what they thought. But he thought it wise to comply with their wish, hoping that sending back their king would make them faithful. He told the king to take care of his kingdom and be loyal to him and the Romans, accompanying him with a handshake. The king then begged Caesar not to send him back but Caesar sent him off, moved by the king's words. The king was glad to be gone and fought a fierce war against Caesar, causing joy among Caesar's allies who saw his weakness. But Caesar's behaviour was not one of weakness, but of great wisdom.

25

When the people of Alexandria learned that the return of their king had not made them stronger nor weakened the Romans, and that their king was despised and weak, they were discouraged. A rumor spread that a large group of troops was coming to help Caesar, but the Alexandrians decided to intercept the supplies coming by sea. Caesar found out about this and ordered his fleet to get ready, led by Tiberius Nero and the Rhodian galleys. Euphranor, their admiral and the key to their success in battles, led them. But on this day, fortune was not on his side. He sunk one of the enemy's ships but was surrounded by Alexandrians without any backup. He alone fought bravely and died with his victorious galley.

26

Mithridates of Pergamus, a man of noble lineage and renowned for his bravery and military strategy, arrived at Pelusium with a vast army he had assembled in Syria and Cilicia, thanks to his skill and the support of those provinces. Achillas, who was well aware of the site's significance, had taken it over and stationed a formidable garrison there. Nonetheless, Mithridates attacked it with great vigor, replacing his exhausted men with fresh ones and pressing the assault with unwavering determination, eventually capturing the fortress on the same day. After leaving a garrison there, he led his forces to Alexandria, conquering and winning over all the provinces he passed through, for the conqueror always holds sway.

27

Delta, the famed Egyptian province named after a Greek letter due to the Nile's division into two channels that gradually distance themselves before joining the sea, saw a fierce battle. The king sent soldiers to stop Mithridates from passing the river, hoping for victory or at least to prevent his union with Caesar. The first wave of soldiers aimed to claim the glory of victory but Mithridates defended his fortified Roman-like camp and then attacked them when they advanced imprudently. Despite his initial success, the following troops prepared to attack again.

28

A message arrived to Caesar from Mithridates' courier, relaying the news of the happenings. Ptolemy marched on to vanquish Mithridates, whilst Caesar's goal was to rescue him. The king decided to employ the swifter boats of the Nile, possessing a grand fleet prepared to aid him. Caesar refused the river's path, avoiding a clash with the foe's naval force, and pursued the African coastline, effectively linking up with Mithridates' winning troops before Ptolemy could strike. The king's camp was located atop an elevation hedged in by a field, fortified by the placement of defenses on three sides, and bordered by the Nile on one. The remaining side was both sheer and unreachable, providing cover from the morass.

29

A narrow river with steep banks stood between Ptolemy's camp and Caesar's route, emptying into the Nile. The king, warned of Caesar's approach, dispatched his cavalry and skilled light-armed soldiers to prevent crossing and engage from a position of safety. Our men were dismayed by the persistence of the Alexandrians. Yet, some German cavalry searched for a ford and swam across where the banks were low. The legionaries crafted a makeshift bridge out of felled trees and pushed to the other side. The enemy fled, but few made it back to the king as most were slain in the pursuit.

30

Caesar marched his army towards the Alexandrian camp, but found it too well fortified to be attacked without putting his troops at risk. Instead, he took a nearby fort, not for its strategic value, but to create a distraction and catch the enemy off guard. The Romans then engaged in an intense battle with the Alexandrians, with two approaches to the camp. The first was heavily guarded, while the other allowed the enemy to easily wound the Roman soldiers with constant projectile attacks.

31

Caesar watched as his soldiers fought fiercely but struggled to advance on the difficult terrain. He noticed the high point of the enemy camp was unguarded, and he commanded some cohorts, led by the brave Carfulenus, to attack from that direction. With few defenders, our men quickly overwhelmed the Alexandrians, causing them to flee in panic. As our soldiers entered the camp, they slaughtered many of the enemy, who tried to escape by throwing themselves over the rampart and into the river. Though the king managed to escape on a ship, it sank under the weight of his followers.

32

Caesar won the battle and marched to Alexandria with his cavalry. He expected the Alexandrians to give up fighting after hearing of his victory and they did. They surrendered, throwing down their weapons and assuming the posture of suppliants. Caesar accepted their submission and walked towards his own quarter where his party greeted him with universal congratulations.

33

Caesar, now the master of Alexandria and Egypt, left the government in the hands of Ptolemy's heirs and pleaded with the Romans not to allow changes. He chose the youngest son, alongside Cleopatra, whom he had always protected, to be the new king after the eldest son's death.

To prevent any disturbances, he banished the younger sister, Arsinoe, who was previously tyrannized by Ganymed. With only a few days of administration, the king and queen did not have a solid foundation of power and were not favored by their subjects due to their loyalty to Caesar.

To ensure their protection, Caesar left the sixth veteran legion in Egypt, and he himself left for Syria with the rest of his forces.

34

While events unfolded in Egypt, King Deiotarus reached out to Domitius Calvinus, who Caesar had tasked with governing Asia and the surrounding regions. Deiotarus pleaded for him to not let Pharnaces ravage the Lesser Armenia, which was his kingdom, or Cappadocia, which belonged to Ariobarzanes. He believed they couldn't execute Caesar's orders nor pay the debts unless they were saved from these circumstances. Domitius understood the need for funds to cover war expenses, but he also felt that it would be disgraceful to Rome's people and Caesar's triumph, as well as to himself, to let a foreign prince usurp the territory of allies and friends. Thus, he sent an envoy to Pharnaces, commanding him to leave Armenia and Cappadocia with no further insults to the Romans during these Civil War times. Domitius planned to have more weight in this decision, and thus led an army by himself. He met with legions already in Asia, taking two of them to Egypt at Caesar's request, and moving with the thirty-sixth legion. Deiotarus added two more trained with their discipline and a hundred horse, while Ariobarzanes furnished another hundred horses. At the same time, P. Sextius reached out to C. Plaetorius for the recently established legion in Pontus, and Quinctius Partisius traveled into Cilicia to draw auxiliary troops. Domitius ordered that all these forces gather in Comana quickly.

35

His embassadors brought news from Pharnaces, who claimed the right of inheritance to the Lesser Armenia and was willing to submit to Caesar's commands. C. Domitius knew Pharnaces had left Cappadocia out of necessity and was more determined to keep Armenia; Pharnaces insisted on leaving Armenia too. Domitius marched along the hills, dividing Armenia and Cappadocia, to prevent surprises and get provisions.

36

Pharnaces sent some folks to make peace with Domitius, but he said no, because he cared about Rome's power and helping its friends. After traveling for a long while, Domitius stopped by a city called Nicopolis, which was in a flat area surrounded by mountains. Pharnaces hid some people and horses in a narrow path between the city and Domitius' camp. He also spread out some cows and people to make it look like everything was normal, so Domitius wouldn't know about the trap.

37

As the design progressed, he persisted in sending envoys to Domitius in hopes of luring him with peace and friendship. Domitius remained in his camp, swayed by the prospect of peace, allowing Pharnaces to miss his opportunity and retreat, fearing his ambush would be exposed. The following day, Domitius set up camp near Nicopolis and our men dug the trenches. Pharnaces arranged his army in battle formation, with a single front line and triple reserves guarding his wings. The center was set up in single files, with two gaps on the sides. Domitius stationed some troops to stay armed near the rampart, while the rest fortified their camp.

38

That night, Pharnaces intercepted the couriers with news of Caesar's danger in Alexandria. He urged Domitius to send help quickly and join him in Syria. Pharnaces knew that delaying the battle would be advantageous, assuming Domitius would soon depart. Thus, he dug two ditches and placed his army between them, leaving his cavalry on the wings.

39

Domitius was worried for Caesar, but also for himself. He couldn't retreat without looking like a coward or asking for the conditions he had refused. So, he led his troops out of the camp and lined them up for battle. The thirty-sixth legion stood on the right, the Pontus on the left and the Deiotarus in the center with a narrow front; the other cohorts supported the wings. Both armies advanced and the battle began.

40

Both sides signalled and engaged in sharp and varied conflict. The thirty-sixth legion charged and drove the king's cavalry to the walls of the town, attacking their infantry from behind. Meanwhile, the legions of Pontus were overwhelmed and borne down by a shower of darts. The legions of Deiotarus hardly resisted, and the victorious forces of the king turned towards the thirty-sixth legion. Although surrounded by the enemy, the thirty-sixth legion formed themselves into a circle and retreated to a mountain. The legion of Pontus was almost fully cut off, and the thirty-sixth retreated with the loss of about two hundred and fifty men. Several Roman knights were killed in the battle. Domitius retreated with the remains of his army through Cappadocia and into Asia.

41

Pharnaces, filled with triumph, believed Caesar's struggles would end in his favor. With his army, he marched into Pontus and took control as a merciless ruler. In his quest for personal glory and power, he conquered towns, seized property and brutally punished citizens for their youth and beauty. With no opposition, he claimed his father's kingdom as his own.

42

We got a big check in Illyricum just as Caesar's quaestor Q. Cornificius defended the place all summer. He was smart and careful, didn't do anything too crazy, and managed to capture some forts that had been causing trouble, giving the loot to his soldiers. Even though the province was in bad shape, the soldiers were thankful for what they got. When Octavius showed up with a bunch of ships after the battle of Pharsalia, Cornificius teamed up with some loyal locals and together they took most of the enemy ships. When Cornificius heard that the remaining enemies had gone to Illyricum to regroup, he wrote to Gabinius to come with reinforcements just in case, and to also be ready to go to Macedonia if Pompey kept causing trouble.

43

Gabinius, in his reckless confidence, marched into Illyricum in the harshest winter season, despite the province's lack of provisions and disaffection towards him. He was forced to wage war on necessity's terms and suffered many setbacks, even losing many soldiers and high-ranking officers. Though he made it to the city of Salona, his troubles did not cease and he died soon after. Octavius saw this as an opportunity to conquer the province, but fortune and the valor of others turned the tide against him.

44

Upon learning of Octavius' alliance with barbarians and attacks on our garrisons, Vatinius received urgent letters from Cornificius, urging him to come to the aid of the province. Though weakened by illness, Vatinius, with great determination and valor, overcame all obstacles, including his own sickness, harsh winter conditions, and a sudden need for preparation. With only a few galleys but a significant number of veteran soldiers, he sailed for Illyricum, attaching beaks to additional vessels in the port to create a makeshift fleet. Without delay, he subdued several maritime states that had sided with Octavius and confronted him near Epidaurus, forcing him to lift the siege and joining the garrison to his own forces.

45

Octavius arrived at Tauris, confident in his fleet's strength and knowing Vatinius had only small barks. But Vatinius, determined to pursue Octavius, followed him and encountered a surprise attack. Ordering his soldiers to arm themselves, Vatinius prepared for battle. The two fleets faced off, Octavius with better organization, and Vatinius with fierce soldiers.

46

Vatinius, faced with a smaller and weaker fleet, left his fate to chance. He bravely attacked Octavius in his mighty four-banked galley with such force that it shattered his vessel's beak. The battle raged fiercely, especially around the two great commanders. In the tight waters, Vatinius's brave soldiers had the upper hand as they leaped onto enemy ships and fought them head-on. Octavius's galley sank, and many others suffered the same outcome. Some soldiers perished on the ships, while others were tossed into the sea. Octavius, wounded, swam to his brigantine after his boat sank, and with the night and strong winds on his side, he fled with a few ships that managed to follow him.

47

After the victory, Vatinius withdrew and entered the port where Octavius had set sail from. He didn't lose a single ship. He captured a quinquereme, two triremes, eight two-banked galleys, and many rowers. The next day, he repaired his fleet and sailed to the island of Issa, thinking Octavius had gone there after being defeated. The city on the island surrendered to him. Vatinius found out that Octavius had left for Greece with a few small boats and planned to reach Sicily and Africa. Vatinius quickly restored the province to Cornificius and forced the enemy fleet out of those waters. He returned to Brundusium victoriously, with his army and fleet in good shape.

48

During Caesar's siege of Pompey in Dyrrachium, his victory at Old Pharsalia, and his dangerous campaigns in Alexandria, Cassius Longinus was left as propraetor of the further province in Spain. Due to his natural disposition or a hatred he had developed for the province after being treacherously wounded there, he became disliked by the people. Sensing their discontent, he gathered the soldiers and promised them a hundred sesterces each to gain their affection. When he became master of Medobriga and Mount Herminius and was declared imperator by the army, he gave them another hundred sesterces each, along with many other gifts. These seemed to increase the army's good-will but weakened their military discipline over time.

49

Cassius sent his army to winter quarters and settled in Corduba to dispense justice. In debt, he burdened the province, justifying his demands by his generosity. He taxed the rich without mercy, ignoring their protests and using minor offenses to extort. All methods of gain were employed, regardless of honor or dignity. None were safe from accusation, and their private fortunes were plundered along with their reputations.

50

Longinus, serving as both proconsul and quaestor, incurred the wrath of the province through his rapacious acts. Even those who executed his orders despised him, and the addition of a costly fifth legion and increased cavalry only furthered the hatred towards him. The province was given no relief.

51

Meanwhile, orders from Caesar came, telling him to take his army to Africa and march through Mauritania towards Numidia. King Juba had sent help to Pompey and was expected to send more. These letters pleased him, giving him the chance to plunder new lands and a wealthy kingdom. He then went to Lusitania to gather his legions and auxiliaries. He assigned some men to arrange for corn, ships, and money, so that he would not be delayed upon his return. Cassius was always diligent when his own interests were at stake.

52

With his army amassed and situated near Corduba, he delivered a speech to the soldiers informing them of Caesar's commands and promised a reward of one hundred sesterces upon reaching Mauritania. The fifth legion was to remain behind in Spain. After concluding his address, he made his way to Corduba. While en route to the hall of justice that same day, a man named Minutius Silo, dressed as a soldier, presented him with a piece of paper. As Cassius read the note, Silo took advantage of the moment, stabbing Cassius twice before being set upon by the remaining conspirators. Munatius Plancus ended the life of the lictor, who was closest to Longinus, and injured Q. Cassius, his lieutenant. Joining forces with Plancus were T. Vasius and L. Mergilio, both natives of Italica. Finally, L. Licinius Squillus pounced on Longinus and dealt several minor wounds as he lay helpless on the ground.

53

At that moment, his guards approached him, always armed with darts and accompanied by several Beronians and veterans who attended to him. They encircled the remaining conspirators who were marching towards him to complete the assassination. Calphurnius Salvianus and Manilius Tusculus were among them. Cassius was brought home, and Minutius Silo was caught as he slipped on a stone while trying to flee. Racilius retired to a nearby friend's house, waiting to hear about Cassius's fate. L. Laterensis, believing that he was already killed, hurried to the camp to congratulate the newly raised legions, who he knew despised Cassius. Hearing the news, they appointed him praetor and put him on the tribunal. All the natives and long-term residents of the province of the second legion, who shared a great antipathy towards Cassius, supported the decision.

54

Meanwhile, Laterensis received word of Cassius' survival. Though saddened by the news, he quickly composed himself and made his way to Cassius. The thirtieth legion, upon learning of the situation, rushed to Corduba to aid their leader. The twenty-first and fifth legions followed suit, leaving only two legions in the camp. Fearing isolation and the possibility of revealing their positions, the second legion joined the others. However, the newly formed legion remained steadfast, unmoved by any threats.

55

Cassius seized all conspirator's accomplices and sent the fifth legion back to the camp, keeping the other three. Minutius confessed and revealed L. Racilius, L. Laterensis, and Annius Scapula, who had great authority in the province and Cassius's trust. Cassius wasted no time and ordered their execution. His freedmen then tortured Minutius and Calphurnius Salvianus also gave evidence, adding to the list of conspirators. Some believed justice was served, while others believed they were coerced. L. Mergilio was also tortured. Squillus accused many who were sentenced to death or who paid a fine for redemption. Cassius pardoned Calphurnius for ten and Q. Sextius for fifty thousand sesterces, revealing himself to be as covetous as he was ruthless.

56

Days later, letters arrived from Caesar, informing him that Pompey was defeated and escaped alone. This news brought both happiness and sadness. He felt joy for Caesar's victory but also regretted that the end of the war would mean an end to his looting. So he was unsure of what to hope for: either triumph or unrestrained debauchery. Upon recovering from his wounds, he demanded immediate payment from all his debtors and obliged those taxed too low to pay more. Additionally, he conscripted Roman citizens to serve in his army, causing much outrage as the soldiers were sent overseas. This generated vast wealth but also increased animosity. He inspected the fleet in Seville, where he stayed for a while to gather those who hadn't paid their fines yet, rousing bitter complaints and protestations.

57

Meanwhile, L. Titius, a military representative of the native legion, sent word of reports that the thirteenth legion, led by Q. Cassius, had mutinied and killed some of the challenging centurions while encamped at Ilurgis. They had defected to the second legion, who were marching another way towards the Straits. With this information, he traveled by night with five cohorts of the twenty-first legion and caught up with them the next morning. He waited there for a day to plan his next steps, then went to Carmona to find the thirtieth and twenty-first legions, along with four cohorts of fifth, and all of the cavalry gathered there. He heard that a new legion had taken four cohorts near Obucula and forced them to join the second legion. They had appointed T. Thorius, an Italian native of Italica, as their leader. Calling a meeting promptly, he dispatched Marcellus to Corduba to secure the city and sent Q. Cassius to Seville. In a few days time, news reached him that the Roman citizens had risen up in revolt in Corduba. Furthermore, the two cohorts of the fifth legion who were stationed there had joined forces with them, whether voluntarily or not. Annoyed by these uprisings, Cassius left and moved to Segovia. He called together an assembly to take the pulse of the troops and learned that their allegiance was not to him, but to Caesar, even in his absence. They were prepared to face any peril to reclaim the region.

58

Thorius led his skilled soldiers towards Corduba, wanting to avoid any appearance of sedition against him or the troops. He also sought to counter Q. Cassius' authority, who had amassed soldiers for Caesar's cause. Thorius publicly claimed he aimed to reclaim the province for Pompey, maybe because of hatred for Caesar or love for Pompey, whose name still held sway over the legions once led by M. Varro. The soldiers bought into the ruse, even inscribing Pompey's name on their bucklers. When the citizens of Corduba approached them, they pleaded not to enter as enemies, since they shared a mutual dislike for Cassius and only refused to act against Caesar.

59

The soldiers, touched by the emotions of the masses, deemed it unnecessary to invoke the name of Pompey to inspire rebellion against Cassius. Marcellus and the people of Corduba would not join their cause, despite their efforts. In response, the soldiers removed Pompey's name from their shields, appointed Marcellus as their leader, and united with the citizens of Corduba. Cassius, camping nearby with a view of the town, sent messages for reinforcements and continued to devastate the surrounding area.

60

The soldiers serving Marcellus were stirred to action after an insult was cast upon them. They wanted to fight the enemy before they could raze the valuable property of Corduba. Marcellus, wary of a battle that could harm Caesar, allowed the troops to cross the Guadalquivir and face the enemy. Cassius did the same, but refused to leave an advantageous position. Marcellus urged his soldiers to retreat back to camp, but Cassius attacked with his cavalry and caused much damage. After realizing their mistake, Marcellus relocated to the other side of the Guadalquivir, where they met the enemy often but did not engage due to the uneven terrain.

Marcellus was a strong commander, leading experienced soldiers into battle. Cassius, however, relied more on his troops' loyalty than their bravery. They were encamped near each other when Marcellus seized a strategic location to deprive the enemy of water. Longinus, fearing he would be besieged, quietly left his camp at night and swiftly marched toward the town of Ulia. There, he believed he would be safe from attack due to the town's position on high ground and strong defenses. Marcellus pursued and set up camp nearby, but chose not to engage Cassius or let him roam freely. Instead, Marcellus enclosed both Ulia and Cassius within his lines and began building redoubts. Cassius, anticipating a shortage of provisions, sent out all his cavalry to cut off Marcellus's supplies.

62

King Bogud arrived with his troops, a legion and some cohorts, after receiving letters from Cassius. In Spain, the civil strife was causing division, with some supporting Cassius and more siding with Marcellus. Bogud engaged in fierce skirmishes with Marcellus at the fortified position but was unable to seize it.

63

Lepidus arrived in Ulia with thirty-five cohorts, horsemen, and auxiliaries from the nearby province aiming to settle the dispute between Cassius and Marcellus. Marcellus surrendered immediately while Cassius remained within his fortifications, either because he believed his cause was just, or because he thought Marcellus's surrender had already biased Lepidus in his favor. Lepidus stationed his troops in Ulia, joined forces with Marcellus, and prevented a battle. He invited Cassius to his camp and promised to remain impartial. Cassius took his time to think but eventually asked for the destruction of the circumvallation and free passage. The truce was reached, and the guards withdrew, but King Bogud unexpectedly attacked one of Marcellus's nearby forts and killed numerous soldiers. Lepidus intervened and stopped further violence.

64

Cassius went to Carmona, leaving a clear path for himself, while Marcellus and Lepidus marched towards Corduba together. Meanwhile, Trebonius arrived to take control of the province. Cassius, upon hearing this, sent his legions and cavalry to winter quarters, and made his way to Melaca with his belongings. He quickly embarked despite the winter season, claiming to avoid relying on Marcellus, Lepidus, and Trebonius for his safety, though rumors suggest he was really securing his ill-gotten wealth. The wind favored his journey until a storm at the river's mouth caused his ship to sink, and he perished.

65

On reaching Syria from Egypt, Caesar learned that the government in Rome was in chaos, with tribunes causing disruptions and military tribunes disobeying orders. He knew he must act quickly to restore order, but first he focused on pacifying the provinces through which he traveled. He rewarded those who deserved it and settled disputes, gaining the loyalty of local rulers. In some areas, he faced more trouble, but he remained resolute in his mission to protect the people and the republic.

66

He left after only a few days and put his friend Sextus Caesar in charge of Syria and its legions. He took his fleet and sailed to Cilicia. He called for the states to gather in Tarsus, the province's strongest and most beautiful city, where he settled all issues concerning the province and neighboring countries. He wasted no time and marched quickly through Cappadocia, stopping at Mazaca only briefly before reaching Comana - a sacred and ancient temple. He granted the priesthood to Lycomedes of Bithynia, who had inherited it from his ancestors, a line that had lost the scepter. Ariobarzanes was confirmed as king while his brother Ariarates was given protection. He continued his march with the same swiftness.

67

As he neared the boundaries of Gallograecia and Pontus, Deiotarus - who was tetrarch of the province as well as king of Lesser Armenia, but had his authority challenged by other rulers nearby - cast off his royal garb and donned the attire of a common man, nay even that of a criminal. In a supplicating manner, he approached Caesar to seek absolution for supporting Pompey with his army and following his orders at a time when he could not find refuge under Caesar's wing. Deiotarus argued that it was his duty to follow the lead of the current governors, without attempting to adjudicate the disputes amongst Rome's people.

68

Caesar reminded him of his past services and decrees, and stated that his defection was inexcusable due to his industry and prudence. He forgave his current fault due to their past friendship, respect for his age, and the intercession of his friends. He returned his royal habit and ordered him to join with his cavalry and legion. The controversy about the tetrarchate would be postponed to a later time.

69

Arrived at Pontus, his forces were scarce and undisciplined, except for the veteran sixth legion he brought from Alexandria, reduced to under a thousand men from harsh wear and tear. He only had Deiotarus' legion and two others who fought in the recent Domitius-Pharnaces battle. Pharnaces' ambassadors arrived to plead submission, assuring Caesar no hostility and no aid to Pompey given, unlike Deiotarus whom Pharnaces pardoned.

70

Caesar spoke calmly to the embassadors, promising justice for
Pharnaces if he kept his word but warning them not to mention
Deiotarus or overstate his own act of refusing aid to Pompey. He never
believed that personal favors could make amends for public harm to
the province, yet he was willing to pardon the past injuries inflicted on
the Roman citizens in Pontus. However, since one cannot restore the
dead or dignity to those stripped of it, he wanted Pharnaces to leave
the province, return the revenue farmers, and give back what was taken
from the Romans and their allies. Only then would he accept any gifts
from a triumphant general, including the golden crown Pharnaces had
sent him. Finally, Caesar sent the embassadors on their way.

71

Pharnaces made many promises, but Caesar, eager to leave, knew he
could not trust him. Pharnaces dragged his feet, delaying the departure
and trying to dodge his obligations. Caesar saw through his ploy and
knew he had to act swiftly. Without hesitation, he chose to settle things
with a battle.

72

Zela, a town of Pontus, sits fortified in a plain, upheld by a natural
elevation. Massive mountains surround it, with valleys carving through.
The highest of them, praised for Mithridates' win, Triarius's loss, and
our army's destruction, rests only three miles away, with a ridge nearly
touching the town. Pharnaces settled his soldiers there, fixing the
fortifications that once helped his father.

73

Caesar set up camp five miles from the enemy, recognizing that the valleys that protected the king's encampment would serve to protect his own, so long as the opposing forces did not take hold of them first. To secure his position in this regard, Caesar ordered for bundles of fascines to be brought within the confines of his intrenchments. Then, in the early morning, just before sunrise, Caesar quietly led his legions to the same post where Mithridates had previously defeated Triarius. Arriving there undetected, Caesar ordered that his soldiers use the army servants to bring all the fascines to the same location, thereby ensuring the soldiers could remain focused on the task at hand. This was important, as the valley dividing Caesar's location from that of the enemy was only a mile wide.

74

Pharnaces saw it and the next day he brought out all his troops in formation in front of his camp. Caesar, because of the disadvantage of the ground, thought he was organizing them to keep many of his men under arms, or because the king was confident he would defend his position by force instead of fortifications. Caesar thus kept only his first line in formation and ordered the rest of the troop to continue with their work. However, Pharnaces, impelled by the fortunate location that his father had, favorable omens, discovery of the small number of our armed men, veteran soldiers who defeated the twenty-second legion, and despising our troop, which they had defeated, was determined to fight. Caesar initially found Pharnaces' impudence laughable since he had crowded his army into such a narrow place. Pharnaces, however, continued to march and began to climb the steep hill on which Caesar was posted.

75

Caesar was taken aback by the brazenness and confidence of his enemy's sudden attack. Nonetheless, he rallied his troops, withdrew them from their posts, and prepared them for battle. The surprise attack initially instilled fear, and the soldiers were thrown into disarray by the scythed chariots. But the enemy's charge was quickly halted by the barrage of darts hurled towards them. With our army still coming into formation, we fought with the advantage of our location and the gods' assistance, who guide the fates of war, even when human effort seems futile.

76

We fought hard and fierce, but finally gained victory on the right wing where the sixth legion stood. The enemy was defeated there. The battle in the center and left was long and uncertain, but with the help of the gods, we eventually triumphed and drove them down the hill. Many were killed, and those who escaped had to throw away their weapons. They could not benefit from the high ground they had once easily climbed. Our victorious soldiers advanced up the disadvantageous ground to attack their fortifications, which they quickly overcame. The cohorts left by Pharnaces to guard it resisted but our men prevailed. The majority of the army was killed or taken prisoner. Pharnaces managed to escape with a few horse, but only because of the attack on the camp which gave him a chance to flee without pursuit. If it weren't for that, he would have surely fallen into Caesar's hands.

77

Though Caesar was already accustomed to victory, the joy he felt at the present success was incredible. The war had come to a swift end, perhaps giving him even greater pleasure as a result. He remembered the danger he faced and this heightened his delight in achieving an easy victory in a particularly difficult situation. Having recovered Pontus without much trouble, he left the soldiers to take the enemy's spoils and proceeded with some light horse. He then ordered the sixth legion to return to Italy to receive the honors and rewards they had merited, and sent home the auxiliary troops of Deiotarus. Finally, two legions remained with Caelius Vincianus to protect the kingdom of Pontus.

78

He marched through Gallograecia and Bithynia into Asia, settling disputes and establishing boundaries as he went. He made Mithridates of Pergamus king of Bosphorus, a man of royal upbringing and allegiance to Rome. He also gave him the tetrarchy of Gallograecia, previously held by Deiotarus. Caesar settled all affairs promptly and efficiently, returning to Italy earlier than anticipated.

AFRICAN WAR

As the narrative unfolds in the African War, readers are thrust into the heart of Caesar's campaign in North Africa, where the remnants of the Pompeian forces regroup and pose a new threat to his dominance. This enthralling account captures the intrigue, strategic maneuvering, and relentless determination that characterized Caesar's pursuit of victory against formidable adversaries in a foreign land. Embark on this riveting journey, as the stage is set for high-stakes battles, dramatic showdowns, and the indomitable spirit of both the Romans and their African foes, all vying for supremacy in the ever-shifting landscape of power and ambition.

1

Caesar marched steadily towards Lilybaeum without rest, arriving
fourteen days before the calends of January. He aimed to leave
immediately, even with limited forces of one legion and six hundred
horse. He set his tent by the sea, determined to show his readiness to
sail at all times. Ignoring the contrary wind, he kept his soldiers and
mariners on board, as the enemy appeared overwhelming. Juba led four
legions, with countless cavalry and light-armed soldiers; Scipio led ten
legions, backed with a hundred and twenty elephants and many fleets.
Despite this, Caesar remained confident and resolute. As the days went
by, more galleys and transports joined him, and new troops arrived
from every corner. The fifth veteran legion and two thousand horse
reinforced his ranks.

2

With six legions and two thousand horse at his disposal, he swiftly
embarked the troops on galleys and the cavalry on transports. After
dispatching most of the fleet to Aponiana, he remained in Sicily to
auction off some confiscated properties. With Allienus in charge of the
island, he ordered the remaining troops to embark as quickly as
possible. Setting sail six days before the calends of January, he caught
up with the rest of the fleet and, favored by the wind, arrived near
Africa within four days. With only a few galleys in attendance as the
transports were scattered, he sailed past Clupea and Neapolis, leaving
numerous towns and castles behind.

3

Arriving before Adrumetum, enemy garrison led by C. Considius, and
Cn. Piso with cavalry of Adrumetum and 3,000 Moors appeared on
shore towards Clupea. Caesar waited for fleet, then landed 3,000 foot
and 150 horse. Encamped before town, refrained from hostility or
plunder. Townspeople manned walls and assembled at gate with
garrison of two legions. Caesar rode around town, returned to camp.
Some criticized his lack of instructions to captains, but Caesar relied on
fortune to find a safe port for the fleet.

4

In the interim, L. Plancus, a lieutenant of Caesar, sought permission to negotiate with Considius and urge him to see reason. Permission being granted, he dispatched a letter to Considius through a captive. Considius, upon receiving the letter, inquired as to its source, and upon learning that it came from Caesar, the Roman commander, he scoffed and declared that the only general of the Roman forces he recognized was Scipio. He then ordered the messenger to be executed in his presence and handed the unopened letter to a trusted supporter, instructing him to deliver it to Scipio at once.

5

Caesar waited for a day and a night outside the town but Considius never replied. The rest of the soldiers had not arrived, and his cavalry was weak. The town was heavily fortified and hard to attack. Caesar did not want to risk injury or fatigue, especially since rumors of enemy horses arriving to assist the town were spreading. It was wiser for Caesar to avoid besieging the town and risking being surrounded by cavalry.

6

As he withdrew his men, the garrison made a sudden attack. Juba's cavalry arrived to get their pay, taking over the camp that Caesar had evacuated, and harassing his rear. The legionaries halted and despite their small number, the cavalry bravely charged the vast enemy horde. In an incredible turn of events, the Gallic horse drove the two-thousand Moors behind their walls with less than thirty fighters. Caesar resumed his march but kept a few veteran cohorts and cavalry with him to ward off repeated sallies from the enemy. As they advanced, the Numidians grew less eager to pursue. Delegates from several towns and castles appeared on the road offering help. On January 1st, Caesar's camp was established at Ruspina.

·7

He moved on and arrived at the city of Leptis, which enjoyed the freedom of being governed by its own laws. There, emissaries from the town welcomed him with an offer of submission in the name of its people. Caesar stationed his centurions and guards at the gates to restrain his soldiers from violent acts against the inhabitants. His camp was set up by the shore, a little ways away from the town. News reached him, by chance, that some of the ships had arrived, and had disclosed that the rest of the fleet had sailed towards Utica, unsure of which course to take. Caesar was unable to travel inland or leave the sea due to the fleet's mistake. The cavalry was sent back to their ships to prevent the country from being plundered, and fresh water was taken on board. In the meantime, suddenly, the Moorish horse attacked where the party had been getting water from the ships, and wounded many with their darts, killing some. These barbarians were known to lie in ambush with their horses among the valleys, and launch sudden attacks, avoiding hand-to-hand combat in a plain.

8

Caesar sent letters and messengers to Sardinia and neighboring regions, commanding them to provide men, corn, and weapons. He unloaded part of the fleet and sent it to Sicily with Rabirius Posthumus to bring the second group of soldiers. Ten galleys were ordered to monitor the missing transports and maintain control of the sea. In addition, C. Sallustius Prispus was instructed to sail to Percina and take control of the island from the enemy, who had a large quantity of corn. Caesar was precise with his orders, providing no room for excuse or delay. He learned from deserters and locals about Scipio's and his followers' condition; he pitied their foolishness for choosing to serve Juba's cavalry rather than enjoy their wealth and freedom with their fellow citizens.

9

On the third day before the nones of January, Caesar relocated his camp. He left six cohorts at Leptis, under Saserna's command, while he returned with the rest of the forces to Ruspina, where he had come from the day prior. After depositing the army's baggage in Ruspina, he led a small group of troops to gather provisions, demanding the townspeople to accompany them with their horses and carriages. With this strategy in mind, he collected a large amount of corn and returned to Ruspina, possibly intending to protect his fleet's escape route by securing the coastal cities with garrisons.

10

Thus, P. Saserna, brother of the commander of Leptis, was left in charge of the town with one legion, while all available wood was gathered and taken there. Meanwhile, the general departed from Ruspina with seven cohorts, part of the veteran legions that had proven their worth under Sulpicius and Vatinius in the previous fleet. They marched towards the port and embarked in the evening, with the troops left behind wondering about their commander's intentions. The small number of troops, composed mostly of inexperienced recruits, made them anxious about their safety, especially considering they were on foreign land against a powerful enemy supported by countless horsemen. However, they looked to their general's intrepid spirit and unwavering confidence for hope and strength, relying on his skill and talents to lead them through all difficulties.

11

Caesar, having spent the whole night aboard the ship, prepared to set sail at daybreak. Suddenly, the fleet that had caused much worry appeared in view. He commanded his men to leave their ships and arm themselves on the shore while the new fleet entered the port as quickly as possible. He then brought all of his forces, including horse and foot, ashore and returned to Ruspina. There, he set up his camp and led thirty cohorts without baggage into the country to forage. Caesar's plan was finally revealed: to sail secretly to assist the lost transports, away from the enemy's view. He did not want his soldiers left behind to know of this, as he feared that they would be intimidated by the vastness of the enemy's numbers.

12

Caesar's scouts and advanced horse reported the enemy's presence just three miles from his camp. A great cloud of dust soon rose, prompting Caesar to order his limited horse and archers to advance. Meanwhile, his thirty cohorts, four hundred horse, and one hundred and fifty archers marched in orderly battle formation. Caesar himself led a small party to confront the enemy, commanding his soldiers to prepare for battle upon sighting them in the distance.

13

Labienus and the two Pacidii led the enemy, with a large cavalry front mixed with Numidians and archers. Caesar's army mistook the cavalry for infantry and were outnumbered. Caesar arranged his army in a single line with archers in front and cavalry on the wings, instructing them to avoid being surrounded. He expected to face only infantry.

14

As they waited for the signal, Caesar remained still, aware that his meager troops would have to rely on cunning rather than might to face the much larger opposing forces. Suddenly, the enemy cavalry began to stretch out, circling the hills and weakening Caesar's own horse, and then closing in on them. Our men struggled to hold their position against the overwhelming number of enemies, as both sides moved in to engage. The enemy cavalry, backed by a few lightly armed Numidians, charged forward, bombarding our legions with darts. Our troops readied themselves for the counter-attack, as the enemy horse fell back, only to rally themselves and charge again with increased vigor.

15

Caesar saw his troops were at risk from a new mode of battle. The foot soldiers had followed the enemies' horses, moving beyond their own colors, which left them vulnerable to deadly Numidian darts. Meanwhile, the enemy's horses were able to fly away from the infantry's javelins. Caesar gave orders for the soldiers to remain within four feet of the ensigns. Labienus's cavalry circled Caesar's few, outnumbered cavalry, forcing them to retreat due to their horses' injuries. The enemy pressed closer, and Caesar's legions were soon enclosed in a circle, fighting for their lives.

16

Labienus rode boldly to the front of the battle, head uncovered, urging his troops forward while taunting Caesar's legions, "What's this? All fired up by his words? He's made a sorry mess of you. My heart goes out to you." The rebuke riled one soldier, "I'm no raw recruit, Labienus, but rather a veteran of the tenth legion." Labienus, quick to challenge, demanded, "Where are your colors, then?" The soldier responded by hurling his helmet to the ground, revealing his face and, with all his might, tossing a javelin that struck Labienus' horse in the chest. "By this spear, Labienus, know that it was a soldier of the tenth legion who threw it." The entire army was struck with fear, especially the fresh troops, now focused solely on defense against the enemy onslaught with little thought of anything else.

17

Caesar spied the foe's plan and maneuvered to expand his battle line. He instructed his cohorts to turn to the right and left, breaking the enemy's circle. Then he attacked a separated section with foot and horse, causing them to flee. Caesar refrained from pursuing too far, wary of ambush, and returned. The rest of his troops also succeeded in forcing the enemy to retreat, wounded and beaten. The foe fell back to their camp, still in battle formation.

18

Meanwhile, M. Petreius and Cn. Piso brought eleven hundred exquisite Numidian horses and a significant amount of infantry to aid the opposition. The enemy regained their bravery upon sight of this reinforcement, attacking the rear of the legions as they backed off, aiming to prevent them from reaching their camp. After witnessing this, Caesar commanded his men to turn around and engage in battle in the middle of the plain. However, the enemy persisted in their dodging of an enclosed fight, and since Caesar's cavalry had not yet recuperated from their recent expedition and were weak from thirst, tiredness, injuries, and hence unfit for an intense and prolonged pursuit, which was not feasible owing to the time of day, he ordered his horse and foot to promptly assault the enemy and not cease the chase until they outstripped them beyond the furthest hills and claimed the position for themselves. On a given cue, when the enemy were carelessly tossing their javelins, Caesar rode upon them hastily with his mounted and foot soldiers, sweeping them from the field and across the neighboring hill in mere moments, occupying that location for a while before gradually retreating back to the camp in a disciplined manner. The opposition, who were consequently contested ruthlessly, finally withdrew to their defenses.

19

Meanwhile, many deserters and prisoners arrived at Caesar's camp after the action was finished. They revealed the enemy's plan to amaze our inexperienced troops with a new and uncommon fighting style, then cut them to pieces by surrounding them with cavalry. Labienus intended to lead an army of auxiliaries to weary us with slaughter and defeat us despite our victory. He trusted his army's size more than their bravery, as he heard of the mutiny of veteran legions in Rome and was confident of his own troops' loyalty. He had amassed a large force of cavalry, light-armed troops, and Juba's massive army with 120 elephants, innumerable cavalry, and over 12,000 legionaries. On the day before January's nones, he came against Caesar with an army of 1600 Gallic and German horse, 900 under Petreius, 8000 Numidians, four times that number of light-armed foot, and a multitude of archers and slingers. The battle raged from the fifth hour till sunset, and Petreius left the field after sustaining a dangerous wound.

20

Caesar, meanwhile, fortified his camp with greater care. He reinforced the guards and constructed two intrenchments. One stretched from Ruspina to the sea, the other from his camp to the sea. By doing so, he secured communication and ensured a safe supply of resources. He armed the mariners, Gauls, Rhodians, and others according to the enemy's example, to enable his cavalry. Heeding Scipio's expected arrival with an army consisting of eight legions and three thousand horse, he recruited a great number of archers from the fleet into his camp. He also established workshops, made a great number of darts and arrows, and prepared leaden bullets and palisades. Additionally, he sent for hurdles and wood from Sicily, as the harvest in Africa was insignificant. The enemy had taken all the laborers into their service, stored up the grain in a few fortified towns after demolishing the rest, and forced the inhabitants into the garrisoned places, thus exhausting the entire country.

21

He courted private individuals and secured a small supply, carefully managing it. He personally inspected the works daily, keeping four cohorts on duty due to the enemy's vast numbers. Labienus sent his numerous sick and wounded in wagons to Adrumetum. Meanwhile, Caesar's inexperienced transports roamed aimlessly without knowledge of the coast, attacked by the enemy's coasters and mostly taken or destroyed. Caesar responded by positioning his fleet for convoy protection along the coast and islands.

22

M. Cato of Utica doth not pause to rouse and implore young Pompey, saying to him thus: "Thy forebearer, at thy youthful age, saw the commonwealth weighed down by vile and fearless foes, driving the righteous to their demise or to flee from their land and kin; and, spurred by a mighty heart and a desire for glory, though he be youthful and simply a citizen, he still had the spirit to gather the remnants of his father's legion and uphold the liberty of Rome and Italy, near crushed entirely. He achieved victory over Sicily, Africa, Numidia, and Mauritania faster than expected, earning a grand reputation across all nations and triumphing when still a youth and only a Roman knight. And he did not undertake public service with merely his father's exploits, or his family's pride and renown, or the state's honors and dignities to his name. But thou, on the other hand, with all these accomplishments and thy father's fame, made more pompous by thy personal actions and a mighty heart, shouldst not waste thy energy and fail to join forces with thy father's upholders to render the greatly needed aid to thyself, our republic, and every nobleman?"

23

The boy, stirred by the serious and respectable senator's scolding, collected around thirty boats, both large and small, a few of which were warships, and sailed from Utica to Mauritania, attacking the kingdom of Bogud. He abandoned his belongings, led an army of two thousand, comprising of some freedmen and some slaves, some with weapons, some without, and reached the town of Ascurum, where the king had stationed a garrison. Upon Pompey's arrival, the inhabitants permitted him to proceed to the walls and gates, but suddenly pushed out, causing his troops to retreat in chaos and panic to the sea and their ships. This failed maneuver compelled him to leave that shore, and he did not dock in any other place, preferring to sail straight for the Balearean Isles.

24

Meanwhile, Scipio marched out from Utica with a strong garrison and joined forces with Petreius and Labienus. They set up camp about three miles away from Caesar's forces and their cavalry continuously harassed Caesar's men, cutting off their access to food and water. With no supplies from Sicily or Sardinia, Caesar's situation became dire. The treacherous navigation season and limited land in Africa added to their troubles. However, the veteran soldiers and cavalry had faced similar challenges in their numerous battles and managed to survive by foraging sea-weed, which they washed with fresh water to feed their horses and cattle.

25

King Juba got wind of Caesar's struggles and, seeing his chance, gathered a large army and marched towards his allies without giving Caesar time to regroup. Sitius and King Bogud caught wind of Juba's advance and joined their forces, laying siege and conquering several cities in Numidia, slaughtering the inhabitants. Juba heard of these attacks and decided to abandon his plans of joining Scipio to defend his own lands. He left with his troops, leaving only thirty elephants behind, to defend his kingdom.

26

Caesar's arrival was doubted by many in the province, who believed instead that some of his lieutenants had come with forces recently sent. In order to inform them of his presence, he dispatched letters to all the several states. Instead of continuing to remain inactive, Caesar was moved by the tears and complaints of those who fled to his camp due to the cruelty of the enemy. He resolved to take the field as soon as possible with his troops. He was anxious and impatient for the arrival of the rest of the troops, as he saw villages burned, the country laid waste, the cattle destroyed, the towns plundered, and the citizens either killed or put in chains. His forces were not enough to provide relief to all those who needed it. Nonetheless, he kept the soldiers constantly building up the intrenchments and carrying on his lines right up to the sea.

27

Meanwhile, Scipio devised a method to train his elephants. He arranged them in a line to face the enemy slingers who pelted them with small stones, causing them to turn and charge their own men. Scipio's army stood behind the elephants, ready to throw stones to force them back towards the enemy. However, progress was slow due to the inherent danger of these animals on the battlefield, even after years of training.

28

Two generals near Ruspina, C. Virgilius, a praetorian man commanding in Thapsus, spotted Caesar's lost ships unsure of his location, thought it a chance to destroy, and pursued them with soldiers and archers. Despite being repulsed, he persevered and caught up with one carrying two young Spaniards and a guilty centurion. The young surrendered to Virgilius and were sent to Scipio, who put them to death three days later. The elder Spaniard even begged to die first, and they both met their sentence.

29

The mounted guards of the two camps battled each other in small conflicts. At times, even Labienus' German and Gallic cavalry would engage with Caesar's cavalry, after agreeing not to harm one another. Labienus attempted to ambush the town of Leptis, guarded by three cohorts under Saserna's command. But he failed, as the town was fortified and equipped with war machines. Despite this, he tried again multiple times. One day, a group of enemies positioned themselves at the gate, but when their leader was killed by a crossbow arrow, they fled in fear, freeing the town from further attacks.

30

Scipio arranged his army every day, lining them up about three hundred paces from his camp. They stayed in arms for most of the day, then retreated back to the camp at night. He did this multiple times, while Caesar's army stayed put without any movement. Scipio's calmness and restraint made him feel superior to Caesar and his army. He gathered all his forces, including thirty elephants with towers on their backs, and spread out his cavalry and infantry as far as possible, even going up to Caesar's fortifications.

31

Caesar, upon his observation, silently called back those who sought forage, wood, or worked on fortifications. His cavalry was instructed to hold their position until the enemy was within reach of dart, and then to retreat in good order within the intrenchments. Other mounted soldiers were prepared and armed in their designated locations. Although he did not give these orders personally or from the rampart, his extensive knowledge of warfare enabled him to direct his officers from within his tent, receiving information from his scouts about the movements of the enemy. He was aware that despite the enemy's confidence in their numbers, they would not dare to attack a general who had repeatedly defeated, frightened, and chased them off, who had often pardoned and spared their lives, and whose name alone had the power to intimidate their army. Additionally, he had a high rampart and deep ditch that were difficult to approach, as well as cleverly positioned sharp spikes to keep them at bay. He had prepared a vast array of weapons, from crossbows to engines, for a determined defense, anticipating a likely struggle with few and inexperienced troops. His hesitation to lead his troops into battle did not stem from fear or the size of the enemy army, but from his concern about the nature of the victory. He recognized that he would be ashamed if he triumphed only over the scattered remnants who regrouped after their defeat, after all his successful battles against powerful adversaries. Consequently, he decided to endure the enemy's pride and jubilation until the arrival of some of his veteran legion in the second embarkation.

32

Scipio withdrew from the trenches, seemingly unbothered by Caesar's presence. He gathered his soldiers and spoke of the impending victory, bolstering their confidence. Caesar, meanwhile, kept his soldiers working on fortifications while teaching the new recruits the importance of hard work. Scipio's army dwindled as more and more soldiers deserted and joined Caesar's forces. Among these were some of high status, back from the days of C. Marius. Caesar sent them back to their homes with letters urging their compatriots to join him in the fight against their common foe.

33

Near Ruspina, deputies from Acilla and nearby towns pledge to execute Caesar's orders if given garrisons for safety. Caesar agrees, assigning a garrison led by C. Messius, a former aedile. Considius Longus rushes with eight cohorts to Acilla, but Messius beats him there. When Considius realizes Caesar's garrison controls the town, he retreats to Adrumetum. Eventually, with Labienus' cavalry support, Considius lays siege to the town.

34

Around that time, C. Sallustius Crispus arrived in Cercina with a fleet, as we've discussed before. C. Decimus the quaestor, who was in charge of the magazines on the island, fled with his own men when Sallustius arrived. But the Cercinates welcomed Sallustius, and he found a lot of corn on the island. He loaded it onto all the ships in the port and sent them to Caesar's camp. At the same time, Allienus, the proconsul, sent the thirteenth and fourteenth legions, eight hundred Gallic horse, and a thousand archers and slingers to Caesar from Lilybaeum. This fleet arrived at Ruspina in four days with a favorable wind. Caesar was pleased to receive both provisions and reinforcement of troops, which gave the soldiers energy and removed their worry about food. He let the troops rest and recover before spreading them out to different forts and works.

35

Scipio and his generals were surprised by Caesar's sudden change in war strategy, leading them to suspect powerful reasons behind it. In an attempt to gain intel, they sent two reliable Getulian deserters who wished to pledge their allegiance to Caesar. Praised and rewarded, these deserters soon proved their merit as more soldiers deserted to Caesar's camp.

36

At Ruspina, things were as they were. M. Cato led in Utica and recruited more and more freed-men, Africans, and slaves to send without pause to Scipio's camp. Meanwhile, Tisdra's deputies arrived at Caesar's doorstep, telling him of Italian merchants and their three hundred thousand bushels of corn in their town, needing a garrison for their protection and their stocks. Caesar replied gracefully, gave the word for the garrison they asked for, and wished them well. P. Sitius, on the other hand, moved on Numidia with troops, and took a castle on a hill where Juba had provisions and materials to wage on the war.

37

With two veteran legions and all his cavalry and light-armed troops on the second embarkation, Caesar sent six transports to Lilybaeum to bring the rest of his army. On the sixth day before the calends of February, Caesar ordered his scouts and lictors to attend him at six in the evening. At midnight, he drew out all the legions and marched towards Ruspina, a garrison that had first declared in his favor. With nobody suspecting his plans, Caesar continued his route along the sea, passing a declivity into a fifteen-mile plain bordering a chain of mountains. In Scipio's former watchtower, with guards and outposts stationed, Caesar arrived.

38

After Caesar took the ridge, he constructed forts on the hills in thirty minutes. At the last hill, near the enemies' encampment where Scipio had stationed his Numidian guards, Caesar paused briefly to assess the situation before positioning his cavalry for the best advantage. He then commanded the legions to construct a trench along the ridge from his current position to where he had begun. Seeing Caesar's movements, Scipio and Labienus ordered their cavalry to leave the camp and line up for battle, while their infantry formed a second line less than half a mile from the camp and about a mile from Caesar.

39

Caesar remained calm before the enemy's approach, urging his men forward. However, as the enemy drew near, he saw the need to act. He commanded the Spanish cavalry and light infantry to charge the Numidian guard and secure their position. The attack succeeded, and Labienus moved his forces to aid the Numidians. Caesar then sent his left wing to intercept the enemy, keeping a strategic distance from his own troops.

40

On the plain was a great villa with four turrets. Labienus could not see that Caesar's cavalry had intercepted him. Without warning, the cavalry charged from the rear causing the Numidian cavalry to flee in terror, and the Gauls and Germans who stayed were completely surrounded and met their end. When Scipio and his legions saw this, they fled in confusion. Caesar ordered a retreat and gazed upon the massive bodies of the Gauls and Germans scattered across the field, amazed by their symmetry and size.

41

The following day, Caesar gathered his troops and arranged them for battle on the open plain. Scipio, disheartened by the unexpected setback and the numerous casualties, remained within his protected position. Caesar advanced his army in formation, slowly manoeuvring along the base of the hills, edging closer towards his camp. Caesar's legions were now just a mile away from the town of Uzita, which was under Scipio's control. Scipio, fearing the loss of the town, decided that he would not allow it to fall into Caesar's hands, and he chose to defend it at all costs. He summoned forth his entire army and arranged them into four lines. The first row was composed of cavalry, supported by elephants carrying castles on their backs. Caesar, believing that Scipio was advancing to engage in battle, remained stationed near the town. Scipio, with the town at the center of his front, extended his two flanks where his elephants could be viewed easily by Caesar's army.

42

Caesar waited till the sun set, and still Scipio held his ground. He didn't seem to be looking for a fight, preferring instead to stay in his strong position. Caesar decided not to push any further until the next day, because the enemy had a large group of Numidians guarding the town. It would be difficult to attack both the town and the enemy's flanks, especially since the soldiers had been standing fast since the morning without food. Caesar led his troops back to camp, determined to move closer to the town the next day.

43

Considius besieged eight cohorts of Numidians and Getulians in Acilla, but after watching his work destroyed and learning of a recent cavalry battle, he burned his corn, destroyed his supplies, and left the siege. He split his troops with Scipio and traveled through Juba's kingdom to Adrumetum.

44

One of the transports, from the second embarkation, was lost at sea during a storm. Q. Cominius and L. Ticida were aboard it from Sicily, and it drifted to Thapsus. The ship was overtaken by Virgilius, and those onboard were taken to Scipio. A three-banked galley from the same fleet was also caught in the wind and landed at Aegimurum. Varus and M. Octavius took the ship, which carried veteran soldiers, a centurion, and a few new levies. Varus treated them with respect and sent them to Scipio under guard. When they faced Scipio, he urged them to join the cause of the righteous citizens and offered them life and money. He believed their actions were not born of malice but from the misguided leadership of their commander.

45

Scipio finished his speech with the expectation of gratitude for his gracious offer. One of the prisoners, a centurion from the fourteenth legion, spoke up, addressing him as Scipio, not as a general. The centurion expressed his appreciation for the kindness that Scipio was willing to show to the prisoners, but he couldn't accept it without committing a terrible crime. How could he fight against Caesar, his general, for whom he had served as a centurion for over 36 years and whose army he had contributed to with his valor? Nor could he fight against Caesar's victorious army. He advised Scipio to stop the war, for he didn't understand the troops he was fighting against, nor did he realize the difference between Caesar's soldiers and his own. He challenged Scipio to choose his best cohort and ten of his own comrades, who were now prisoners, to engage them. Then Scipio would see the outcome and better understand what he was up against.

46

The centurion spoke boldly, which angered Scipio. He signaled some officers to kill the centurion, which they did. Scipio ordered the separation of the veteran soldiers from the new ones and had the contaminated soldiers carried away and killed. The new soldiers were divided amongst the legions, and Cominius and Ticida were forbidden to see Scipio. Caesar fired the officers responsible for coastal security, as they neglected their crucial duty.

47

During Caesar's campaign, a wretched tempest terrorized his army one night when the Pleiades had departed. Hailstones of colossal size came crashing down, adding to their misery. What made matters worse was Caesar's habit of relocating his troops every few days, causing them to be unprepared to withstand the brutal winter weather. Even worse still, his army had been prohibited from bringing any utensils, slaves or equipment and had no supplies or tents to protect themselves. With no option of shelter, the storm ravaged the camp, dousing the fires and washing away their rations. In the blink of an eye, the already wretched camp plunged into deeper misfortune as the javelin shafts in the fifth legion spontaneously ignited.

48

King Juba was told of Scipio's cavalry moves, and invited to assist by the general himself. Leaving part of his army to fight Sitius, Juba came with three legions, eight hundred horse, and thirty elephants, along with light-armed troops and a body of Numidian cavalry. Juba set up a separate camp near Scipio's, which soothed the worries of Caesar's men. With Juba's aid, Scipio felt braver, and even led his army in a showy battle with Caesar's troops, before going back to camp.

49

Caesar saw that Scipio had received his supplies and would no longer avoid a fight. He advanced with his troops, secured his lines with redoubts and took control of the high ground. The enemy, confident in their numbers, took a hill nearby to stop our progress. Labienus planned to take this post and quickly moved towards it from his quarters.

50

A valley lay ahead, deep and wide, with rough edges and caves. Caesar must cross this valley to reach the hill he desired, where a dense grove of aged olive trees waited. Labienus, wise to the paths of the land, hid with light-footed soldiers and some cavalry. He held some horsemen back behind the mounds, waiting for the right moment to attack Caesar's foot soldiers from the mountainside. All the while, Caesar and his army were surrounded by danger, unable to move ahead or back. Labienus boasted his troops would find victory in their grasp by pouncing upon them. Caesar, unaware of danger, sent his cavalry forward. Upon arriving, Labienus's men forgot the plan or feared being trampled by Caesar's horse. They emerged in small groups from the rock and started up the hill. Caesar's cavalry chased and took prisoners, then claimed the hill. Labienus and some of his horsemen barely escaped.

51

The mountain cleared by cavalry, Caesar said to entrench himself, assigning task to legions. Then, he ordered communication lines from the greater camp to cross the Uzita plain which was held by Scipio's detachment. His intention was to secure his flanks and prevent enemy horse from surrounding his troops, giving his men chances to speak with enemy and facilitate deserter's escape. By approaching enemy, he also could see if they wanted to fight. Additionally, it was a good place to dig wells because the area was low. While legions were working, part of army fought Numidian horse and foot at trenches.

52

Near dusk, as Caesar withdrew his troops, Juba, Scipio, and Labienus attacked fiercely with their horse and foot soldiers. The enemy cavalry was overwhelmed by the vast numbers of the assault and were forced to retreat slightly. However, Caesar's legions swiftly returned to aid their cavalry, rallying and launching a ferocious charge against the disordered and dispersed Numidians. The Caesar's forces pursued them to the king's camp, inflicting heavy losses and slaying many. Had the wind not stirred up dust and night not come, Juba and Labienus and their whole cavalry would have been lost. Meanwhile, the fourth and sixth legions under Scipio deserted him as did Curio's horse who trusted neither Scipio nor his army.

53

As Caesar and his foes waged war near Uzita, the ninth and tenth legions voyaged from Sicily aboard ships. Upon reaching Ruspina, they spied what they believed to be enemy vessels near Thapsus where Caesar's fleet lay at anchor. Without forethought, they set sail into the open sea, tossed and tormented by wind and hunger. Finally, they made it to Caesar's encampment.

54

Following the landing of these legions, Caesar recalled their previous unruly behaviour in Italy and the misconduct of some officers. He seized the opportunity provided by C. Avienus, a military tribune of the tenth legion, who had filled a ship with his own slaves and horses without taking a single soldier on board while departing for Sicily. Summoning all the tribunes and centurions, Caesar proclaimed that he intended to discipline those who could not control themselves and make a good use of his leniency. Due to their revolts and rapine, he dismissed and ordered C. Avienus to leave Africa immediately, and he did the same with A. Fonteius as a seditious officer and bad citizen. T. Salienus, M. Tiro, and C. Clusinus, who failed to display bravery in war and good conduct in peace, were also dismissed as centurions. Caesar then delivered them to the custody of centurions, with orders to isolate them on a ship with a single attendant slave each.

55

Getulian deserters, sent home by Caesar, returned to their homeland and persuaded their countrymen to revolt against Juba. The king, now facing three wars, had to send six cohorts to defend his borders against the rebels, weakening his army against Caesar.

56

Caesar finished his lines of communication and entrenched himself near the town. He played constantly with warlike machines placed in front of his works to increase the enemy's fears. He also drew five legions out of his other camp. Caesar foresaw the benefit of holding conferences with several persons of eminence and distinction who earnestly requested an interview with their friends. The Getulian horse's chief officers and other illustrious men of that nation, under the cover of darkness, came over to Caesar's camp near Uzita with a thousand horses and servants.

57

Scipio was pissed when he found out about the disaster. He spotted M. Aquinius chatting with C. Saserna and told him to stop yapping with the enemy. Aquinius didn't listen and kept it up. But then, a guard of Juba's came and told him to shut it. Saserna heard this and Aquinius, being scared shitless, quit talking and did what Juba said. It's crazy to think that a Roman citizen, who had some honors and wasn't even exiled, would choose to obey a foreign prince and watch his own party get wrecked rather than return to his country. Juba was even worse, disrespecting Scipio - a man from a great family, with honors, and high rank in the state. Juba told him he couldn't wear his purple coat of mail, which was Scipio's usual outfit. So, Scipio changed to a white robe, bowing down to that arrogant and cocky tyrant.

58

On the next day, they withdrew all their forces from the camps and formed them on an eminence close to Caesar's camp, ordering themselves in battle formation. Caesar also withdrew his men and arranged them in battle formation before his lines, not doubting that the enemy, who had more soldiers and had been reinforced by king Juba, would advance to attack him. He rode through the ranks, encouraging his men, and gave them the signal of battle. He did not think it wise to move far from his lines, as the enemy had a strong garrison in Uzita that was facing his right wing, and advancing beyond that would expose his flank to a sally from the town. The ground in front of Scipio's army was also very rough, which he believed could disturb his men during the charge.

59

The order of battle for both armies must be described. Scipio arranged his own and Juba's legions at the front, along with a reserve body of Numidians who were positioned in such thin ranks and length that they appeared as a line of legionaries, with the wings being the only part that was doubled. The elephants were evenly spaced on the right and left, supported by light-armed troops and auxiliary Numidians. Additionally, all the regular cavalry was on the right, while the left was covered by the town of Uzita, providing no room for the cavalry to extend themselves. To incite confusion in Caesar's army, Scipio placed the Numidian horse and light-armed foot at a distance of a thousand paces from his right, near a mountain, allowing the cavalry to make a longer sweep and encircle the enemy with their darts when the fight began. This was Scipio's strategy.

60

Caesar's battle plan, from left to right: Ninth and eighth legions on the left, main body consisting of thirteenth, fourteenth, twenty-eighth, and twenty-sixth legions, and right wing with thirtieth and twenty-eighth legions. Second line on the right mixed with new recruits. Third line on left, extending to middle legion of main body, creating triple order of battle. Left wing stronger to match enemy cavalry, with all horse and light-armed foot there. Detached fifth legion to support. Archers scattered with emphasis on wings.

61

The armies stood facing each other, only 300 paces apart, without fighting throughout the day, an unprecedented occurrence. Caesar's retreat prompted the unbridled Numidian and Getulian horse to attack his camp, while Labienus's cavalry held Caesar's legions at bay. Without orders, Caesar's cavalry charged against the Getulians and retreated in disorder with the loss of one trooper, twenty-six light-armed foot, and several wounded horses. Scipio celebrated his success, but the next day, Caesar's horse attacked and captured about a hundred enemy stragglers for provisions. Both leaders fortified their positions, with frequent skirmishes between the cavalry.

62

Meanwhile, Varus got word that the seventh and eighth legions had sailed from Sicily. Promptly, he outfitted the fleet he'd wintered at Utica with Getulian rowers and sailors. Then, he set sail and came upon Adrumetum with 55 ships. Unaware of Varus' arrival, Caesar sent L. Cispius with 27 boats to anchor near Thapsus as a security measure for his convoys. He also dispatched Q. Aquila with 13 galleys to Adrumetum. However, Aquila's plans were foiled by a storm that forced him to seek shelter in a nearby creek. In the interim, the remaining fleet before Leptis was left defenseless as the mariners dispersed on the shore. Taking advantage of this opportunity, Varus left Adrumetum and sailed to Leptis, where he burned all the transports at sea, and seized two five-benched galleys without resistance.

63

Caesar received news of the unfortunate incident while inspecting the camp. In response, he mounted his horse and rode two leagues to Leptis, where he boarded a brigantine and ordered his ships to follow. He caught up with Aquila, who was frightened by the number of opposing ships, and pursued the enemy fleet. Varus, taken aback by Caesar's bravery and quickness, turned his fleet and headed for Adrumetum. Caesar, however, managed to retrieve one of his galleys with a crew and 130 of the enemy's men, as well as capturing a three-benched galley belonging to the enemy. The rest of the enemy fleet went to Adrumetum, and Caesar followed the next morning after setting fire to all transports outside Cothon and commandeering any galleys he found. Although he waited for a chance to engage the enemy, he eventually returned to his camp.

64

On the ship rode P. Vestrius, a Roman knight, and P. Ligarius, who fought against him in Spain and joined Pompey in Greece. Caesar gave the order to kill Ligarius for his disloyalty, but pardoned Vestrius because his brother paid for his freedom in Rome. Vestrius also proved that he was once sentenced to death but was saved by the mercy of Varus, with no chance for escape since.

65

In Africa, it was customary to stash corn privately in underground vaults for protection during war. Caesar was tipped off about this by a spy and sent out two legions and cavalry to retrieve some corn. They traveled ten miles and successfully returned with the goods. Upon learning of this, Labienus marched seven miles through the same mountains Caesar had traversed the day before and set up camp with two legions. He anticipated Caesar's repeated attempts to secure corn and laid in wait with a sizeable group of horse and light-armed foot.

66

Upon word of Labienus' trap from deserters, Caesar paused briefly until their awareness waned from repeated attempts. Then one morning, with eight seasoned legions and some cavalry, he marched out by the Decuman gate while a different cavalry group approached the enemy's concealed light-armed infantry, killing five hundred and scattering the rest. Labienus then rode forward with all his cavalry to offer salvation but was almost victorious in their number when Caesar emerged with the legions, lined up and ready for war. This display left Labienus with pause, leading him to call for a retreat. The next day, Juba had all the deserters who fled to their camp crucified.

67

Caesar, lacking corn, summoned his forces back to the camp. He left a few garrisons and commanded two fleets to blockade Adrumetum and Thapsus. He burned the camp at Uzita and marched with his baggage on the left. He arrived at Agar, where they found plenty of provisions. Meanwhile, Scipio pursued him and camped six miles away in three different camps.

68

Zeta was a town not far from Scipio's land, a few miles from his camp, and maybe eighteen from Caesar's. Scipio sent two legions there to get food, but a deserter told Caesar. He moved his camp to a hill for safety and left some soldiers there, while he left at three in the morning with the rest of his troops. He went past the enemy's camp and took the town. He saw Scipio's legions had gone to get more food further away. He went after them, but the entire army came to help so he had to stop chasing them. He caught C. Mutius Reginus, a knight and Scipio's friend, the governor of the town. He also caught P. Atrius, a knight from Utica, with twenty-two camels from king Juba. He left some soldiers there and went back to his camp.

69

As he approached Scipio's camp, which he had to pass by, Labienus and Afranius lay in ambush nearby with their cavalry and light infantry. Caesar sent his cavalry to meet them and ordered the legions to face the enemy, throwing their baggage into a heap. The legions charged and easily pushed back the enemy. But they came back again and again, harassing Caesar's troops, keeping a safe distance. Caesar realized their plan was to force him to camp in a place without water, starving his men and animals.

70

As the sun set, Caesar realized that despite four hours of marching, he had not advanced more than a hundred paces. His cavalry suffered significant losses by trailing behind, prompting him to order the legions to slow down and follow behind. By doing so, his troops were better equipped to sustain the enemy's charge. Yet, the Numidian horse threatened to surround them. Only a few veteran soldiers were needed to incite the enemy to flee, but they would quickly regroup and charge the legionaries with their darts. Caesar proceeded cautiously, halting and marching alternately until they reached the camp safely at seven in the evening, with only ten men injured. Labienus also retreated after exhausting his troops. Scipio, to intimidate Caesar's troops, paraded his legions and elephants before his camp but withdrew them later.

71

Caesar had to train his soldiers differently when facing these enemies. He taught them how to move their feet, when to attack and when to defend, and even how to fake an attack. These enemies were troublesome, with their light weapons killing horses and wearing down soldiers. But Caesar's soldiers were prepared for their maneuvers.

72

Caesar fretted as these events unfolded; whenever he faced the enemy's cavalry without the support of his infantry, he found himself at a disadvantage. The enemy's light-armed foot made it even worse. He feared that his army would struggle more when facing their legions. He suspected that the clash between the two armies would be devastating. The sheer number and size of the elephants also frightened his soldiers. To remedy this, he brought over some elephants from Italy so that his men could grow accustomed to them. Caesar also made sure that his horses were not startled by the sight, cry or scent of these animals. With great success, his men came to comprehend the elephants' strength and weakness. They knew where to aim their darts. The soldiers even grew comfortable enough to touch the elephants with their hands, whilst the cavalry attacked them with blunted darts to desensitize their horses step by step.

73

Caesar was worried and moved with caution, unlike his usual speedy actions. He had to face a crafty foe who was skilled in the art of war, unlike the simple and direct enemy from the champaign country. To prepare his troops, Caesar made them take part in frequent marches and taught them how to pursue and avoid their skilled opponent. He waited for Scipio in an open plain but retreated when he saw that Scipio was still hesitant to fight.

74

As the sun rose high, messengers from Vacca approached, their faces weary and drawn. They begged Caesar for assistance, promising to provide all that was needed for the upcoming battle. Meanwhile, across the land, the gods smiled upon the great leader, for a traitor revealed that Juba had already taken the town and committed unspeakable horrors, leaving nothing but savagery in his wake.

75

Caesar inspected his army on the twelfth day before the calends of April. The following day, he advanced five miles from his camp and stood ready for battle two miles ahead of Scipio's forces. Despite many challenges, the enemy avoided a fight. Caesar led his army back and decamped the next day, marching towards Sarsura. Scipio had a garrison of Numidians and a corn storehouse there. Labienus learned of Caesar's move and attacked the rear with cavalry and light-armed troops. They captured some baggage and thought the legionaries would be an easy target, overburdened as they were with the march. But Caesar had planned for this moment and had readied 300 men in each legion for action. These men fought Labienus and scared him into fleeing. Many of his men died or got injured. The legionaries resumed their march, and Labienus followed at a distance along the mountains' summit to the right.

76

Caesar, arriving at Sarsura, took it without resistance from the enemy who did not dare to attack. He then slaughtered the garrison left by Scipio, including his veteran commander P. Cornelius. After distributing the corn found in Sarsura to his army, Caesar marched to Tisdra where Considius was holding out with a strong garrison and cohort of gladiators. Unable to besiege the town due to lack of supplies, Caesar immediately retreated back to his camp at Agar after marching for four miles. Scipio followed suit and retreated to his own quarters.

Meanwhile in Thabena, a nation located on the edge of Juba's kingdom by the seacoast, the people who were once under the ruler's control rose up against his garrison, murdering them all. They then went to Caesar, seeking protection for their city from the Romans. Caesar was impressed with their bravery and sent M. Crispus the tribune, along with a powerful cohort, archers, and numerous war engines to defend Thabena. Additionally, four thousand foot soldiers, four hundred horses, and one thousand archers and slingers, who were unable to join the rest of the legion due to illness or other reasons, arrived by boat to join Caesar. With this full force, Caesar went into a plain eight miles away from his camp, and four miles from Scipio's camp, to face his enemy in a battle-ready position.

Tegea, a town below the camp of Scipio, housed his garrison of 400 horse. Positioned right and left of the town, Scipio drew up his legions in order of battle on a hill lower than his camp. Caesar, who remained in one place, dispatched some cavalry squadrons, accompanied by light-armed infantry, archers, and slingers to charge the enemy cavalry. When Caesar's troops galloped to engage, Placidius began to surround them. Caesar sent 300 legionaries to aid us, and Labienus kept sending more help. As Caesar observed our cavalry, who were only 400, began to waver under the charge of the 4,000 enemy force, he sent the other wing to assist. They fell upon the enemy, put them to flight, slew or wounded many, and pursued them three miles to the mountains. Scipio retreated to his camp at four in the afternoon without a single casualty. Though in this action, Placidius received a severe head wound, and many of his best officers were injured or killed.

He could not lure the enemy to the plain or move his camp closer due
to lack of water, which made the Africans disrespect him. Therefore,
he departed at midnight before nones of April and traveled sixteen
miles beyond Agar to Thapsus. There, he established his camp and set
up redoubts for security and to prevent any assistance from entering
the town. Meanwhile, Scipio was forced to fight to avoid
abandonment. He followed Caesar's movement and positioned himself
in two camps eight miles from Thapsus.

80

Salt-pits, a narrow pass, Scipio's attempt to help the people of Thapsus,
Caesar's fort-building, and encamping around town. Scipio's
disappointment led to his intrenchment near the sea. Caesar heard the
news and quickly marched his forces to the area, leaving only Asprenas
and two legions at camp. Caesar split his fleet, leaving some in Thapsus
and ordering the rest to approach the enemy's rear. With a sudden
shout, the enemy was forced to face behind them.

81

Caesar arrived at the place and saw Scipio's army in battle formation
before the intrenchments, with elephants on either side and some
soldiers fortifying the camp. He set up his own army with three lines,
placing certain legions on each wing and in the center, flanked them
with cohorts against the elephants. Archers and slingers were put in the
wings, and the cavalry was mixed with light-armed troops. Caesar went
amongst the ranks on foot, urging the veterans on and reminding them
of past victories, and encouraging the new levies to follow suit and
strive for fame, glory, and renown by winning.

82

As he sprinted from row to row, he noticed the foe skulking around
their base, anxious and unsettled. They retreated to the barricade one
moment, only to reemerge in disorderly chaos the next. As more in his
army caught on, his subordinates and volunteers pleaded for him to
initiate the battle. Their conviction was fortified by the pledge of a
conclusive triumph by the immortals. Though he was hesitant and
labored to suppress their fervor, insisting he had no intention of
launching a sudden attack and holding back his troops, suddenly a
bugle blower on the right flank, not with Caesar's consent but forced
by the soldiers, sounded a charge. At that moment, all the cohorts
surged forward towards the enemy, ignoring the efforts of the
centurions who tried to hold them back with force to avoid the charge
conflicting with the orders of the general, but to no avail.

83

Caesar, with his soldiers' fervor uncontainable, cried "good fortune"
and charged the enemy's front on horseback. The archers and slingers
on the right relentlessly hurled their javelins at the elephants,
frightening them so much that they trampled their own men and
dashed through the unfinished gates of the camp. The Mauritanian
horse, also stationed on that same wing, fled in their absence. The
legions turned to face the elephants, took over the enemy's
fortifications, and killed off those who resisted. The remaining troops
fled quickly back to their camp from the day before.

84

The brave soldier of the fifth legion deserves recognition for his
courageous actions. A wounded elephant, driven by pain, trampled an
unarmed man to death. Upon seeing this, the soldier charged at the
elephant with his javelin. The elephant immediately seized the soldier
with its trunk and flung him around, but the soldier did not lose his
composure. He relentlessly attacked the elephant's trunk with his sword
until the animal finally released him and fled in agony.

85

The Thapsus garrison attempted to flee for safety, but were attacked by their opponents and forced to return to the town. Scipio's army was routed, and the legions pursued them without allowing time for a rally. When they arrived at their newer camp and sought to choose a commander, they found no reliable option and ultimately surrendered to Caesar's troops. However, the impact was minimal, as Caesar's veterans were too furious to spare the enemy and even attacked their own comrades. Despite appeals for mercy from Caesar, all of Scipio's soldiers were ultimately killed.

86

Caesar took over the enemy's camps, killed ten thousand soldiers and defeated the rest. He only lost fifty men and a few who were injured. He also captured sixty-four elephants and displayed them with their ornaments and trappings in front of a nearby town called Thapsus. Caesar hoped the enemy would surrender after seeing their loss, so he invited Virgilius to submit. However, since there was no response, Caesar left. The next day, he praised and rewarded his soldiers, thanked the gods, and continued his march to Utica while leaving his troops to continue with the siege.

87

Scipio's cavalry had escaped the battle, heading towards Utica until they arrived at Parada, where the people denied them entry due to Caesar's victory. So they broke in, started a fire in the forum, and threw all inhabitants, along with their possessions, into the flames. Their cruelty, unheard of before, was their way of avenging the slight they'd faced. From there, they headed straight to Utica. M. Cato had arrested the senators previously, and expelled and disarmed the populace, fearing their support of Caesar due to Julian law. The cavalry came to attack them since they favored Caesar, aiming to obliterate their own defeat. But the people, encouraged by Caesar's triumph, pushed them back with stones and clubs. So they forcefully entered the town, killing many while plundering their homes. Cato tried to stop them, but failed, giving each a hundred sesterces for peace. Sylla Faustus did the same and, with them, marched on into the kingdom.

88

Many fled the battle to Utica, where Cato gathered them and urged
them to free their slaves and defend the town. However, some were
too afraid, so Cato gave them ships to flee. He then settled his affairs
and commended his children to L. Caesar before privately taking his
own life. Though the Uticans opposed his party, they respected Cato's
integrity and buried him with honor. L. Caesar capitalized on Cato's
death by urging the people to open their gates and seek Caesar's
forgiveness. Messala guarded the gates as ordered.

89

Caesar marched from Thapsus to Usceta, where Scipio kept a cache of
weapons and wheat with a small guard. Caesar seized the town and
moved on to Adrumetum without resistance, recording the town's
provisions, currency, and arms. Q. Ligarius and C. Considius were
forgiven, Livineius Regulus left in control, and Caesar set out the same
day for Utica. Along the way, L. Caesar begged for his life and Caesar,
being kind as usual, pardoned him, along with others such as Cato's
son and Damasippus' children. Caesar got to Utica that night, outside
the city with only torchlight to guide him.

90

At first light the next day, he entered the room and gathered the
people. He thanked them for their support and chided the Roman
citizens and merchants for their wrongdoing. He let them know that
they need not be afraid, for he only planned to sell their belongings,
not take their lives. He warned them that their items would soon be up
for sale, but they could buy them back by paying a fine. The fearful
merchants were willing to pay any sum, and begged him to set one so
they could repay their debt. So, he charged them two hundred
thousand sesterces, to be paid to the republic over three years. The
merchants happily agreed and gave their gratitude to Caesar, thinking
of it as a second birth.

91

King Juba, who fled from battle with Petreius, came to Numidia after hiding in villages during the day and traveling only at night. Upon reaching his residence in Zama, where his wives, children, and most valuable possessions were located, he was denied entry by the inhabitants due to his declaration of war against the Romans and his plan to burn them all on a pile of wood if he failed. Despite pleading and threatening, the inhabitants did not yield, prompting Juba to retreat with Petreius and a few horse to one of his country estates.

92

In the meantime, the Zamians had dispatched envoys to Caesar who was stationed in Utica. Their message was clear, they had taken a stand and wanted Caesar's assistance before the king could muster an army against them. "We'll defend the town to our last breath," they proclaimed. Caesar was pleased with their determination and agreed to offer his support. He left Utica the following day with his cavalry and headed towards the kingdom. Along the way, many of the king's generals sought his forgiveness and were granted pardon. They all accompanied Caesar to Zama. As news of his leniency spread, the Numidian cavalry grew in numbers and felt a sense of relief under his protection.

93

Considius, the commander at Tisdra, fled with his retinue, Getulian garrison, and gladiator company upon hearing of their defeat and Domitius' arrival. He was murdered by the Getulians for his treasure, while fleeing with few barbarians and all his money towards the kingdom. Meanwhile, C. Virgilius found himself stuck without defense, with his followers dead, and Juba deserted. Caesar entered Utica without competition and Caninius besieged him. With Utica and his children vulnerable, surrendering to Caninius appeared to be G. Virgilius' wisest choice.

94

King Juba, nearly cornered in his own kingdom, shared a meal with Petreius before offering a duel to the death. Though Juba emerged victorious, he lacked the strength to end his own life and was forced to plead with a slave to do the deed for him.

95

P. Sitius defeated Sabura's army, killed the general, and joined Caesar after marching through Mauritania. He encountered and ambushed Faustus and Afranius, leaders of a plundering party of around 1,500 men heading to Spain, capturing or killing most of them. The prisoners included Afranius, Faustus, and their families, but the soldiers mutinied and killed the leaders. Caesar pardoned Faustus' wife, Pompeia, and allowed her to keep her belongings.

96

Scipio sailed with Damasippus, Torquatus, and Plaetorius Rustianus towards the Spanish coast. The winds were cruel, and they were forced to dock at Hippo, where P. Sitius's fleet was stationed. Sitius's larger ships overpowered Scipio's smaller ones, causing them to sink. Scipio and his companions met their end in the depths of the sea.

97

Caesar sold the king's effects and took the estates of those who fought against the republic. He abolished the royal tribunes, changed the kingdom to a province and appointed a proconsul to control it. He rewarded those who wanted to exclude the king in Zama, then left for Utica. There he sold the estates of Juba and Petreius' officers and levied fines from various cities, but he spared their territories. The people of Leptis were ordered to pay oil annually for their alliance with the king. Meanwhile, Tisdra's impoverished people were only required to give corn every year.

98

With all in order, he set out from Utica on the ides of June and three sunrises later found himself in Carales of Sardinia. There, he administered justice by fining the Sulcitani one hundred thousand sesterces for aiding Nasidius's fleet. They were now to pay an eighth to the public coffers, instead of their former tenth. He also seized the property of those who had acted with greater fervor than the others. Setting sail from Carales on the third day before the calends of July, he hugged the coast and after twenty-eight days - often waylaid by unsympathetic winds - he made it back to Rome unscathed.

SPANISH WAR

In the Spanish War, the narrative sweeps readers into the final chapter of Caesar's struggle for supremacy, as he faces the last remnants of the Pompeian forces in the Iberian Peninsula. This compelling account captures the intensity, strategic acumen, and unyielding determination that define Caesar's campaign to quell resistance and secure his rule over the Roman Republic. As you embark on this gripping journey, prepare to be captivated by the intricate web of alliances, fierce battles, and the indomitable spirit of the Romans and their Spanish adversaries, as they navigate the treacherous path toward victory and the ultimate fate of Rome itself.

1

Pharnaces defeated, Africa subdued, the fugitives scattered to young
Cn. Pompey in Further Spain, while Caesar stayed in Italy, minding
games. Pompey sought succor from each state, positioning himself
against Caesar. By force, with a sizable army, he ransacked the
province. Some states offered aid freely, others locked their gates.
Assaulted towns were plundered, even when adorned with citizens
exemplary to Pompey (the father). Such wealth was deemed a crime,
and the soldiers took the spoils. Thus the enemy's ranks swelled with
each success, and Pompey's opponents pleaded for refuge from Italy.

2

Caesar, dictator for the third time, and elected for a fourth, marched
fiercely into Spain. On the way, ambassadors from Corduba, who had
already deserted Cn. Pompey met him. They informed Caesar that he
could easily take the town by surprise, as Pompey's scouts were all
captured and the enemy knew nothing of Caesar's approach. He
quickly alerted his lieutenants, Q. Pedius and Q. Fabius Maximus, to
send him all the cavalry they could gather. Though he came upon them
sooner than expected and was without the cavalry he desired, he
pressed on to finish the war.

3

Sextus Pompey, brother of Cneius, ruled over Corduba, the province's
capital. Cneius himself fought in the siege of Ulia, which dragged on
for months. Upon receiving news of Caesar's arrival, messengers
pleaded with Pompey to send aid to their besieged town. Caesar,
recognizing the people's loyalty to Rome, dispatched eleven cohorts
and horsemen under the seasoned command of L. Julius Paciecus, who
knew the province well. Upon arrival at Pompey's camp, they
encountered a fierce storm and deep darkness, which aided Paciecus in
his strategy. He led his cavalry two by two through the enemy's
quarters to the town and gained entry with cunning tactics. Shouting
loudly, they seized the advantages of the unexpected attack and
captured most of the enemy's men at their camps.

4

Ulia's relief came with Caesar's march to Corduba, as he sent cavalry and heavy infantry ahead, undiscovered by the enemy. When the cavaliers' approach drew out the foes to fight, the foot soldiers joined the fray, pounding them with such force that few escaped. This struck fear in Sextus Pompey, causing him to call for his brother's aid against the imminent capture of Corduba by Caesar. Thus, Cn. Pompey left the verge of Ulia's fall and headed for Corduba to assist his brother.

5

Caesar arrived at the Guadalquivir River, which he found too deep to cross. So, he sank baskets of stones to create a bridge and transported his troops to the camps in three groups. The bridge's beams stretched over against the tower in two rows, and Pompey arrived soon after and encamped directly over against Caesar. A struggle emerged between the two generals, which should first get control of the bridge. This conflict resulted in skirmishes that sometimes favored one side or the other. In a serious engagement on the narrow bridge, many fell headlong, and the losses were pretty even. Caesar persisted in trying to bring the enemy to an equal engagement to conclude the war soon.

6

They avoided the battle, which was why he left Ulia, so he lit fires in the night and went towards Ategua. They had strong defenses there. Pompey found out and went back to Corduba. Caesar attacked Ategua and surrounded it. Pompey heard and started marching. Caesar took many forts to guard against him. Pompey arrived when it was foggy and trapped Caesar's horse, killing most of them.

7

That night, Pompey burned his camp and moved to higher ground between Ategua and Ucubis. Caesar built a mound and readied his machines for an attack. The terrain was mountainous with a river separating it from the plain. Pompey's camp was on the mountains and visible to both towns. His legions were mostly made up of deserters, with only a few trustworthy soldiers. We had greater numbers and courage in our light-armed foot and cavalry.

8

Pompey could prolong the war due to the mountainous terrain and well-fortified encampments of Further Spain. The inhabitants, frequently subject to native incursions, built towers and castles made of earth that overlooked the surrounding area. Even the majority of towns were constructed on difficult-to-reach mountains. This made it troublesome for attackers to lay siege, as seen in the present struggle between Pompey and Caesar. Pompey set up his camp between Ategua and Ucubis with a view of both towns, so Caesar constructed a fortress four miles away on a convenient hill.

9

Pompey saw the strategic importance of the high ground near Caesar's camp, even though it was a distance away and separated by the Rio Salado. He believed that Caesar wouldn't be able to send reinforcements due to the difficulty of crossing the river. So, Pompey attacked the fort in the middle of the night to aid the besieged. Our soldiers shouted and hurled many javelins, causing numerous casualties. As resistance grew, news of the attack reached Caesar, who immediately mobilized three legions. In the ensuing chaos, many of Pompey's soldiers fled and some were captured. Eighty shields were recovered, along with several prisoners such as two... and many others who managed to escape by discarding their weapons.

10

Arguetius came from Italy with the cavalry and five standards from Saguntines. Asprenas, who also reinforced Caesar from Italy, took over Arguetius' post. That night, Pompey burnt his camp and headed to Corduba. Indus, a king who was bringing troops to Caesar, was captured and killed by Spanish legionaries for chasing the enemy too hard.

11

Our cavalry chased the provision-carriers near Corduba's walls, and took fifty prisoners along with some equine. Q. Marcius, a military tribune from Pompey's army, defected to us on the same day. The town witnessed an intense battle at midnight, with fiery projectiles thrown from both sides. After the attack ended, C. Fundanius, a Roman knight, deserted the enemy and joined our camp.

12

On the morrow, two Spanish soldiers, disguised as slaves, were captured by our cavalry. But when they were taken back to camp, they were recognized by soldiers who had served under Fabius and Pedeius, and had left Trebonius. There was no mercy for them, and they were killed by our troops. As the night progressed, the besieged rained arrows and flames upon us, as they do every night. Many of our men were injured. At first light, they attacked the sixth legion as we worked on our fortifications. This sparked a fierce battle with our men coming out as the victors despite fighting from a lower position. The attackers were driven back into the town, many wounded.

13

On the morrow, Pompey commenced a line from camp to Rio Salado. A group of our horse, outnumbered and outgunned, were driven off their post with three of their companions meeting their end. A. Valgius, a senator's kin, betrayed our cause and rode his trusty steed to the enemy's side sans luggage. Our second legion spied one of Pompey's own and meted out his just punishment. A bullet marked with a message of ill tidings was shot into the town, hinting at the siege to come. With the walls weakened, our men seized the opportunity to strike, but the enemy garrison, suspecting an attack, retaliated with a fierce sally. A tower fell to our engine and brought down five enemy men and a boy.

14

Pompey built a fort across Rio Salado without trouble from our men, feeling proud to be so close to us. The next day, he attacked our cavalry and drove back several squadrons and light-armed foot. This happened near both camps, which excited the Pompeians. Our men regrouped and intended to fight back after getting reinforcement.

15

In cavalry clashes, when troopers dismount to attack infantry, things often turn out unequal. Such was the case today. A group of the enemy's light-armed foot suddenly came upon our horses, causing our men to dismount and engage them in infantry combat. But, just as suddenly, our forces turned the tables and became cavalry once again. Though we were driven back at first, reinforcements arrived and we were able to not only kill 123 enemies, but also make some throw down their arms and wound many others. After the battle, the enemy showed their true barbarity by throwing citizens off the walls. This act has no equal in recorded history.

16

As darkness fell, Pompey dispatched an unknown messenger to persuade the garrison to ignite our towers and mound, and launch an attack at the stroke of midnight. With a hail of darts and flames, they ravaged a considerable part of the rampart and surged through the gate in plain view of Pompey's camp, armed with fascines to bridge the ditch, hooks and fire to raze the reed barracks, and silver and lavish attire to distract our troops. Pompey anticipated their victory and stood battle-ready across the Rio Salado, anticipating their retreat. Though our men were oblivious to the plot, their valor outmatched the foe, thwarting their plan and sodomizing their march, seizing their plunder, capturing their weapons and culprits, and slaughtering them the following day. Meanwhile, a turncoat from the town apprised us that Junius, who was overseeing the mine when the people were massacred, revolted against his men's cruel and savage behavior, protesting how they had shown the troops generosity by accommodating them in their homes and shrines, and insisting it was a breach of all Judaic virtues. His remarks impacted the garrison so profoundly, they abstained from the horrendous bloodshed.

17

On the morrow, Tullius, a lieutenant general, and C. Antonius of Lusitania arrived to see Caesar. Tullius stated how he would have been one of Caesar's soldiers, rather than a follower of C. Pompey. He regretted fighting for Pompey and wished to have achieved great deeds for Caesar. He spoke of the meager rewards they received after being reduced to poverty by the ill-fated circumstances. Tullius asked for mercy and for Caesar to be as forgiving to his fellow citizens as he had been to foreign nations. Caesar replied, "I shall show them the same kindness."

Ambassadors gone, Tiberius Tullius reached the town gate without C. Antony, who he then seized and wounded with a dagger. They fled to Caesar. A legion's standard-bearer came to our camp reporting the loss of thirty-five men in a skirmish, unspoken of in Pompey's camp. A slave killed his master and escaped to inform Caesar of the city's defensive plans. Two brothers deserted and told us of Pompey's plan to retreat to the sea, despite soldiers objecting. Some couriers were caught and Caesar used them to set fire to a tower. A messenger died attempting the task. A deserter told us of Pompey and Labienus being angry about the massacre of the citizens.

19

The tower fell at night, and there was a fight under the walls. The besieged burned two towers using the wind. The next day, a woman jumped off the wall and came to the camp. Her family planned to do the same, but they were caught and killed. A letter was thrown over, saying that L. Minatius would serve Caesar if he spared his life. Deputies went to Caesar, offering to surrender the town if their lives were spared. Caesar agreed and was hailed imperator on February 19th after taking control of the town.

20

Pompey heard the town surrendered and moved to Ucubis to build defenses. Caesar followed suit. A Spanish soldier deserted to us and tattled that Pompey questioned people on their loyalties. A slave who killed his master was caught and burned. Eight Spanish centurions defected to Caesar. We lost a skirmish and some of our foot were wounded. We caught enemy spies and executed them.

21

The next day, a group of the enemy's cavalry and light-armed infantry defected to us. While our men were out getting water, eleven of their horse attacked and killed some of our men, taking eight troopers as prisoners. The day after that, Pompey executed seventy-four people suspected of supporting Caesar. The remaining suspected individuals were taken back to town, but one hundred and twenty managed to escape to Caesar's side.

22

Afterwards, the Bursavola deputies arrived - the same ones Caesar had captured at Ategua - and were sent back to their town with Caesar's own ambassadors to relay the events of the massacre to their people. However, upon their arrival, our deputies, all Roman knights and senators, were too afraid to enter the city. After much back and forth communication, the Bursavolans pursued and killed all of our deputies except for two who made it back to Caesar. Later, the people of Bursavola sent spies to confirm the reports, and they even considered stoning the cause of the deputies' murder, but were restrained. Yet in the end, the man was the cause of their destruction, as he obtained permission to go to Caesar, privately gathered troops, returned in the night, and massacred all the inhabitants. He sold all their goods and killed their leaders, bringing the town to submission. The soldiers on Pompey's side were not allowed to leave without being unarmed and some abandoned hope, deserting from our camp and taking refuge in Baeturia. Anyone who deserted from our camp was forced to join the light-armed infantry, with pay of only 16 asses per day.

23

The day after, Caesar moved his camp closer to Pompey's and began to draw a line towards the river Salado. While our men worked, enemies attacked and wounded many without resistance. Ennius says, "our men retreated a little." Two centurions from the fifth legion then passed the river, restored the battle, and fought valiantly. One fell from the multitude of darts, while the other retreated but stumbled and died. The enemy crowded together, and our cavalry drove them back to their intrenchments. Many of our men were wounded, but none of them fell, except for the two centurions who sacrificed themselves.

24

On the following day, our forces and Pompey's withdrew from Soricaria, and we continued with our works. Pompey, realizing that our fort had cut off his communication with Aspavia, about five miles from Ucubis, deemed it necessary to engage in battle. However, he did so from an advantage point of a hill. Despite both parties seeking the higher ground, our men were quick to drive them down into the plain, granting us an advantage in the fight. The enemy gave up on all fronts, and we inflicted significant damage on them. The mountain, not their bravery, had protected them, and our small number of men would have deprived them of any relief had night not set in. We avenged the deaths of the two centurions from the previous day, with 324 light-armed foot and 138 legionary soldiers falling to our hands, in addition to their armor and spoils.

25

On the following day, Pompey's cavalry advanced towards us, their usual custom being to engage on level ground. They began skirmishing with our men while they worked, and the legionaries called out to choose a field of battle, pretending they wanted a fight. Our men left their encampment on the hill and advanced into the plain, but none of the enemy dared to face us except Antistius Turpio. He boasted that he was stronger than anyone on our side and offered us a challenge. Pompey's army watched as Q. Pompeius Niger courageously approached Antistius like Memnon against Achilles. The battle was intense, and both combatants had glittering bucklers. However, the Pompeians were frightened by our horse's cries during the fight, and they fled with many casualties.

26

Caesar rewarded the Cassian troop with thirteen thousand sesterces and distributed ten thousand more among the light-armed foot. The cavalry commander received five golden collars. Three Roman knights of Asta, A. Bebius, C. Flavius, and A. Trebellius, came to Caesar with their horses adorned in silver, informing him that all of the Roman knights in Pompey's camp conspired to join him, but were seized and thrown into custody. Letters intercepted that day from Pompey to Ursao expressed his success and desire to end the war quickly, protecting towns and forcing the enemy into engagement. He planned to send new troops and cut off enemy supplies.

27

Afterwards, while our men scattered around, horses grabbed some olive grove timber and were killed. Several slaves fled and told us that since Soritia's fight on March 7th, the enemy remained in constant danger, and Attius Varus was selected to protect the lines. That same day Pompey left, camping in an olive grove close to Hispalis. Caesar, before moving out, waited till midnight, where the moon started to show. He ordered friends to burn the abandoned fort of Ucubis at his departure and meet in the larger camp. Then he besieged Ventisponte, which gave in, and went to Carruca, setting up camp across Pompey who burned the city after the stronghold refused to open the doors to him. A soldier who killed his brother in the camp was also whipped to death. Caesar then reached the plains of Munda, pitched his camp against that of Pompey, and kept marching.

28

The day after, Caesar got word from his spies that Pompey had been ready to fight since midnight. This caused Caesar to raise the standard and prepare his army for battle. Pompey had informed his loyal followers in Ursao that Caesar was hesitant to engage in the open field due to his inexperienced troops. This made the city even more loyal to Pompey. Pompey thought that he could win the entire battle based on this belief and the geographic advantages of his position in the hills, without any intervening plains.

29

An accident occurred during this time that should not be overlooked. The two camps were separated by a five-mile plain stretched out between them. Pompey had an advantage with the town's location and the terrain providing double defenses. A rivulet flowed through the valley, causing difficulties for anyone trying to approach the mountain as it formed a deep morass on the right. Caesar believed that when he saw Pompey's army in formation, they would come down to the plain for battle. The day was calm and clear, perfect conditions for the engagement. Our men were happy about the opportunity, but some still felt a sense of unease as their fate was uncertain. Caesar marched onto the battlefield, confident that the enemy would do the same, but they were hesitant and did not leave the shelter of the town's walls. As our men held their position in battle formation, the flat terrain tempted them to come down and fight, but Pompey's army remained on the mountain near the town. We hastened towards the rivulet while they stayed in the same place.

30

Their army, a force of thirteen legions, arranged itself with the cavalry on the wings and six thousand light-armed infantry, along with a similar number of auxiliaries. Our side only had eighty heavy-armed cohorts and eight thousand horse. When we arrived at the edge of the plain, right where the real trouble awaited us, the enemy, stationed above, was waiting. Caesar noticed this and made it clear to his men where they were. This prevented any rash acts from his troops that could have resulted in unpleasant consequences. The army, however, grumbled, as though they had been denied a guaranteed victory. This delay, in turn, inspired the enemy, who then assumed that Caesar's troops shirked from a fight because of fear. They m ade a bold move, and while in a relatively safe spot, they advanced. The tenth legion held their usual place on the right, the third and fifth positioned on the left, and the cavalry and auxiliary troops in between. The battle began with a deafening cry.

31

Our men showed great bravery, but the enemy held the high ground and fought fiercely. Arrows and darts filled the air as both sides fought valiantly, with the tenth legion on the right attacking the enemy and forcing them to bring reinforcements. Our cavalry on the left also joined the fray, and the battlefield was filled with the sounds of clashing armor, groans of the wounded, and shouts of combatants. Nevertheless, our forces were victorious, routing the Pompeians and slaying over thirty thousand. The enemy lost many officers and soldiers, and we gained thirteen eagles and seventeen prisoners. The battle was fought on the feast of Bacchus, and it was a great triumph for our side.

32

Pompey's army, now dead and gone, had retreated to Munda in hopes of defending their ground. But we had no choice but to invest the town. We piled the corpses of our enemies high to use as our fortifications and fashioned their weapons into stakes. It was a grim sight, but it was all we had. We knew we had to strike fear into our foes, so we hung their shields on the stakes, put their heads on swords and lances, and planted them around the works. We wanted them to know the extent of our might.

As our attack began, young Valerius rode to Corduba to inform Sextus Pompey of our plans, and he left under the guise of seeking peace. Cn. Pompey took a different route, heading towards Carteia where he could find his fleet. When he got close, he sent one of his men to get a litter, pretending he was sick. When he was carried into town, his followers came to him, eager for his command. Pompey left the litter and put himself in their hands.

33

After Munda, Caesar headed to Corduba, where some enemy survivors mocked his men from a guarded bridge. Caesar crossed the river and set up camp while Scapula, who had caused a slave revolt, tried to save himself in Corduba. When besieged, Scapula hosted a grand dinner, gave away his belongings, and had one of his freedmen kill him and set fire to the funeral pyre.

34

Caesar arrived and the conflict between the factions of him and Pompey caused a rift in the inhabitants. Legions of former deserters and slaves pledged allegiance to Caesar, but the thirteenth legion defended the town, prompting the other faction to seek Caesar's help. The battle caused the town to be set ablaze, leading to the death of many. Meanwhile, those trapped in Munda made an attempt to escape, but failed.

35

Caesar went to Hispalis, and the city asked for forgiveness. They declared their ability to protect themselves, but he still sent troops and Caninius to the city. Pompeians within the city sent Philo to Cecilius Niger for help, who arrived at night and seized control of the gates, leading to a battle for the city.

36

Deputies from Carteia arrived boasting the capture of Pompey, hoping it would make amends for previously shutting their gates against Caesar. Meanwhile, Lusitanians plundered Hispalis, yet Caesar refrained from pressing too hard, fearing they would set fire to and destroy the town. Council decided to let the Lusitanians escape, but our men foiled their plan by setting fire to their ships in the Guadalquivir river. Marching on to Asta, the town submitted. Many soldiers who had escaped from the long-besieged Munda eventually surrendered and were formed into a legion. They plotted a massacre in the camp but were found out and put to death outside the rampart.

37

As Caesar conquered other towns, the Carteians argued over young
Pompey. One group supported Caesar, while the other favored
Pompey. The Pompeian supporters overpowered the others, causing a
massacred. Pompey himself suffered injuries, but managed to escape
on twenty galleys. Upon learning of Pompey's escape, Didius pursued
him with his fleet and stationed cavalry and infantry along the coast.
Pompey left Carteia hastily without water, forcing him to stop on the
way, where Didius caught up to him after four days and burned his
remaining ships.

38

Pompey, injured and on the run, sought refuge with friends in a strong
and natural fortification. Pursued relentlessly by troops with inside
information, he was eventually cornered in a well-defended post.
Despite attempts to storm the location, the enemy held strong and we
were forced to lay siege. The enemy eventually fled upon seeing our
preparations, and Pompey escaped.

39

Pompey, he was hurt and hobbling, couldn't escape fast in that rough
terrain. Our forces raided his stronghold, causing slaughter and
shutting off his supplies. He took refuge in a cavern, hiding from us,
until his location was revealed by captives. In the end, he was killed and
his head was shown in Hispalis while Caesar was nearby in Gades.

40

Young Pompey died. Didius, filled with pride, retired to the nearest fortress to fix some vessels. The Lusitanians who survived from the battle came together and advanced towards Didius. Although he concentrated on keeping the fleet safe, Didius had to leave his fort to hold back the enemy's repeated attacks. They started to fight daily which ended with an ambush. Enemies split into groups, set fire to the fleet, and lured Didius's followers into the ambush. Didius fought bravely but he and most of his soldiers were surrounded and killed. Some people fled by taking boats while others chose to swim to reach the galleys. Caesar returned to Hispalis from Gades. The Lusitanians took everything that belonged to Didius and his men.

41

Fabius Maximus, who continued the siege of Munda with great zeal, caused the enemy to sally out and be repulsed with great loss. Our men took advantage of this opportunity and captured the town, along with approximately fourteen thousand prisoners. They then retreated to the exceedingly strong town of Ursao, which was difficult to conquer due to its natural and artistic fortifications. The besieged had a strategic advantage, as the only spring within eight miles supplied the town. Moreover, the necessary wood for building towers and machines had to be obtained from a distance of six miles. To increase the difficulty of the siege, Pompey had cut down all the timber in the area and collected it within the walls. This forced our men to bring needed materials from Munda, the nearest town they had subdued.

42

At Munda and Ursao, amidst transactions, Caesar gathered the citizens upon his return from Gades to Hispalis. He spoke of his time as quaestor, serving their province above all others, and doing all within his power for them. During his praetorship, he abolished taxes imposed by Metellus and became their patron, defending their private and public rights. Despite rendering his consul services, they showed ingratitude throughout both the preceding and recent war. They violated the law of nations, assaulted Roman magistrates, remained enemies of peace, and displayed cowardliness in war. He questioned their victory against ten legions of Rome, even if his destruction occurred. The book's end remains lost.

◆◆◆

EPILOGUE

As the dust settled following the Spanish War, Julius Caesar emerged as the undisputed ruler of Rome. With the last of the Pompeian forces vanquished and his adversaries scattered or eliminated, Caesar's grip on power tightened, and the Roman Republic was forever altered. Yet, the consequences of these sweeping changes would not be without their own perils.

Though Caesar's victories brought a measure of stability and unity to the Roman world, they also heralded the end of the Republic and the dawn of a new era. The triumphs and tribulations that characterized Caesar's military campaigns not only shaped the lives of those who fought and suffered during these tumultuous times but also laid the groundwork for the rise of the Roman Empire.

In the years that followed the Spanish War, Caesar implemented numerous reforms, seeking to address some of the long-standing issues that plagued the Republic. However, his consolidation of power and the changes he enacted would ultimately sow the seeds of his own demise. The Ides of March, 44 BCE, saw Caesar assassinated by a group of conspirators, including some of his closest allies, who believed that the only way to save the Republic was to eliminate the man who had come to embody its dissolution.

In the wake of Caesar's death, Rome was plunged into a new cycle of civil wars, as the remnants of the Republic grappled with the forces of change and the shifting tides of power. Eventually, Caesar's grand-nephew and adopted son, Octavian, would rise to prominence, defeating his rivals and ushering in a new era of Roman history. As the first Roman emperor, Augustus, Octavian would establish the Pax Romana, a period of relative peace and stability that would last for centuries. The legacy of Julius Caesar, his military prowess, political acumen, and the consequences of his actions, would continue to shape the course of Roman history and, by extension, the Western world.

The narratives of Caesar's military campaigns, from the conquest of Gaul to the Civil Wars and beyond, provide invaluable insights into the mind of one of history's most influential leaders. These accounts reveal not only the strategies, ambitions, and motivations that drove Caesar's actions but also the complex interplay between conquest, diplomacy, and the indomitable spirit of the people who found themselves caught in the crossfire of history.

As the pages of time continue to turn, the lessons gleaned from the annals of Caesar's conquests continue to resonate, offering a fascinating glimpse into a pivotal period that forever transformed the world. Through the study of these captivating chronicles, we are reminded of the enduring impact of individual ambition, the power of collective action, and the inescapable influence of history on the human experience.

Summaries

Commentarii de Bello Gallico (Commentaries on the Gallic War):

- Caesar's initial involvement in Gaul due to migration of the Helvetii (58 BC)
- Defeat of the Helvetii and the Suebi, led by Ariovistus
- Confrontation with the Belgae tribes, notably the Nervii (57 BC)
- Caesar's expeditions to Britannia (55 and 54 BC)
- Revolt of the Eburones, led by Ambiorix, and the massacre of the Roman legions (54 BC)
- Campaigns against the Treveri, led by Indutiomarus, and the Menapii (53 BC)
- Uprising of the Gallic tribes under the leadership of Vercingetorix (52 BC)
- Siege of Alesia and the surrender of Vercingetorix, leading to the end of the Gallic resistance
- Pacification of Gaul and mop-up operations against the remaining opposition (51-50 BC)

Commentarii de Bello Civili (Commentaries on the Civil War):

- Breakdown of the First Triumvirate (Caesar, Pompey, and Crassus) and escalating political tensions (50 BC)
- Caesar's crossing of the Rubicon River, marking the start of the civil war (49 BC)
- Caesar's rapid advance through Italy, leading to Pompey and his supporters fleeing to Greece

- Caesar's siege and capture of Massilia (modern-day Marseille) in southern Gaul (49 BC)
- Caesar's campaign in Hispania against Pompey's legates, Lucius Afranius and Marcus Petreius (49 BC)
- Caesar's return to Italy and his crossing of the Adriatic Sea to pursue Pompey (48 BC)
- The Battle of Dyrrhachium, where Caesar suffered a tactical defeat but avoided a complete rout (48 BC)
- The decisive Battle of Pharsalus, where Caesar defeated Pompey's larger army (48 BC)
- Pompey's flight to Egypt and his assassination upon arrival by Ptolemy XIII's advisors
- Caesar's arrival in Egypt and the beginning of his involvement in the Alexandrian War

De Bello Alexandrino (On the Alexandrian War):

- Caesar's arrival in Egypt after the Battle of Pharsalus and the presentation of Pompey's severed head by Ptolemy XIII's advisors
- Caesar's decision to intervene in the Egyptian civil war between Ptolemy XIII and his sister Cleopatra VII
- Cleopatra's secret meeting with Caesar, leading to their alliance against Ptolemy XIII
- The Alexandrian War: a series of skirmishes, sieges, and naval battles in and around the city of Alexandria
- Caesar's efforts to secure grain supplies and reinforcements from Asia Minor and other Roman provinces
- The involvement of Mithridates of Pergamum and his forces, supporting Caesar against Ptolemy XIII
- The Battle of the Nile (47 BC), where Caesar's forces defeated Ptolemy XIII's army

- Ptolemy XIII's death by drowning while attempting to flee across the Nile
- Cleopatra's ascension to the Egyptian throne as the sole ruler, with her younger brother Ptolemy XIV as a nominal co-ruler
- The birth of Caesar's son by Cleopatra, Caesarion, and the establishment of a political alliance between Rome and Egypt

De Bello Africo (On the African War):

- Caesar's pursuit of the remnants of the Pompeian faction after the Battle of Pharsalus (48 BC)
- The Pompeian forces, led by Metellus Scipio, Cato the Younger, and King Juba I of Numidia, regrouping in North Africa
- Caesar's arrival in Africa with his legions (46 BC)
- Initial setbacks for Caesar due to the harsh environment and successful guerrilla tactics employed by the Numidian cavalry
- Caesar's consolidation of his forces and securing the support of local tribes, such as the Musulamii
- The capture of several important towns and strategic locations, including Thapsus, which served as a base of operations
- The decisive Battle of Thapsus (46 BC), where Caesar's forces defeated the combined army of Scipio and Juba
- The aftermath of the battle, with the suicides of Cato the Younger at Utica and King Juba I of Numidia
- The capture and execution of Metellus Scipio, effectively ending the organized resistance of the Pompeian faction in Africa
- Caesar's return to Rome and his celebration of a triumph for his victory in Africa

De Bello Hispaniensi (On the Spanish War):

- The last remnants of Pompeian forces, led by Gnaeus Pompeius and Sextus Pompeius (Pompey's sons), continuing their resistance in the Iberian Peninsula (45 BC)
- Caesar's arrival in Hispania to confront the Pompeians and secure the western provinces for Rome
- Initial skirmishes between Caesar's forces and the Pompeian army, with both sides trying to gain strategic advantages
- The siege of Corduba (modern-day Córdoba) and its subsequent capture by Caesar's forces
- Caesar's attempt to win over local tribes and secure their support against the Pompeians
- The decisive Battle of Munda (45 BC), where Caesar's forces faced a numerically superior Pompeian army
- Caesar's victory at Munda, resulting in the death of Gnaeus Pompeius and the end of organized resistance by Pompey's supporters
- The capture and execution of the remaining Pompeian leaders, while Sextus Pompeius managed to escape
- Caesar's return to Rome, marking the end of the civil war and the beginning of his brief tenure as the sole ruler of the Roman Republic
- The consolidation of power in Caesar's hands, paving the way for the eventual transformation of the Roman Republic into the Roman Empire under his adopted son and heir, Augustus (Octavian)

✦✦✦

About The Author

Valerius Vogan is a history enthusiast and enigmatic writer with a penchant for the avant-garde. Fusing his love for ancient Rome with a modern, hacker-inspired approach, Vogan decodes the past to make it accessible and engaging for contemporary readers. Often found scouring the digital world for hidden historical gems, Vogan combines cutting-edge research techniques with his creative writing flair, crafting immersive narratives that transport readers back in time.

Printed in Great Britain
by Amazon